WHO'S IN CHARGE?

WHO'S IN CHARGE?

A TEACHER SPEAKS HER MIND

SUSAN OHANIAN

Boynton/Cook Publishers
HEINEMANN
Portsmouth, NH

Boynton/Cook Publishers, Inc.
A subsidiary of Reed Elsevier Inc.
361 Hanover Street
Portsmouth, NH 03801–3912
Offices and agents throughout the world

Library of Congress Cataloging-in-Publication Data

Ohanian, Susan.
    Who's in charge?: a teacher speaks her mind / Susan Ohanian.
        p.   cm.
    ISBN 0–86709–339–0 (acid-free paper)
    1. Ohanian, Susan.   2. Teachers — New York (State) — Biography.
3. Teaching.   I. Title.
LA2317.O34A3   1994
371.1'0092 — dc20   94–5586
    [B]   CIP

Editor: Robert W. Boynton
Production: Vicki Kasabian
Cover design: Diana Coe

Printed in the United States of America on acid-free paper
98 97 96 95 94   EB   1 2 3 4 5

For Hans,
Who taught me about paragraphs.

Contents

Introduction   ix

TEACHING   1

Stacks of Letters   5
Love, Leslie   10
The Tantalizing Vagueness of Teaching   15
Collaboration, Silence, and Solitude   18
Notes on Japan from an American Schoolteacher   34

LEARNING   51

P. L. 94–142: Mainstream or Quicksand?   53
To 'Pete,' Who's Lost in the Mainstream   63
Question of the Day   69
Will You Recognize the Ready Moment?   80
Okay to Be Different   87

CURRICULUM CHOICES TOUGH AND EASY   93

To Hell with Rip Van Winkle   96
Reading for What?   110
Smuggling Reading into the Reading Program   120
When the Reading Experts Gather, What's Their Real Agenda?   127
Beware the Rosy View!   134
How Today's Software Can Zap Kids' Desire to Read   141
Who's Afraid of Old Mother Hubbard?   146
Ruffles and Flourishes   155
A Plea for More Disorderliness   159
Literature Has No Uses   163

HIERARCHIES, OR WHO'S IN CHARGE?   169

The Paper Chase   172
There's Only One True Technique for Good Discipline   178
'Yes, But Where Are Your Credits in Recess Management 101?'   185
Huffing and Puffing and Blowing Schools Excellent   195
On Stir-and-Serve Recipes for Teaching   207
'Just the Facts, Ma'am': Tests vs. Intuition   215
Testy Thoughts of May   218
Not-So-Super Superintendents   221
What Makes Whittle Qualified to Do High School TV News?   227
Inside Classroom Structures   230

Envoi: *Thirteen Ways of Looking at Mastery Learning*   245
Credits   247

Introduction

$W_{HO'S}$ I_N C_{HARGE}? is a chronicle of my struggle over the past twenty years to find and articulate my teacherliness. My language is a parlance born of loneliness and indignation. For over twenty years I found myself isolated by the stony silence of my colleagues and insulted by the shrill rabble-babble of the media notion of schooling.

"They've got it all wrong," I kept complaining every time I read an article about education. "Can you do better?" my husband pestered and prodded. I decided I could. Every article I wrote grew from the desire to do it better, to tell the teacher's story.

Being published did not make my teaching any less lonely. Every time one of my articles was published, I'd send a copy to the superintendent, put one in the principal's box, put another in the faculty room. Even administrators and teachers who liked me were disinclined to talk about the issues I raised. At first, the silence was numbing, but later, as it grew deeper, the surrounding silence provoked me to find a bolder voice and taught me to be my own best audience.

Writing a ten-page teachers' union newsletter each month helped me learn to look closely at the daily lives of teachers and children. Because writing that newsletter taught me to look at language as a weapon as well as a defense, it put me in charge of my professional life.

Certainly when I took on my first teaching job I hadn't thought about language as a weapon. Even so, it didn't take me half an hour into someone else's lesson plan to know that something was wrong with the language in that New York City classroom.

I started my teaching career one late October — with a master's degree in medieval literature and an emergency credential. I had no student teaching or other pedagogese in my back pocket. Nonetheless, I quickly saw that round-robin reading of "Paul Revere's Ride" made no sense, that *Silas Marner*, *Johnny Tremain*, and "Ode to a Daffodil" made no sense. The malevolence of a policy that fills classrooms with language that excludes students has been the focus of my writing ever since.

That first year taught me that it's better to ask for forgiveness than to beg for permission. After the "Paul Revere" disaster, I asked the department chair if we really really had to "do" *Silas Marner*. He was a decent fellow; he understood the problem. Outside the school, parents carrying hate slogans picketed the newly-integrated building and hoodlums terror-ized the subways on which I needed to ride home. Inside, *Silas Marner* made no sense to the students or to me. Nonetheless, the department chairman stipulated, "Yes, do it. Every teacher should teach it at least once."

At the time I was too desperate to detect irony. Twenty-five years later, I wonder. I wonder if he knew that the experience would convince me to spend the rest of my career searching for a better language for my students. Ever since, whether I'm teaching tenth graders or third graders, I insist on filling their school days with a language that will touch their hearts and minds, a language that will make them laugh, weep, ponder, shiver, and wonder, a language that will make them want to read some-thing else.

During that first year, as green as I was, I knew I had an obligation to counter the effects of the official school language. I didn't have much time for preparing lessons because I was up past midnight every night typing short stories and novel excerpts onto ditto masters. That smudged purple typescript was dreadful to read, but the students seemed to like the idea that I was offering them some of my favorite words. A group of 8 tenth graders figured that if I could type the words of Shirley Jackson, Bernard Malamud, Eudora Welty, James Thurber, Ray Bradbury, and T. H. White, then maybe I could type their words too. Each day they'd present me with an installment of a story set in a large urban high school. I'd go home and type, and the next day I'd distribute the new episode—filled with intrigue, romance, deception, violence, retribution.

Teenagers from all over our school of three thousand began showing up at my classroom door requesting copies. Before long, I was using so much duplicating paper that I came to school early to pilfer any paper in the main office that wasn't nailed down. Eventually the secretaries locked the cupboards, and I had to buy paper. A ream of my own. Finally I lim-ited each day's print run to 125 copies—available only to students in my classes. Today, I don't have a single copy of any of the episodes. Some student always talked me out of my last copy.

Because I was a green teacher, I didn't know how to build on that student language. Build on it? I didn't even know how to let it into the classroom. Students wrote their stories—which were far more influenced by soap operas and the *National Enquirer* than by *Silas Marner* or *Julius Caesar*—outside of class. I was their typist and editor—outside of class. I quite literally distributed the dittoed copies at the classroom door. Then we went inside our classroom and worked on what we perceived to be the real and necessary curriculum. In Jim Herndon's words, we concerned our-selves with the way things were "'spozed to be." Even when I began devoting one day a week to silent reading from paperback books and magazines that I scrounged from used-bookstores, it never occurred to me or my students that we could let their out-of-school writings into the classroom.

Even though I was required to teach *Silas Marner*, nobody seemed to care that magazines and paperback novels took up more and more of our class time. I don't know whether I was left alone because schools, by and large, have no trouble incorporating mutually exclusive principles or simply because I didn't send students to the office. The fact of the matter is that most schools treat teachers with a curious mixture of nit-picking and neglect. I remain grateful that they nitpick the inconsequential and neglect what matters. When we get *standards* and everybody has to agree on curriculum, then we'll be in trouble.

Writing about schools has helped me learn firsthand about the Bill of Rights. I am here to bear witness that a teacher *can* be heard if she is willing to speak up. I continue to wonder why teachers are so secretive about, even protective of, the bizarre conditions under which we work. Nobody can stop us from telling the truth about our lives, nobody, that is, except ourselves. If you ask for permission, you are doomed. But if you write about your classroom—about the texts and traditions, about the administrators who annoy you and the texts that block you, your public words will provide a protective shield. As long as you show up for hall duty and keep your attendance cards in order, nobody will bother you. Teachers need to remember one thing: if your principal or your curriculum coordinator or your assistant superintendent in charge of curriculum likes consonant blends, basal texts, interactive response journals, or whole-class novel study units—or *Silas Marner*—she is protected by the U. S. Constitution. But so are you. So are you.

At the time I was writing basal-bashing articles, teachers in my district were receiving negative ratings from a petty tyrant because at the moment of official evaluation they weren't on the exact page in the text their lesson plan indicated they would be. Since my lesson plans didn't indicate use of any basal pages at any time, I anticipated an interesting showdown. It never happened. The petty tyrant found an excuse for staying out of my classroom. All year. No administrator ever questioned why I didn't use a basal. My evaluations were sterling. As a matter of fact, I was named my district's first Teacher of the Year. I turned out to be my district's only Teacher of the Year, but that's another story.

I admit I found satisfaction documenting in a public forum the indignities inflicted on me by several tyrants, including the assistant superintendent in charge of curriculum. I never told her she was full of it; I just wrote about what she did. And my public words protected me. The assistant superintendent in charge of curriculum never admitted to reading what I wrote, but she backed off. Way off. For my last five years in the district we rarely saw each other; we never spoke. Sad to say, in my district being left alone was the best I could hope for.

Not that my district was the only institution to ignore my writing. Two of my early articles were rejected both by *Language Arts* and *Reading Teacher*. In both cases I knew the experts were wrong and so I persisted. If a teacher stops believing in her voice just because the experts, be they assistant superintendents in charge of curriculum, professors, or editors, don't give her a vote of confidence, then she will soon find herself mute.

A teacher has to be tough and tenacious. If she is going to write about things that matter (and why would anyone take the trouble to write about things that don't matter?), then her toughness has to be industrial-strength. I'm as thin-skinned as the next person, but somehow, I find being the object of four pages of letters-to-the-editor denunciation in *Phi Delta Kappan* an exhilarating experience. And how many people can lay claim to a full-page denunciation in *Education Week?* Imagine getting so many of the good professors out of their ivory towers long enough to pay attention to a teacher's words, to take a teacher's language seriously.

When everybody agrees, nobody is thinking much. I say three cheers for those singular periodicals still willing to let unorthodox voices be heard, periodicals that don't construct their tables of contents from focus group responses. I say three cheers, too, for my enemies, the people who care enough to write nasty letters.

Maybe I have a certain fondness for denunciatory letters-to-the-editor because that's how I got my start. The guest on a TV news show was taking cheap potshots at teachers, so I wrote a letter to NBC News and sent a copy of the letter to *New York Teacher*. They printed it as well as numerous responses that came in from teachers. A few months later an editor from *New York Teacher* phoned, asking me if I'd like to write a book review for them. My heart sank when he sent a demographic study, but, given the chance to be heard, I wasn't about to be picky about the topic. I read the book three times before I found something to write about, but once I started I came up with fifteen hundred words. They sent another book, and my commentary on that one ran three thousand words. As I became more confident, I began choosing my own books. So I'd get paid $10 to spend three months writing a review of a book that cost me $14.95. Fifteen years later my finances haven't improved: a local newspaper pays me $35 for a monthly opinion piece.[1]

---

[1]Even at the risk of being labelled a footnote writer, I want to offer a cautionary note. I know of several teachers who, having found their voices, followed my example and left the classroom to take up careers as writers. Should anyone else consider such a step, please know that in writing as in teaching, an idealist needs to cultivate a sense of practicality. When I left the classroom to write, I went to a full-time job as staff writer for an education magazine. When I left that position to become a freelancer, I had over

The *New York Teacher* reviews took three months to write, and then I'd spend another month pestering the editor to find space to publish the review. Eventually, it was the length of the reviews, not the opinions, that shut me out of *New York Teacher* pages. It was the first of a number of battles I've had with editors who believe in focus groups, editors who embrace the *People* and *Current Affair* credo for educational publishing, editors who insist that teachers don't read.

Writing the reviews was both good practice and good sustenance. I learned I wasn't talking to myself, after all; I learned that people who cared about children and about pedagogy were listening — and supporting my efforts. The enthusiasm of *New York Teacher* readers turned me into a writer. My second-favorite story is about a famous physicist getting off a plane and asking my husband, who had invited him to speak at a local Einstein centenary, "Are you related to that opinionated Ohanian in *New York Teacher?*" My favorite story is about Bob Boynton, who read one of those early reviews and wrote me. He's been egging me on ever since.

I used to think it a pity that we teachers don't have a specialized, even arcane, vocabulary — words, like those of doctors and lawyers, that would mystify and daze the public. Speak plainly and you get no respect. But then a wash of nasty terms — facilitators, closures, outcomes, empowerment, shared decision making — flooded the field and I knew I had to fight to keep my own language clean. Bad language is a signpost for bad pedagogy. Behavioral objectives, for example, sound ugly and are, of course, a lie. Who would be so arrogant as to claim that a student *will?* I have taught high school dropouts, seventh graders, and third graders: I know that the best you can say on a given day is that a student *might*. Furthermore, I'd just as soon clean my refrigerator — or my desk — as facilitate anything, and I don't engage in interactive response journal communication either. If someone asks me if I favor process or product, the answer is yes. I don't like words that seem to imply we teachers are more organized than we need to be or that we have already arrived or that we even know precisely where we're trying to get. We must be wary of words that carry exclusivity, words that set people up as *us* and *them*, words that are so easily co-opted by the educational-industrial complex. We must look not to the political or mercantile interests of our profession for the words and deeds of our craft but

---

two hundred articles in a wide variety of periodicals to my credit. I also had experience in the commercial ed-biz world. The simple truth of the matter is that writing opinion pieces is a passion and maybe an obsession; it is not a way to make a living. Most years I don't even break even. Here is the economic reality of opinion piece writing: I spent one week in Orlando doing research for "Not-So-Super Superintendents." *Washington Monthly* published the piece and sent me a check for two hundred dollars. When I protested that the plane fare alone was over three hundred dollars and that I'd spent a week in a hotel, the editor told me that when their writers are out of town working on a story, they stay with friends. Knowing the financial realities, would I still go after that piece? You bet.

to Emerson's threads on the loom of time: Illusion, Temperament, Succession, Surface, Surprise, Reality, Subjectiveness.

When Bob Boynton asked me to gather a collection of my essays, he suggested I might go through and eliminate repetitions. But I discovered that I love and cherish the repetitions. I can't tell Leslie's or Michael's or Jack's stories often enough. A story gains new meaning in changing contexts, takes on nuances not apparent in the first telling. Early on I wrote about what David Hawkins calls the miracle of "the bird in the window," that unexpected wonder that interrupts your carefully planned lesson and leads you and your students to new possibilities — if you are ready for and worthy of the bird. I became aware that I'd used the metaphor more than once when my husband complained, "Not the bird again," and I decided that maybe it was time to look for new metaphors. Then, in 1993, which had to be a decade after the last time I mentioned the bird, at the conclusion of a talk in Norfolk, a teacher came up and said, "Your writings have touched my life — especially that bird in the window." So there. Some stories are worth repeating; some metaphors can last a lifetime.

I hope that I have found a language that gives people no place to hide. Teaching is a calling requiring compassion, courage, and craft. I mean craft both in the sense of skill and in the sense of cunning. I hope readers find this to be a crafty book. In acknowledging that our craft is a messy, complicated, eccentric, and, yes, magical, undertaking, I try to show why we must use our language to speak up. In the end, I know that just as stories can sustain you, silence can kill you — like that terrible scene at the end of Kafka's *The Trial* when Joseph K. dies voiceless.

You don't become a teacher simply by being there in the school. You don't become a writer by keeping a diary. The teacher-writer needs a voice of her own as well as a room of her own. For me, that voice begins in annoyance and anecdote. I write to set things straight, to make a difference. Mine is a language of incident looking for righteousness.

Because I'm a teacher and therefore of a class that's overlooked and underrated, I have to keep a close eye on a language that is apt to careen between the cranky and the self-congratulatory. It is fear of these two parts of my language that have made writing this introduction so tough. I have procrastinated for over a year, wondering why the book even needs an introduction: don't the words already speak for themselves? All I can hope is that the words do for the reader what they do for me: cause some laughter, some tears, and a few intellectual goose bumps. I hope the words leave the reader with some knotty questions. As a teacher and as a writer I end up working where I don't know the answers ahead of time and often not afterward either. I hope that people of good heart and sound mind find something here that pinches a bit, that makes them want to argue with me. If they do, I'll know I've done my job.

TEACHING ....

In a sense I've been telling one story for more than twenty years. Children change; I move from high school to middle school back to high school and on to third grade. But things remain more the same than different. In my first year of teaching I asked why I should teach *Silas Marner* to students. Nearly three decades later, I'm still asking that question: Who chooses the language in our classrooms? For whose benefit is the language of schools employed?

As a reader, I have grouped the pieces in each section according to an internal coherence. As a writer looking back, I am struck by how differently certain pieces use language. My work seems to divide into what I call the sweet and the sharp. Sometimes I very deliberately craft stories to pull at the heartstrings; they celebrate being a smart teacher of good heart. This is the language of "Stacks of Letters" and "Love, Leslie." These are my "good news" pieces, words born of the desire to talk about the daily experience of teaching—to share a good idea, to celebrate the spirit of children and the good heart of teachers.

"Stacks of Letters" will always be special to me. It was my entrée into the mass-market education press, and it changed my career forever. I saw "Stacks of Letters" as a curriculum article, an upgraded "What can I do on Monday?" piece. I was so convinced that my letter-writing idea was stupendous that after I dropped it into the mailbox to *Language Arts*, I sat back and waited for their congratulatory acceptance. I was paralyzed with anticipation, unable to write a thing during the three months it took to get their mass-produced rejection notice. Then I sat around for another three months licking my wounds. How could NCTE [National Council of Teachers of English], the professional organization to which I felt such loyalty, fail to recognize the merit of my idea? Finally, I decided to give the article to *Reading Teacher*. That's how I looked at it: trying to decide who else might be worthy of this gift of a terrific idea. It took the folks at IRA [International Reading Association] another three months to reject the piece, and of course, instead of writing during that time, I waited.

The second rejection surprised me—and made me angry. I began to suspect a professorial conspiracy. After all, I had everyday classroom evidence that this idea was the best of my career. I began to suspect that the simplicity of the idea was its downfall when it came up against the ivory tower. Exchanging classroom letters with children required no special degree, no staff development training, no professional handbook, no three-hundred-dollar box of laminated activity cards. Anybody of good heart could do it. Faced with multiple rejections, my convictions solidified. It never occurred to me to stop sending out this article or to junk it up with such *interactive journaling* educationese that, a decade and half later, delineates the classroom exchange of letters.

Learning accepted the article right away and sent me seventy-five dollars. I nearly wore the check out for pulling it out and looking at it. My husband said it was a good thing they didn't know me, didn't know I'd pay them to put my words in print. But *Learning*'s acceptance was the beginning of tortured impatience: I grabbed every issue, expecting to see my article. Finally, after a year, I wrote them, asking "What's going on? Where's my article?" I'm glad I didn't know then what I found out a few years later about editorial offices: editors sometimes buy articles that they never publish; editors sometimes lose articles; editors often rewrite articles.

The article was published eventually, and the words in it were mine. I didn't moan and groan when I saw they'd cut it in half, mainly because I couldn't grin and moan at the same time. For three days I read it over and over, grinning more broadly with each reading. There's something hypnotic about seeing your words in print on slick paper for the first (or the fiftieth) time. The humor is still fresh after the fourteenth reading — at least for me. For my husband, one reading was enough. After the third day he asked me, "How can you still laugh over it? After all you wrote it!" I told him I wanted to buy lots of magazines and paper the walls with my article. I was only half-kidding. A decade or so later I still think an article would make great wallpaper. I wouldn't overdo it: just one room.

A footnote to "Stacks of Letters" is that it provoked more reader response than any article I have ever written. Teachers, guidance counselors, and parents didn't write to the editor; they wrote to me, expressing gratitude for an idea that changed their lives with children. Even though I know that nostalgia is the eighth deadly sin and that I'm in danger of sliding into it, I am proud that I hung on to my belief in a good classroom practice, that I didn't give up in the face of repeated rejections from the bigwigs. I'd never have become a writer if the teacher in me hadn't already learned how to hang tough, to hold on to convictions in the face of discouragement.

A decade later, when the editors of *The Whole Language Catalog* asked me to contribute a piece, I knew immediately that I wanted to write about my letter exchanges with children once again. This time I wrote about the letters Leslie and I shared. Leslie is a child I've written about a lot, the child to whom I gave a bigger part of my heart than any other, the child-woman whose present-day letters still evoke my tears of joy. Certainly Leslie's letter-writing story brings the pedagogy full circle.

The language of "The Tantalizing Vagueness of Teaching" is different. It is a gentle call to arms, asking that teachers make their voices be heard. "Collaboration, Silence, and Solitude" and "Notes on Japan from an American Schoolteacher" are not so gentle. Here is the language of a teacher trying to come to grips with big ideas, a teacher circling around a topic as she struggles to find out what she knows; it is the language of a teacher willing to admit that teaching is an ambiguous craft, that it has its dark side. I struggle with this ambiguity for months as I work on one of these big pieces. I am a slow writer; the road to finding out what I know is torturous. Flannery O'Connor put it this way: "I don't know what I think until I read what I say."

If pieces like "Stacks of Letters" and "Love, Leslie" come from the heart, then "Collaboration, Silence, and Solitude" and "Notes on Japan from an American Schoolteacher" come from the head. I make my presence known in these articles; I show off a bit, wanting the reader to know that teachers are in charge; they are savvy and tough-minded, forces to be reckoned with.

I developed my writing method for these meaty pieces while writing book reviews for *New York Teacher*. If I was reviewing a book, say, by Jonathan Kozol, I would reread every book he'd ever written; if I was reviewing a book about testing, I might not read everything written about testing, but I'd try. Before I went to Japan, I read twenty books, trying to learn about every aspect of Japanese thought, art, and everyday life. Once I arrived in Japan, I filled several notebooks with everything that I saw, everything I heard, everything I ate. Hey, one never knows what might come in handy. I came home worrying that I had lots of notes but no article. And so I did what I always do when I'm desperate: I read thirty more books. I can point to one funny line in "Notes on Japan from an American Schoolteacher" that came from reading half a dozen books on Zen Buddhism. One good line is reward aplenty. As a matter of fact, single lines often come far before any sense of the piece itself. I had good lines written on index cards that made a stack half an inch thick before I found my hook into the piece. In the end the hook was, of course, not sociology, not philosophy, not even good lines, but the students, the children I observed in the Japanese schools. I don't downgrade the background preparation; without it the hook would have come up as empty as most media coverage of education. Knowing schools is never enough. A writer has to earn her expertise over and over, just as a teacher renews her expertise every day.

Finding the hook took more than a year of struggle. Occasionally I'd give up on the article and write some curriculum materials on safe topics:

Japanese art, poetry, and social customs. I knew that the trip to Japan hadn't been necessary to write a poster study guide, but for a long while that was the best I could do. Because I'd cultivated different voices as a writer, when one voice failed, I had another to fall back on. The fact of the matter is that educational publishing is much more eager for the words of the journeyman writer who can crank out activities than for the words of the writer who insists on digging deeper.

In the end, my Japanese hosts, prominent industrialists, were not happy with the article I wrote. They had anticipated a piece celebrating the terrific haiku and origami I'd seen in their schools. They were decidedly uncomfortable when I talked about the deeper significances of Japanese classroom practices. Telexes flew, and my Japanese hosts had to be reminded of such concepts as freedom of the press. I finally agreed only to remove any mention of which Japanese corporation sponsored the American students' and teachers' trip. The irony of the matter is that my piece is in no way anti-Japanese. It is, in fact, eminently more respectful of Japanese culture and traditions than are the sycophantic pieces written in the food-tastes-better-when-eaten-with-chopsticks mode. A number of Japan experts have told me I got the Japan part right. The teacher in me knows I got the American part right.

When Jim Collins, the editor of the *Vital Signs* series, invited me to write a piece for his issue on collaboration, I was delighted. I love being given a topic. Before Jim called with the topic, I'd pretty much avoided getting close to collaboration talk because I didn't like the self-righteous smugness of the language surrounding it. I accepted Jim's invitation because I knew he would let me say what I ended up needing to say. "Collaboration, Silence, and Solitude" is the result. It was excerpted in *Education Week* and provoked the nastiest bit of public diatribe I've ever encountered. My answer is to say the best thing a teacher or writer can say: *I stand by my words.*

Stacks of Letters

I TEACH WHAT is called a language arts tutorial class of thirty middle-grade students who have been given every label from "culturally deprived" and "learning disabled" to "minimally brain dysfunctioned" and "slow learner." Professional journals offer many articles and ads to help me deal with my students. Curriculum innovators put forth all kinds of ideas about how to teach these children. I find most of these materials and methods either too esoteric or too dull.

The innovators seem to cluster at two extremes. At one end are the "find the poet in every child" adherents. Every other day, kids are exhorted to write five words on how it feels to be a butterfly. At the other end of the extreme are those who entreat us to teach practical "life skills." I think of them as proponents of the phone book curriculum.

I don't knock the idea of looking for the poet in every kid. My own classroom has its share of colorful butterflies hanging from the ceiling, five words dangling from each. And I, too, have students fill out job applications, read driver's manuals, and wear out countless phone books with exercises on how to use the Yellow Pages and locate emergency numbers. Phone books and butterflies are useful, even necessary, pedagogic ploys, but neither of them do much to improve a child's writing skills.

One day I looked at all the writing my kids did and realized that none of it *involved* them; it had no meaning for them. So I asked myself: What kind of writing has meaning to me? And I realized that the first thing I do when I get home from school is rush to the mailbox. My father writes to me every day, and I rely on his letters. Even when his news is just a summary of weather conditions and a comment about weeding the garden, his note, for a few moments, gives me a personal link to someone three thousand miles away.

So I set out to introduce my class to letter writing. The students were stunned at the idea of writing a letter to me. Most of them had never written a letter, and few had ever received one. They could see me, talk to me, touch me. Why write?

A Metamorphosis

I remember Barry's first letter very well: "I HATE writing letters. My weekend was terrible." Barry was sent to my tutorial class two months after school had started. He was sullen, withdrawn, uncommunicative, and so antagonistic about being in my class that I decided to leave him alone, to let him find his own way gradually. But I did insist on letters. I answered him:

> Dear Barry,
>   My husband would sympathize with you. I have never seen anyone who hates to write letters as much as he does. After being married to him for more than ten years, I have finally given up trying to force him to write his parents. I write to them instead. However, Barry, I am not ready to give up on you. You just need some practice.
>   What was so terrible about your weekend? I'll tell you what was terrible about mine. I HATE snow! My driveway is so long to shovel, it makes me sore just to look at it.
>
> Your friend,
> Mrs. Ohanian

> Dear Mrs. Ohanian,
>   I love shoveling snow. Shoveling snow gives you strong muszels. My snow-mobile blew a clutch. And I had to buy a new one.

> Dear Barry,
>   Do you go snowmobiling when the weather is this cold? Michael wrote that he went ice fishing. I think he is crazy. What do you think?
>
> Your friend,
> Mrs. O.

> Dear Mrs. O,
>   When you ride a snowmobile you don't get cold because the heat from the motor keeps you warm. But when you go ice fishing you get cold because you are just standing there. Or sitting.

Our letters continued in this fashion: I was careful to sign every letter "your friend"; Barry didn't even sign his name. I was also careful to ask Barry a question in every letter, and he always answered it. Then one day he asked *me* a question: "What do you do during the summer when there is no school?" Instead of writing him the answer, I took the chance of speaking to him directly (up to this point all our communication had been on paper). I said, "Wow, Barry, your question really makes me wish for summer." We talked for ten minutes about what we liked to do in the summer. Other kids joined the conversation. Barry had never before talked to any of them. Soon after that, Barry started working in my class, and teachers in his other classes reported a metamorphosis in his behavior and study habits.

I know that writing has been therapeutic for Barry. He started out writing, "I HATE writing" and proceeded to write every day, telling me about his snowmobile, his fort, about the fact that his father lives in the country and his mother and stepfather live in the city. There may not be a poet in Barry struggling to get out, but there is a country boy struggling to become reconciled to the city:

> Dear Mrs. O,
>   I like the country a lot. I was born on a farm. A BIG farm.
>   In the summertime we have a BIG BIG garden. We have a tracktor. In our garden we have corn, tomatoes, strawberries, carrots, potatoes, and other things.
>
> Your friend,
> Barry

Humor, Advice, Empathy

People look at Michael's spelling and can't see his charm. Once I complained to him about the snow in January and he replied, "I take the months as thae come." His family was planning a trip to Florida and he wrote, "I'm getting excited about florada coming so soon. I herd that thae are cansuling flits to save on gass. I don't no fi they wod cnsul our flite. I hoep thae don't." Because of illness, his family had to cancel the trip. Michael wrote me, "Now I'm not going to florada I can onle wish you the best of luk of your trip to calafrna and hop the wethur is gud."

Although writing is difficult for Michael, he is a regular correspondent. I showed some of Michael's notes to a graduate professor of humanities, who did not find anything charming or amusing in them. Michael's mother, however, read his letters and felt hope. She had no idea Michael could read and write letters of any kind. As she was leaving my classroom she said, "Maybe he'll write you from the Senate one day."

The letters are important to many of the kids' parents. Barry's mother and stepfather came to school to check his progress. I showed them two packets of his letters. They sat down and read them aloud to each other, enjoying shared memories. Joey's mother read her son's entire packet of letters and asked me in disbelief, "You mean he could read what you wrote? You didn't have to read it to him?" My kids' comprehension has amazed me too. I don't write letters with a "carefully controlled" vocabulary. In the beginning the kids claimed they couldn't read my handwriting, couldn't understand the big words. Now I am seldom asked to decipher any of my letters, and I know they are reading them because they are responding. Some days I watch them chuckling over my notes and concentrating on their answers, and I feel as though I should hold my breath in the presence of a miracle.

I never know when I will strike a nerve. One day I couldn't think of a thing to write to Kevin, so I asked, "What happens at a stock-car race? I've never been." Kevin, who always complains when asked to write, wrote all period and asked to stay after class to finish his reply. His answer, in very small handwriting, filled six pages.

Debbie has a speech impediment and came to us from a training school for wayward girls. She sat and glowered at me for three months before we started the letter project. From the first day, she has been one of my most enthusiastic letter writers, always asking about my husband and my cats. I once asked her about her favorite dessert, and she copied down the recipe so I could try it for myself.

Occasionally I have students write to each other. Each child chooses a different period, writes a note and puts it in an addressed envelope. We hang the envelopes from the ceiling with strings. There is always great excitement when students come into class and discover they have mail. Their excitement lasts for an exchange of three or four letters, whereupon the students run out of things to write about, complain about each other's bad penmanship and spelling, and ask me to start writing to them again instead. But it is fun for a short time now and again.

The Rewards of Persistence

Our letter-writing project has achieved a number of things. It has taught the children in a real way that a letter is a good means of communication. It has increased student fluency. It has even induced more positive attitudes in students, which delights me. Many who started out just answering my questions eventually began to copy my style and insert such comments as: "I liked your last letter" or "I hope you have a good weekend."

If the business of a language arts teacher is to develop a child's reading and writing skills, imagination, intellect, and empathy, what better way is there to strengthen these abilities than through letter correspondence? Too many teachers assign too many tedious chores. If they tried a few of these assignments themselves, they'd never require them again. In this writing project, I am as involved as the students. The kids see me chuckling over their letters; they see me writing replies while I'm on hall duty. They call out to me, "Have you got to mine yet?" Because I sometimes get tired of writing letters, I can sympathize when a student writes, "I really can't think of anything to say today." Usually I'll write back, "I know what you mean. Today is slow for me too."

Several colleagues have expressed concern that all this letter writing must be very time-consuming for the teacher. I cannot deny that; but it is also very rewarding. When I tire of writing letters, I need only remind myself that it must be at least a hundred times easier for *me* to write a letter than it is for Michael.

Other colleagues have liked my idea and have introduced letter writing into their own classrooms. Without exception, they have been enthusiastic about the results. You cannot teach writing from static merchandise—from a shiny box of story starters or a thick workbook or a set of dittos. I have been teaching for fifteen years—first grade through college—and I have tried many different techniques to inspire students to write clearly, powerfully, meaningfully. Each day I am astounded anew at the effects my letter project has had on these seventh and eighth graders—and on me. John Donne put it very well centuries ago: "Letters mingle souls."

Love, Leslie

LESLIE AND I started third grade together. I arrived from ten years of teaching seventh graders. For a while, we didn't know where Leslie came from. She arrived carrying a hastily scrawled note from the secretary, "Leslie is deaf. We are trying to get her folder." My third-grade colleagues and I held a mini-caucus in the hallway: "Can she hear at all? Can she speak? Do you know what to do?"

Of course we had a right to be angry and the Special Ed supervisor would soon know it, but anger and apologies don't sharpen pencils, so I smiled and said, "Welcome to our class." Leslie stared at me, her face solemn. A tear ran down her cheek. She put her head down on her desk and didn't look up for an hour.

Leslie didn't say a word to me or the other children for two days. I soon discovered, however, that she and I could communicate. I gave everybody a small spiral notebook with a welcoming note inside. My note to Leslie, like the others, explained that I would write her every day and I hoped she would write me back every day. Leslie read my note and suddenly her solemn little face broke into a wide grin. She grabbed a pencil and wrote:

Dear Mrs. O,
Thank you thank you thank you for writing to me. I will write you every day. I will write you 2 times a day. I will write you 10 times a day.
Good bye.

That note cheered me up. Now I knew something important about Leslie. Not only could she read, she could write with a real voice, and she liked repetition and exaggeration. I put a copy of *Pinkerton, Behave!* on her desk along with my next note, saying, "You write like Steven Kellogg, so I think you will like his book."

Leslie was thrilled, showing my note to Dougie, whose desk was next to hers—her first attempt to communicate with another child. "Wow! Can I have that book when you finish, Leslie?" he asked. Leslie grinned and nodded. So now we knew some more important things: Leslie could lip-read, and she was willing to reach out to other children. I knew things were going to be all right.

Suddenly I realized that although it might be important to continue nagging the Special Education Department "for the principle of the thing," I needed to face up to the fact that no expert was going to step forward and tell me what I needed to know about Leslie.

I remembered what Ned O'Gorman wrote in his lovely little book *The Wilderness and the Laurel Tree:* "A teacher will learn about children by watching them first of all; not by reading about them or talking to experts about them."

So during my first week in third grade, I resolved to stop giving myself excuses, to stop fantasizing that I could teach Leslie better if only I had information about her previous schooling, if only I had detailed guidance on how to teach the deaf, if only I had special equipment. *If onlys* don't sharpen any pencils. Instead, I resolved to watch Leslie and base my plans on what I saw.

In her next note Leslie wrote, "Thank you for that funny dog book. It is a nice story and I love the pictures but I like cats better. Do you have any cat stories?"

Now the kid was talking my language. Asking me for cat stories is definitely carrying coals to Newcastle.

Long before Leslie's special equipment arrived, a microphone for me and a receiver for her, we knew she could talk. During that first week, I wrote her a note about my cats and she responded with a note about her cats. I looked up from her note and asked, "What are your cats' names?" Leslie told me.

"Leslie can talk!" exclaimed Dougie.

"Of course I can talk!" Leslie was indignant. "What did you think?" There was a moment of silence as we all stared at her. I hugged her. "We weren't sure. You've been here two days, and you haven't said a word."

"I was scared," she whispered. "I'm handicapped and I've never done this before. And besides, I didn't know if you could understand the way deaf people talk." This was a litany Leslie repeated all year long whenever she faced something new. She cried, stamped her foot, and wailed, "I'm handicapped."

Leslie was spoiled, overprotected; she cried a lot. She was also brave, determined, exuberant, strong-willed, loving; she laughed a lot. I spent a lot of time hugging her, wiping her tears, finding special books to delight her, writing her notes. And she wrote back. Neither of us missed a day.

Dear Mrs. O,
  Thank you for showing me that new book. I love pretty books. Even if I don't read them I still love them.

Dear Mrs. O.
  Rumpelstiltskin makes me so happy I get goose bumps.

Dear Mrs. O.
   I love you so so so so so much. Millions and billions and trillions and super de dooper.

Like her classmates, Leslie sprinkled her notes with snippets from books she loved. This one is quite an accomplishment: Leslie has squeezed in allusions to e.e. cummings, Wanda Geig, and Dr. Seuss.

   Leslie gave me many gifts during our year together: she taught me important lessons about handicaps and bravery and kids' ability to stick together and help one another. And Leslie showed me that unlike most writing assignments that are completed and then forgotten, personal notes live forever. In May she wrote, "What kind of soup did you eat on 3/16/83?" I was a bit puzzled until I flipped back in her notebook and saw that on 3/16/83 I'd written to her that I'd cooked a big pot of soup.

   When Leslie and her classmates couldn't think of anything to say, they'd go back through the spiral bound notebooks, rereading old notes, trying to find something they could use as a springboard for new communication. They loved to look back and count all the notes they'd written, and then report their findings in very large letters, "THIS IS THE 85th NOTE I'VE WRITTEN YOU!!!!!!!!!!"

   I like to reread notes too. There's no way that Leslie would part with her notebook in June. "It's my souvenir of third grade!" she announced. But she lent it to me to photocopy, and it's my souvenir too.

Dear Leslie,
   My cat begged and begged for turkey for dinner. So I gave him some. I hate to see a cat cry.

Dear Mrs. O,
   I love it when your cat cries. I laugh a lot. Goodbye.

Dear Leslie,
   I love it when you laugh. When you laugh, you are beautiful.

Dear Mrs. O,
   I know you think I'm beautiful. My pop does too. My pop says I'm beautiful and my mom says I'm beautiful and I am happy. My mom and me love you. Jesus loves you too.

I wrote Leslie that my husband baked muffins and she answered,

Dear Mrs. O,
   What kind of muffins did he make? Fill in the answer here _____ . Were they good? _____ Did he clean up his mess? _____ Did the cats like the muffins? _____
   P.S. This is your homework.

12

In one note I asked Leslie what kind of ice cream she liked and she started laughing—and writing. She wrote and wrote, shrugging off any other work with the insistence she was writing a very important note and needed time to finish it.

Dear Mrs. O,
    I like lemon ice cream, vanilla ice cream, butterscotch swirl ice cream.

On and on her list continued—thirty-one flavors that she copied from a menu I'd given the class. Leslie thought it was a wonderful joke—and a lovely surprise—as she painstakingly wrote the entire list in her newly-acquired cursive. So did I.

Even more lovely to behold was the way the benefits of letter writing moved outward from the teacher's desk. One spring day Leslie, who was very proud of her artistic talents, drew a beautiful picture on the board. Carol, participating in a math contest nearby, accidentally erased Leslie's picture. Leslie had hysterics, and nobody could have hysterics the way Leslie could.

Carol felt unhappy she had caused the crisis but soon became aggrieved at all the fuss. Carol sat at her desk. She picked up a book but obviously wasn't reading it. We all tried to go on with our work. After Leslie ran out of sobs and sighs she buried her head in her arms on her desk. After half an hour of this, Carol wrote a note to Leslie:

Dear Leslie,
    I am sorry I erased your picture. It was a nice one. I like you and I like the way you draw and I want to still be your friend.

Carol folded this note up into a tiny square and made an envelope for it, which she then sealed shut with half the tape in my dispenser. Then she pushed the note under Leslie's elbow.

Of course Leslie couldn't resist it and soon became engrossed in getting all that tape off the envelope. She was thrilled with the note—showed it to me and immediately started a reply:

Dear Carol,
    It's OK. I want to be your friend still. You can come to my birthday party. Don't worry. Your friend, Leslie, LOVE.

These children were no more than two feet away from each other during the crisis. They never exchanged a spoken word but settled their differences and soothed their wounds through the note exchange.

One dismal day during my annual February panic, when bureaucratic nonsense combined with the conviction that winter would never end and that I hadn't taught the kids a thing, Leslie hugged me as she left the room. Very earnestly she said, "Now don't you worry. It's OK. We're going to get it. You are doing a good job." And her note that day recounted a new adventure with her cat. She added, "P.S. A lot of people love you."

No, we aren't always aware of just what we are teaching. I didn't know my February desperation was so obvious to the children. I hadn't guessed my love for Leslie would be returned tenfold.

When, in November, Leslie's parents began to panic, fearing that "regular" school was too difficult for her, when they wanted to put her back in a sheltered environment for the handicapped, I fought against it. I used her notes as proof of her ability to cope and even triumph in public school. In June, Leslie's mother wrote me a lovely thank you letter. In it, she said, "I was going to phone you, but Leslie insisted that I write. She said if I write it down you will know that I really mean it, that when you really care about a person you write them a letter."

Leslie still writes. In the spring before she graduated from eighth grade, she wrote to tell me she was in a regular program and on the honor roll. She said she owed her academic success to me and to Jesus. I gladly accept my half of the credit because I'm the one who taught her knock-knock jokes. But that's another story. . . .

The Tantalizing Vagueness of Teaching

In 1916, ROBERT FROST wrote his friend and fellow poet Louis Unter-meyer that a poem "begins as a lump in the throat." Frost also noted that a poem is "at its best when it is a tantalizing vagueness." I feel the same way about teaching.

That's why I become uncomfortable and even irate when committee-persons insist that a good teacher's performance can be charted and graphed, and then rewarded accordingly.

If someone appears in my doorway and says, "I'm going to examine your anticipatory sets," I wonder if I have the right to make one phone call first. Teachers have been polite too long to managerial types, fellows with bulging briefcases of checklists with terms like *praise as positive reinforcer, demonstration of mastery, time on task,* and other slimy slugs of that ilk.

We are teachers. Teachers. Teachers. We traffic in words and ideas and feelings and hopes, not in goods or systems, not even in five-tiered career ladders. I hear the blizzard of words spewed forth about teacher compe-tency and I want to ask, "Why me?"

Do we see such high-level scrutiny of other professions—of doctors, for example? After all, their collegial cover-ups are notorious—and life-threatening. Yet I can't pick up my morning newspaper and find out what my surgeon's operating mortality rate is. Nor do I know what percentage of his diagnoses are correct. Would the AMA sponsor the idea of box scores for doctors' performances—or merit pay?

But if teachers can prove they are competent, say our education man-agers, society will pay them accordingly. Hah. American values simply aren't skewed that way. Sports figures might easily get $500,000—or $5,000,000—to hit around a little white ball. But teachers can't command much—mainly because we don't have any special skills that are observ-able. What we do looks fairly easy; most people feel they could do the teaching part, though they acknowledge that putting up with the kids all day might be a bit difficult. Our real skills, of course, are secret. Nobody ever knows when we hit a home run or a grand slam, and that's why we can never be paid what we're worth.

It doesn't take the perception of a parsnip to realize that teachers didn't enter the calling to get rich. Yet these education managers persist in ignoring—and even eliminating—the very qualities that did lead us into the fold. They talk a lot about skills, for example, but don't mention a sense of humor or a tolerance for ambiguity or an enjoyment of children.

Behaviorists have long insisted that they can deliver the carefully delineated subskills of learning. Now they are marketing a similar package for teaching. Some administrators label this move to standardize teaching as a clarion call for excellence. A lot of us veteran teachers see it as an ultimately catastrophic worship of systems at the expense of people.

I am particularly bothered by the growing popularity of teacher evaluation forms that are supposed to be objective, systematic, impersonal. Such forms tell no more about essential teacher qualities than do a box of jujubes. The time is past due for teachers to stand up and say, "No! Your checklists and timetables run counter to what goes on in a vital, stimulating, nurturing classroom." The time is past due for the professors of education to step down from their ivory towers and to become involved in what's happening in the schools. If they form one more committee or draft one more recommendation, let it be on the importance of human relations in the classroom. Let them form a task force to protect teachers . . . and children.

The education managers who hand out competency tests and who write up official classroom observations make a critical mistake. They insist that prospective teachers should prove what they know. But we veteran teachers realize that the hard part of being a teacher has nothing to do with facts. Yes, teachers need to know where the apostrophes should land, but more important, they need to be nurturing human beings. They must be optimistic and enthusiastic about the possibilities of the children in their care. They must be flexible and able to bounce back after sixty-three defeats — ready and even anxious to try again.

I'm not much interested in seeing how a teacher carefully structures her lesson so that the kids stick to the objectives and the bell always rings in the right place — just after she makes her summary and gives the prelude for what will come tomorrow. I want to find out if that teacher is tough and loving and clever and flexible. I want to be sure she's more nurturing than a halibut. . . . What does she do when a kid vomits (all over those neat lesson plans)? Or an indignant parent rushes in denouncing the homework? Or the worst troublemaker breaks his arm and needs special help? Or the movie-projector bulb burns out, and the replacements have to come from Taiwan? Or somebody spots a cockroach under her desk?

A teacher's talents for dealing with crises aren't easily revealed on an evaluation report or rewarded on a salary schedule. And neither are those special moments that a teacher savors. So don't yield to the number crunchers — even when they dangle a golden carrot in front of you. Remember that the most wonderful joys of teaching happen in the blink of an eye and are often unplanned and unexpected. You can miss their importance and lose their sustenance if your eyes are glassily fixed on the objective you promised your principal you'd deliver that day. When you maintain a sharp eye and the ability to jump off the assigned task, the rewards are many—when a child discovers a well-turned phrase; or a mother phones and says, "Our whole family enjoyed the homework. Please send more"; or the shiest child in the room announces *she* wants to be the narrator in the class play; or the class bully smiles quietly over a poem. Our joy is in the daily practice of our craft, not in the year-end test scores or the paycheck. When outside experts ignore this, then we must stop and remind ourselves. We must talk, not of time on task but of the tantalizing vagueness and the lumps in the throat, the poetry and true purpose of our calling.

Collaboration, Silence, and Solitude

AMAZING AS IT seems, eight years ago microwave popcorn didn't exist. Today it rates half an aisle in my supermarket and the annual per capita consumption tops forty-six quarts. We are witnessing a similarly rapid rise in the collaboration curve, going from 2.8 mentions per 10,000 words in educational journals in 1982 to 1,345 in 1989. As we enter this new decade, collaboration ranks second only to journal keeping as the badge of right-minded professionalism.

Teachers can never sit back and take it easy. Just when we think we've outrun the systems analysts — the Mastery Learning folk and their seven-step lesson-plan kin, we find ourselves in danger of being pedagogically mugged by guys wearing white hats. We have university research projects, ed-biz-whiz consultants crisscrossing the country, and warm, fuzzy teacher-support groups telling us we aren't whole if we aren't working in teams. Zealotry runs high. Disagree with a collaborationist and more than likely you'll find yourself trying to prove you aren't a fascist.

For some, instant conversion to the collaborationist/cooperative mode does not require a lot of preparation. *Item:* At a recent whole language conference I picked up a bit of flotsam called *Whole Language Lesson Plan* in which the teacher-author establishes a category called *Cooperative Learning Activities* and insists that "anything you would ask one student to do can be accomplished cooperatively."

Indeed.

Item: In a recent book on collaboration published by one of our major professional organizations, I read that "teachers should imitate the practices of scientists, scholars, journalists, and businesspeople" and encourage their students to write collaboratively.

Freeman Dyson, Jeremy Bernstein, Stephen Jay Gould, P. B. Medawar, where are your collaborators? And are the ghostwriters hired by Donald Trump, Lee Iacocca, et al. the collaborative model to which we aspire? It is worse than simplistic to claim that if we want our students to think like scientists we should stick them in groups. When *New Yorker* writer Ved Mehta was asked about the relationship between creativity in the sciences and in the arts, he observed, "What a good writer shares with a good scientist is a sense of the ironic, an ability to look at the same thing everybody else is seeing and see something different, something surprising, something fresh. In that way the good scientist and the good writer are both skeptics, and both have a capacity for wonder" (Shekerjian 1990, 175).

It takes a very single-minded skepticism to survive a committee. Can we expect an eight-year-old or a thirteen-year-old or a forty-five-year-old to be that hard-nosed? Mandated classroom collaboration seems designed to breed conformity rather than a sense of irony.

Item: Collaboration is a hot item and travels under a variety of aliases. School district managers, for example, have learned to subvert union activism by instituting a collaborative model called shared decision making. I have in front of me the minutes of a meeting of a joint administrative-teacher group called the Shared Decision-Making Steering Committee. The group got together to discuss the four-step procedures for creating and disseminating "Shared Decision written communications." Of course, nobody chaired the meeting; it was facilitated. And the minutes demonstrate what can happen when you let a committee into your life:

1. The General Steering Committee will determine if a communication should be issued.
2. A subcommittee will be formed to develop the communication (involving at least one member from the Steering Committee).
3. The subcommittee will report back to the Steering Committee for discussions, alterations, and general approval of the survey.
4. The communication will be distributed to the full building membership.

I assure you that this is an exact, word-for-word rendition of this committee report. One thing about being a chronicler of education: you don't have to invent a thing. Parody is nigh impossible: the real McCoy is bizarre enough to defy exaggeration. Too often in education we jump on bandwagons and end up parodying ourselves.

Does it come as any surprise that district administrators are fully supportive of this sort of thing? In a district where not one teacher was sent to a statewide writing conference held less than twenty miles away or a regional whole language conference little more than twenty miles away, administrators send teachers hundreds of miles out of town to be turned into facilitators of shared decisioning. It makes sense. Keep folks busy enough figuring out rules and regulations for putting memos in teachers' mailboxes and there won't be much time left for meddling with the curriculum, reforming the scandal of special education, or agitating for better working conditions.

This district has a long history of training teachers in how to be other-directed. Following on the heels of teacher inservice training in assertive discipline, Madeline Hunter, mastery learning, shared decision making, computer-assisted instruction, critical thinking, differential mentoring, and creative visualization, this district has recently instituted teacher inservice training in cooperative learning. The same teacher-leaders — no, make that facilitators — who trained everybody to stand in front of the mirror and practice saying, "I like the way you . . ." are now gearing up for training sessions on classroom chair rearrangement. Honest.

The collaborative learning process, as folks like to say in ed-speak, looks good to some people for the same reason they hankered after file drawers full of behavioral objectives, seven-step lesson plans, and the M & M theory of crowd control: they are in desperate need for a technique that will get those kids to behave. And no matter how you wrap it up, all these neat and tidy programs become little more than mechanisms for social control.

I guess the thing that distresses me most about the collaborationists is that they don't seem to get around to talking much about *what* they teach; they seem concerned only with something they call group process, group interaction. And so collaborationists join a long queue of ed-biz-whiz systematologists crisscrossing the country peddling their wares. They don't need NCTE or IRA because they look neither to the right nor to the left at the matter being learned — nor at the kids doing the learning; for them method is all. A spoonful of togetherness makes the curriculum go down. And calms the restless.

The first time somebody tried to force me to write collaboratively was at the New York State Writing Conference. According to the program, two presenters were going to talk about how they collaborate to teach writing in an urban middle school. After some preliminary moaning over the fact that we couldn't get our chairs into a circle, the presenters told us to get out our pencils and open our notebooks because we were going to write for ten minutes. "We're going to recreate the feelings of terror, anguish, and impotence we experienced in our youth when the teacher demanded we *write* and we stared in terror at the blank page," announced the group leader, an earnest-looking type straight out of the L. L. Bean catalogue. "And then we'll share. And collaborate to produce better writing."

Neither common courtesy nor the ignominy of creating an uproar in front row center could keep me in my chair. I stepped on thirteen toes and eighteen shopping bags stuffed with publishers' wares while scrambling to make my escape. As I neared the door, the group leader commented in a patient, sorrowful-but-understanding tone about teachers who are so threatened by the thought of exposing themselves in writing that they can't even *stay* in such a session.

Indeed.

I guess writing conferences are ever in danger of turning into mini-EST sessions, and I've since gotten pretty savvy about avoiding gatherings that attempt to practice Primal Pen Therapy. Writing is the way I make my living. And I take it so seriously that even for the sake of politeness, I refuse to engage in little ten-minute scribble-and-share games. I marvel at the exhibitionism of these collaborative writing groups popping up everywhere. Maybe someday the National Science Foundation or the National Association of Pigeon Fanciers or a group of similar public spirit will fund a study to determine the ratio of sharing to publication. Writing is so crummy on the nerves that unless you're writing a letter to your mother or your Congressman, why would you do it except for publication?

For me, to talk about a piece is to kill it, and not even my husband and best editor ever can take a peek until I've been through sixty-three drafts and prepared the final copy eight times. Sometimes, even after all that, I'm still too touchy to risk talk. I just send it off and a distant editor becomes the first reader. Writing is the most private thing I do. It is entirely solitary. I don't start to write a piece until I've thought about it a month . . . or a year. I spend a lot of time avoiding writing. But once I've finally forced myself to start writing, I'd maim anybody who tried to sneak a look after I'd been at it for only ten minutes. And the only person's writing I am interested in taking a look at ten minutes—or ten hours—after he's started is Calvin Trillin's.

Franz Kafka wrote to Felice Bauer, "You once said that you would like to sit beside me while I wrote. Listen, in that case I could not write at all." Kafka went on, "One can never be alone enough when one writes . . . there can never be enough silence around one when one writes . . . even night is not night enough."

What a chilling and accurate refutation of the collaborationist chorus singing hosannahs to writing as a social act: *one can never be alone enough . . . even night is not night enough.*

Nicole, an eight-year-old in Georgia, agrees with Franz Kafka. Sally Hudson-Ross, professor of language education at the University of Georgia, presented tapes of her interviews with Nicole the writer at the 1989 NCTE Spring Convention in Charleston. A third grader, Nicole writes prolifically at home but doesn't write much at school. For one thing, all the talk at school bothers Nicole. She says she needs quiet when she writes and as soon as someone starts talking in the classroom, "It's like an eraser that comes up to you and goes 'Swish!'"

Nicole also points out that she doesn't like reading her writing aloud: "I just don't like the idea of other people hearing what I write." Sally asked Nicole why she likes to write but many of the other kids don't. "What would you tell them about why they should like to write?"

"They shouldn't like to write," insists Nicole. "If they like to write, they like to write. If they don't, they don't."

Nicole is my kind of person. I confess I'd let a lot of teachers off the hook about writing. A teacher's competence should not be judged by the pile of personal journals she keeps. Likewise, not everybody wants to sit around in groups baring her soul. There should be room for the private person in our schools. We should stop haranguing teachers about twisting themselves into somebody else's model of teacherliness.

A book with collaboration in the title recently published by one of our major professional organizations dismisses the notion of one person sitting down all alone to write as a "romantic ideal." Indeed. Dr. Seuss disagrees. "You can get help from teachers, but you are going to have to learn a lot by yourself, sitting alone in a room."

But the idea of sitting alone in a room with a piece of paper is a very scary notion for 99.83 percent of the people in this country, teachers being no exception. And as for reading, how many of the people we know, the people who run our schools, the people we elect to Congress and the White House, are much different from that Vladimir Nabokov character who, "had he been condemned to spend a whole day shut up in a library, would have been found dead about noon"?

When I taught third grade, we started the day with fifteen minutes of sustained silent reading. That's what it said in my plan book, anyway. I thought I'd have to tie those kids into their chairs to keep them there five minutes. And even when they became convinced that I'd have to see blood gushing before I'd let anybody move from the chair to go to the nurse or call his lawyer, they didn't read: they sat quietly and watched me read. For months. It was a scary time for me, but I kept reading and I buttressed myself with a stubborn faith in kids and good books. Eventually, that faith flowered. By March those children were complaining that they were "right in the good part" when I called a halt to silent reading at the end of an hour each morning.

When I tell this story as the miracle of third grade, a lot of people are upset. When did I teach? they ask. How did I make myself accountable for learning, how did I assess the children's progress during that hour of silence? Some questions aren't worth heeding. If I answer at all it's with talk of miracles. One miracle is obvious: in a rigorously grouped school, this crew was the bottom, the rotten readers of third grade. Kids repeating the grade, kids labeled with all sorts of dysfunctions, and kids mainstreamed out of special ed were all reading on their own for an hour a day. The other miracles were individualistic, twenty-one separate, magical connections made with books. And I tell their individual stories every chance I get.

Nonetheless, that hour of silence makes a whole lot of people nervous. And I know why. Not many people believe you learn to read by reading. It's too simple. And if truth be known, not many adults can sit and read on their own for an hour every day. And not many teachers can keep quiet for an hour a day.

As a part of a big university teacher-training grant, I was once tested on my tolerance for ambiguity. Certainly no one who has ever seen me in a classroom or taken a look at my office would be surprised that I came out exhibiting a very high tolerance for ambiguity. A straight-row, lesson-plan-in-place, learning-outcomes-on-the-chalkboard teacher I ain't.

There was no surprise, either, that my as-organized-as-a-new-deck-of-cards, team-teaching partner, the person with whom I worked in the same seventh- and eighth-grade classroom for six years, came out on the same test exhibiting almost no tolerance for ambiguity. We came close to being a pedagogical Odd Couple and yet we taught together in a cordial, supportive manner and I think we did a bang-up job.

There's a lot of talk these days about learning styles. How about teaching styles? For six years, my cohort and I taught side by side, and although there was a lot of give-and-take between us, I wouldn't say we collaborated. She taught what she taught the way she wanted to teach it. I did likewise. We worked out a system that seemed to suit us and the students in our care.

If I hadn't already known it, those six years of team teaching showed me that there are different teaching temperaments. There's no one best teaching style any more than there's any one best learning style. What a teacher needs to do is find the teaching style that suits her temperament and then hone that style, gnaw her own bone, ignoring the clamor of bandwagons that go careening by. In Jung's words, "The shoe that fits one person pinches another; there is no recipe for living that suits all cases." But the consultant cooks keep trying to lure us with yet another dish.

If I sometimes wonder how come I still can't hyphenate words even after six years of hearing my partner teach the sixteen rules of syllabification, I remain grateful that she turned my eclecticism into lesson plans that passed muster. And besides, she's the one who showed me *Flat Stanley*.

I suspect all this collaboration mania was probably invented by editors, and teachers had better be very wary about letting themselves think too much like editors, the guys who also invented committee meetings, *People* magazine, and 93 percent of the stuff on television. I'm pretty sure editors are also responsible for PopTarts, the designated-hitter rule, and Call Waiting, but I can't prove it.

Collaboration is, after all, just a fancy name for committee, and as C. Northcote Parkinson once observed, like the House of Representatives and a den of thieves, a committee is a noun of multitude. And no good ever came from a multitude. I have nothing against people getting together and patting each other on the back. Teachers need all the kind strokes they can get, and what they do in their spare time is certainly their own business. But when collaborationism moves into the classroom, I worry. We're not talking here about kids chatting, kids working on a project together, kids

23

going off to read their stories to younger children. We're talking about systematized schemes with the teacher grading each segment as an Olympic judge scoring the compulsories in figure skating. Most formalized classroom collaboration plans handed down from the universities turn out to be little more than elaborate crowd-control devices training kids to subordinate their quirky individualism to the corporate good.

I read of strategies to train children to "perceive that they can obtain their goal if and only if the other people with whom they are joined can obtain their goals," but I see no acknowledgment of a down side to forcing youngsters into an other-directed, gray-flannel mold of group value judgments. Maybe nobody reads David Reisman any more. And I wonder, are the same fellows who collect paychecks for teaching kids to "just say no" to peer pressure in drug education also getting paid for training kids to think they can find success only in peer-group process? All in the same week?

Some folks posit collaboration as the opposite of ugly, roughneck competition. Not so. Nobody talks much about the training necessary for the gradebook explosion that follows in the wake of the imposition of cooperative learning groups. Although a degree in statistics is not essential to figuring out individual and group improvement bonuses each week in the Johns Hopkins cooperative learning model, for example, it wouldn't hurt to have a sister-in-law who's a C.P.A. And the bonuses are important because that's where the payoff comes as so-called cooperative groups compete against one another for top billing, first-prize certificates, pizza parties, and the like.

For me the opposite of collaboration is not competition but quietude. And silence doesn't sell. There's no pizzazz in silence.

Nonetheless, silence is necessary. Oxford lecturer in psychiatry Anthony Storr (1988, 28) argues that "some development of the capacity to be alone is necessary if the brain is to function at its best, and if the individual is to fulfill his highest potential." Storr insists solitude is necessary for "learning, thinking, innovation," that solitude promotes insight as well as change, and that although everyone needs some human relationships, "everyone also needs some kind of fulfillment which is relevant to himself alone."

Maybe, instead of commending to our students a corporate committee model of collaboration, we should share with them *Mississippi Solo*, Eddy Harris' account of paddling a canoe—alone—the 2,350-mile length of the Mississippi River, from its beginnings in Lake Itasca in Minnesota to New Orleans. Or how about *Equator*, Thurston's Clarke's account of his three-year travels around the world along the equator? Both of these travelers meet plenty of people along the way, but in each case the journey is highly individualistic, the quest more interior than exterior.

In his *Pre-History of the Far Side,* cartoonist Gary Larson notes that the cartoonist's world is a silent one: "the cartoonist never hears laughter, groans, curses, fits of rage, or anything" (1989, 155). The cartoonist works alone. Although, as Larson himself admits, the book is not for the "humoristically squeamish," it does give us a revealing peek at the conflict between a creator's wackiness and committeespeak, his editor's public concerns. As we see how a Larson cartoon goes from idea to publication (or extinction), we get a glimpse of one person's solitary creativity.

Maybe kids and their teachers need to know about General John E. Hull. He was in charge at the American Air Force base at Iwakuni, Japan, on a May morning in 1955 when twenty-five Japanese women, badly crippled and disfigured by the atomic blast at Hiroshima, were to begin their trip for medical help in America. They were already aboard the U. S. Air Force plane when an aide dashed up to General Hull with an urgent cable from Washington. Not wishing to risk repercussions should the Hiroshima women encounter medical complications, a committee at the State Department had ordered the flight canceled. For a long moment, General Hull said nothing. Then he handed the cable back to his aide. "Unfortunately, I don't have my reading glasses with me," he said. "Be sure to remind me to read this later." And the plane took off (Barker 1985, 82).

I want my students to know such stories, stories of personal quests, individual creativity, and conscience, stories of one person standing up and obfuscating bureaucracy and group-think, one person refusing to take time for a committee vote.

Collaborationists insist "there is no type of learning task on which cooperative efforts are less effective than are competitive or individualistic efforts." They assert that cooperativeness is positively related to a number of indices of psychological health: emotional maturity, well-adjusted social relations, strong personal identity, and basic trust in, and optimism about, people. In contrast, individualistic attitudes are related to a number of indices of psychological pathology: emotional immaturity, social maladjustment, delinquency, self-alienation, and self-rejection (Johnson et al. 1988).

Indeed.

Some strange things happen in the name of collaboration. Along with a lot of talk about "increased self-esteem" and "bright kids learning to appreciate the special talents of slower kids," and "disabled kids becoming the peers of nondisabled kids," and "potential for upward mobility, and powerful synergistic reactions," there's the inescapable fact that when teachers in California collaborated to come up with a core book that every ninth grader should read so that every kid—slow, accelerated, and in-between—would have something in common to discuss, the result in a whole lot of districts was *Great Expectations*. Honest. Who could make that up? And nobody seems to be asking how people—kids and teachers—can live with that choice. I fear that all kids—slow, medium, and in-between—who are force-fed *Great Expectations* may never willingly pick up a book again. In the matter of choosing books, as in so much else, I agree with Thomas Jefferson who, in 1789, wrote to Francis Hopkinson, "If I could not go to Heaven but with a party, I would not go there at all."

For years I've kept an observation of Ann Berthoff's taped on one of my file drawers: "Pedagogy always echoes epistemology: the way we teach reflects the conception we have of what knowledge is and does, the way we think about thinking" (1981, 11). My close encounters with students over the years have affirmed that statement again and again, and I keep it in front of me as a constant reminder that not only is it true that we are what we teach, but the kids are what we teach too. And there ain't no system, no matter how we pretty it up with psychological platitudes or shove it in with bonus points, that can shortcut or systematize the power and control relationships that surround what we teach. You can't buy your control relationships prepackaged any more than you can buy your true curriculum. Some things you have to earn.

And not a year goes by that those of us in the ed-biz don't have some new terminology traps laid before us. The collaborationists provide some humdingers. I'm all for increased self-esteem and I'd probably be for powerful synergistic reactions too, if only I knew what they were. But when people start making claims about systems that ensure "bright kids learning to appreciate the special talents of slower kids," I get very nervous. I'd like to ask the same question Michael Dorris (1989) raises about his learning-disabled son Adam's education. If talented, right-thinking teachers can really produce powerful synergistic reactions and set up groups that inspire bright, nondisabled kids to appreciate the special talents of slower, developmentally dysfunctional kids, then in all the years of Adam's schooling, how come no school chum ever phoned up and talked to Adam? How come nobody ever invited Adam over?

Dorris' question broke my heart. I read it and wept, because every year I welcomed half a dozen children just like Adam—with the same good heart as Dorris acknowledges in Adam's teachers. Dorris' book cuts through the right-thinking clichés and raises profound questions about the purposes and possibilities of our classrooms. It forces us to consider retrenchment, to acknowledge that we might have laid claim to more territory than we can handle. Maybe it's past time to deflate the rhetoric, to look beyond the hubbub and hoopla, beyond what William Gass calls sword-rattling simplicities that "lie on the tip of every tongue like a bubble of spit" (1984, 22). Collaborative learning isn't going to cure plantar's warts. And it isn't going to get Adam friends.

According to one cooperative learning teacher-training manual, students are trained to "perceive that they can reach their learning goals if and only if the other students in the learning group also reach their goals." The manual continues: "Thus, students seek outcomes that are beneficial to all those with whom they are cooperatively linked. Students discuss the material with each other, help one another understand it, and encourage each other to work hard." Surely any experienced junior high teacher — or anybody who has worked on any adult committee — stands amazed at the crockful of presumption buried in that assertion. I don't believe that assumption works even with the brightest, most cooperative of students — or with the best of teachers. It just makes me tired. I think of that line by Garrison Keillor: "I began sleeping twelve to sixteen hours a day in order to have a little time by myself."

And remember Kafka: *There can never be enough silence.*

While collaborationists insist we must train, say, thirteen-year-olds in a model making them dependent on one another, I think of Sara Lawrence Lightfoot's discovery as an adolescent of "the advantages of not fitting in" (Shekerjian 1990, 206). Lightfoot cultivated this "otherness" and became only the second black woman to be a tenured professor at Harvard as well as a recipient of one of the coveted MacArthur "genius" awards. What a thought: teachers helping oddball thirteen-year-olds to capitalize on their quirks rather than training them to iron out idiosyncracies for the good of the group.

Collaboration consultants address the issue of obnoxious students who aren't effective collaborators by advising teachers to "ensure that students see the need for the skill" by putting up bulletin boards and posters. Honest. According to this theory such bulletin boards prove to the student that the teacher considers the skill important.

Indeed.

Some proponents of collaborative learning make their case on the grounds that our students come to us from families wounded by drugs, divorce, unemployment, lack of traditional values, and so on. And they posit the school as the only institution left to redress these evils. I'm not sure it's altogether easy to figure out just what the world needs. Maybe, just maybe, the world needs a few more people who can stand on their own two feet, people who can walk away from the comfort of the crowd. If you're in the bonus-points racket, perhaps it is at least as legitimate to give bonus points to kids who can set their own goals and achieve them on their own as to give them to the group-thinkers.

Wendell Berry (1983), Kentucky poet, farmer, and teacher, writes often of the accountability of words and of deeds faithful to words. If we "stand by our words," insists Berry, then we must speak in specifics about this child and this curriculum. When we are unable to stand by our words, we use abstractions, making use of the slippery language of public relations. And committees.

I think of Jack. Jack, definitely not an abstraction, wouldn't have been impressed by any bulletin boards displaying my values. Jack wouldn't have survived even ten minutes in a collaborative learning group. And nobody in the group would have survived Jack either. Surviving Jack was my job. He was a foul-mouthed, obnoxious pest. And he carried with him the fetid stink of the long unwashed. Bad enough that Jack was my problem; why should he be the burden of his classmates? Why should other kids be forced to sit with him and *perceive that they can reach their learning goals if and only if* Jack reached his? In the end, Jack's fellow students couldn't save him and neither could I. All I could do was hope that Jack would save himself.

When I found out that Jack was intrigued by Scrabble, I gave him a *Harper's* article about Scrabble hustlers in New York City. Jack was impressed by the money they made and because the article mentioned that serious Scrabble players liked the extra word lists provided in the *Funk and Wagnall's Dictionary*, he began pestering me to get that book. I pointed out that I was sure our *American Heritage Dictionary* would be adequate for his needs but he managed to convince me to order *Funk and Wagnall's*.

Once it arrived, Jack retired to a corner of the classroom with the Scrabble board — for six months. And I left him there. My supervisor deserves credit. Having hired me to teach, he then allowed me to be responsible for my students. He had faith in me and I had faith in Jack. Sort of.

There was a certain amount of tension — and needling. My supervisor would look around the room and say, "Jack still at the Scrabble?" I won't pretend that my smile didn't become a bit forced by the third or fourth month and desperate by the fifth. But I guess if I have one tenet in teaching it is that no one can *make* a resistant high school student — or a third grader, for that matter — learn anything. You can't threaten or cajole anybody into learning. You can't collaborate them into learning either. You can only provide an environment for possibilities — and hope.

Jack spent six months playing Scrabble against himself — muttering, cursing, reading the dictionary. A few weeks into this solitary marathon I did needle him into reading for half an hour a day. We had a bountiful supply of paperbacks, and Jack eventually went on buying trips with me, becoming an avid mystery fan along the way. Some California core teachers may be dismayed that he never went near Dickens and never read the same books as anyone else. Not at the same time, anyway. But I'd rather see a kid read Dick Francis with pleasure — and know he may be tempted to pick up another book when he's out of school living his life — than see him fake his way through Dickens and fear the experience has squashed any desire to go near a book again. Some days Jack would lose himself in a book for an hour or two before returning to his solitary Scrabble training. He told me he read more books in the first three months in my classroom than he'd read in ten years of more conventional school.

During this time, Jack did none of the more traditional work that occupied the other students. None of his classmates asked me, "How come?" How come they were doing assignments and Jack wasn't? Pure and simple, kids want to be regular, want to fit in. Jack was so weird that nobody wanted to be like him.

But make no mistake about it. Jack was engaged in work, very difficult work. His real work was silent and internal; it involved coming to grips with himself and his own deepest needs. His work involved first changing his view of himself and later figuring out where he might find a place for himself in the world.

Finally Jack decided he was ready. He challenged me to a Scrabble match, and he won by three hundred points. After this triumph his school day began to change. For one thing, his fellow classmates took another look. Some of them wanted to see if they could beat him at Scrabble, and after their defeat they asked him for lessons. And I pounced, negotiating some new ground rules with Jack. He could play Scrabble with someone only after he'd done three hours of required academic work and only if he hadn't driven us—me or his fellow students—to screaming fits with his obnoxious horsing around.

About a year and a half after Jack entered my classroom, I appeared as a character witness for him in court—much to the annoyance of the district attorney. Yes, he'd stolen the items, and yes, he admitted it, but he'd also turned his life around to such a degree that he was on the verge of graduating from high school. A few months later, Jack asked even more of me. Never in my life would I have believed that I'd write a letter to a Marine Corps sergeant commending someone I cared about into their service. Not until I met Jack. But students force teachers into reorganizing their priorities and prejudices. Jack insisted that the Marine Corps was his ticket to turning his life around, and I had to figure that Jack knew best. And I wrote the letter.

I'm sure Jack was a reject in school from the first day he entered kindergarten. Certainly I have never encountered a child who looked or smelled worse, a child so ill-cared-for that he had trouble learning to care for himself. All the collaborative peer-group-think in the world couldn't have gotten Jack to the point of being able to do regular school work or qualify for the Marines. What he needed was to beat his teacher at Scrabble. And he did it. All by himself.

The funny thing about Jack—or Donna or Charles or Chris or David or Jennifer or Leslie or LeRoy or Heywood or Sylvia or the scores of others who have left their mark on me — is that the point of any story I tell depends on how I choose to frame it. Who knows? Maybe the kids would remember it differently. Maybe they'd remember the moments they worked together, not the times they sat by themselves.

Certainly my students at every grade level worked together every day, but that working was fluid, vague, and transitory. There was nothing so formal or permanent as learning groups "seeking outcomes that are beneficial to all those with whom they are cooperatively linked." Nothing so idiotic as announcing to groups of kids what the "cooperative learning outcomes" will be for the day. It's taken me close to fifteen years to figure out what Jack's learning outcomes were; I sure couldn't have announced them ahead of time.

That's not to say that I wouldn't have loved to write in my plan book that a learning outcome for Leslie from October to March was learning to read a knock-knock joke. If I'd known at the time that it was so important, maybe I would have written it down. But the truth of the matter was that, as with most of my teaching, I didn't realize until months and even years later how important the event was. What William Stafford says of poetry is equally true of classroom significances: It's "the kind of thing you have to see from the corner of your eye. You can be too well prepared for poetry. A conscientious interest in it is worse than no interest at all, as I believe Frost used to say.... If you analyze it away, it's gone. It would be like boiling a watch to find out what makes it tick" (1978, 3).

I have written a lot about Leslie, a third-grade deaf child to whom I gave more of my heart than to any other student. Leslie had never been in public school before and it was a painful, terrifying, and ultimately joyous experience — for her and for me.

I'm convinced the greatest good a teacher can do for her students is to help them find a book that will knock their socks off. For Leslie, the first knocking-socks-off book was *Rumpelstiltskin*. Her whole class loved that book. I had five copies and the kids read it to one another in small groups; they went off alone and read it silently. Charles, an emotionally disturbed boy mainstreamed into our classroom, read *Rumpelstiltskin* sixteen days in a row. And then I stopped counting.

Leslie wrote me a note, "I love Rumpelstiltskin. Every time I read it I get goose bumps." And when Leslie encountered *Amelia Bedelia*, her joy was even more profound. She bought her own personal copy through the book club and when it arrived she jumped up and down and then burst into tears.

But what Leslie really wanted was knock-knock jokes. Leslie cried buckets over knock-knock jokes. The class was wild about them. We ended silent reading each day with somebody reading two or three jokes and the knock-knocks were hands-down favorites. And they eluded Leslie. She would wail, "What's so funny? Why is everybody laughing?" And some days she'd get mad and stamp her feet. And she'd cry. And cry.

For months, at odd moments during the day different children would wander over to Leslie and try to help her "get" the point. Anna persisted more than anybody else. A lovely, quiet, shy child whose father berated her for being slow, Anna was repeating third grade. She put up with Leslie's tantrums, helped her find her place, and was a true friend. And every day Anna patiently sat with Leslie and tried to explain knock-knock jokes.

And then one day in March Leslie was sitting all by herself. And she picked up the knock-knock joke book. She read one, clutched the book to her chest, and jumped up. "I get it!" she yelled. "I really get it!" And she read it to us at eighty decibels. Then the other kids cheered and Leslie burst into tears. And so did I. But Leslie recovered quickly—and yelled, "Let me read another one!"

So is this a story of class collaboration or of an individual child overcoming all odds? I don't know. Does it matter? Why do some folks insist we're competent and professional only when we can affix labels and categories to the fabric of our work with children?

Leslie wrote me a couple of years ago that she was graduating from eighth grade—regular classes—on the honor roll. And she said she owed her success to me and to Jesus. I went to her graduation, thrilled to accept my half of her success. After all, those were my knock-knock joke books. But I didn't teach her. Leslie learned—sometimes with others, but mostly all by herself.

A lot of collaborationists travel under a *no-fail* banner. By combining kids into collaborative safety zones, we supposedly reduce the risk of individual failure. We're urged to form *success teams*, teams that will "cheer you up, cheer you on, help you out, keep you going, and refuse to let you lose."

Indeed. I'm not the first person to point out that without risk, without failure, there is no learning.

Item. Consider Charles Darwin, who, with nobody cheering him on, spent forty-four years of his life thinking about earthworms. In his typically methodical fashion he made the following notation:

> Worms do not possess any sense of hearing. They took not the least notice of the shrill notes from a metal whistle, which was repeatedly sounded near them; nor did they of the deepest and loudest tones of a bassoon. They were indifferent to shouts, if care was taken that the breath did not strike them. When placed on a table close to the keys of a piano, which was played as loudly as possible, they remained perfectly quiet. (Quammen 1988)

What a wonderful image: Charles Darwin alone in his study with a tin whistle and a bassoon and a piano, trying to get a rise out of worms. As science writer David Quammen, who relates this incident, points out, "That sort of stubborn mental contrariety is as precious to our planet as worm casting. It is equally essential that some people *do* think about earthworms, at least sometimes, as it is that *not everyone* does. It is essential not for the worms' sake but for our own" (1988, 11–13).

Have you noticed that there is nowadays a movement afoot to get all us teachers thinking about the same things at the same time? I don't much care whether the movement is Mastery Learning or Writing Process or Core Literature or Collaborationism: unanimity brings bad things down on itself. When we all think alike, we don't think enough: our ideas become fat and lazy and self-satisfied. When that happens we are in great danger of teaching the method instead of the child.

In Jane Yolen's beautiful picture book, *Owl Moon*, a young girl and her Pa go owling, which means they go out on a cold winter's night, long past her bedtime, in search of the Great Horned Owl. The little girl has waited a long time for this night. She knows there are no guarantees: sometimes there is an owl but sometimes there isn't. And even though she has to run to keep up and she gets very cold, she doesn't say a word because

> If you go owling
> You have to be quiet
> and make your own heat.

The owl does come finally and the young narrator concludes:

> When you go owling
> you don't need words
> or warm
> or anything but hope.
> That's what Pa says.
> The kind of hope
> that flies
> on silent wings
> under a shining
> Owl Moon.

I feel the same about classrooms as Jane Yolen feels about owling: My students and I need to know when to be quiet; each of us needs to learn to make her own heat; we need a lot of hope.

References

Barker, Rodney. 1985. *The Hiroshima Maidens*. New York: Viking.

Berry, Wendell. 1983. *Standing by Words*. Berkeley, CA: North Point Press.

Berthoff, Ann E. 1981. *The Making of Meaning.* Portsmouth, NH: Boynton/Cook.

Brown, Jeff. 1964. *Flat Stanley.* Illustrated by Tomi Ungerer. New York: Harper & Row.

Clarke, Thurston. 1988. *Equator.* New York: William Morrow.

Dorris, Michael. 1989. *The Broken Cord.* New York: Harper & Row.

Gass, William. 1985. *Habitations of the Word.* New York: Simon & Schuster.

Harris, Eddy. 1988. *Mississippi Solo.* New York: Harper & Row.

Johnson, David, et al. [1984] 1988. *Circles of Learning: Cooperation in the Classroom.* Reston, VA: Association for Supervision and Curriculum Development.

Kafka, Franz. *Letters to Felice.* New York: Schocken.

Larson, Gary. 1989. *Pre-History of the Far Side.* Kansas City: Andrews and McMeel.

Quammen, David. 1988. *The Flight of the Iguana.* New York: Delacorte.

Shekerjian, Denise. 1990. *The Uncommon Genius.* New York: Viking.

Stafford, William. 1978. *Writing the Australian Crawl: Views on the Writer's Vocation.* Ann Arbor, MI: University of Michigan Press.

Storr, Anthony. 1988. *Solitude.* New York: Free Press.

Yolen, Jane. 1987. *Owl Moon.* Illustrated by John Schoenherr. New York: Philomel.

Notes on Japan from an American Schoolteacher

EDUCATION EXPERTS — the people who observe classrooms from afar, tote up standardized test scores, and then declare us a nation at risk — have discovered Japan. And Japan has a peculiar effect on foreigners. Some people take one look at fried fish heads or one bite of sea urchin and forever after make sure they know the way to *Maku-donarudo* (McDonald's). Others don silk kimonos and lyrically maintain that chopsticks make food taste better. I don't think a visitor should go so far as George Bernard Shaw, who steadfastly refused to take off his shoes when entering Japanese homes and schools, but surely there is some cultural baggage we cannot abandon just because our Japanese hosts are so gracious and their children so appealing.

Too many education experts return from their whirlwind tours of Japanese schools and issue educational imperatives. Neither our schools nor those of the Japanese are well-served by quick and shallow veneration of their students sweeping the school corridors, making clever origami figures, or winning international mathematics competitions. One needs to dig a little deeper, to think about the cultural values that produce our schools — and theirs.

I, too, have been to Japan. I, too, have admired the sight of polite, orderly students, efficient teachers, and immaculate buildings. One image that sticks with me is all those shoes neatly lined up in open cubbies just inside the doorway of a junior high school in Tokyo. Anyone who has taught seventh or eighth grade in a large metropolitan school in the U. S. can appreciate what a stunning sight that is. My students padlocked their lockers and I my desk — and still our possessions were stolen.

When I entered that Tokyo school, carrying a (borrowed) dripping umbrella, I was told to leave it in an open receptacle near the shoe cubbies. My immediate reaction was panic. I clutched the umbrella tighter and thought, "I can't do that." The elegant umbrella had been lent to me by the executive of a large Japanese corporation just ten minutes after we met. I was responsible for it. What would it do to East/West relations if I lost it? School officials assured me that at the end of the day the umbrella would be where I left it. And it was.

Nonetheless, if we are to take education seriously—both Japanese and American—we must look beyond the surface features of a clean, well-ordered, and honest place. I watched Japanese students at work and at play; I met with teachers, principals, the head of the parent-teacher organization, and members of the Tokyo Board of Education. I spent a weekend in the home of the principal of a technical high school. I talked with a teacher at a night school for dropouts. And from all this I gleaned neither theory nor agenda for changing American education. What I gleaned are a few anecdotes.

Sixteen years as a teacher in public school classrooms convinced me that one good anecdote is worth a thousand lesson plans and ten thousand standardized test scores. A good anecdote is worth a million words spewed forth from the ed-biz-whizzes who ride the policy-making circuit with an ever-changing bag of patent nostrums. One year, they're selling vouchers; another year, career ladders. Right now, they're demanding of American teachers, "Why can't you be more like the Japanese?" To answer that question, I offer a few anecdotes.

For part of my stay in Japan, I traveled with a group of seventh- and eighth-grade American students and their art teachers. On the day we were invited to visit a junior high in Tokyo and to participate in their classes, we traveled to the school in separate taxis. I happened to arrive before the rest of my group, at about the same time as a cheerful, chattering, well-behaved, and uniformed bunch of Japanese students. It was raining fairly hard as these students and I walked up to the school, and I was impressed by how orderly they were—no pushing, no shoving. If there was teasing, it was of a very gentle sort. No teachers were standing guard to prevent mischief or mayhem, and none were needed.

As soon as they got inside the front door, the students put their umbrellas in the open receptacles and their shoes in the cubbies, changing into sneakers or slippers. (Think of how much easier it would be to keep our schools clean if we didn't allow children or teachers to walk through the school in muddy shoes.)

The principal and the vice principal rushed up to me, smiling. "Early," said one.

I smiled back. "That's okay. I'll just wait here."

"No," said one of the gentlemen, looking at his watch and shaking his head. The two men conferred, obviously upset. Just then a Japanese business executive who was also visiting the school appeared. He spoke with the school officials and then explained their problem to me. "They have planned an opening ceremony. The brass band will play your national anthem."

"That's nice," I smiled.

"But the ceremony will be spoiled if you stay here. They want to greet you officially as you walk up to the school. So you need to leave until it is the right time."

It was raining. But I saw I was going to mess up a carefully planned ceremony if I didn't leave. So I walked out into the rain and down the street, taking shelter under an overhang half a block away—out of sight of the school entrance. Fifteen minutes later, the rest of my group arrived. We walked up to the school and were accorded our official welcome: smiles, handshakes, exchange of business cards, and a spirited rendering of "The Star Spangled Banner."

The Japanese like timetables. They like things to run on schedule—be it the bullet train, an official visitor's welcome, or their children's education. From the time they enter school, Japanese children know they are part of a group. And that group must learn on schedule. The teacher does not permit anyone to move ahead nor acknowledge that anybody might have fallen behind. Moreover, the Japanese child learns from the beginning that he or she is a member of a *right-handed* group. One of our American left-handers, a spirited twelve-year-old, was not permitted to use her left hand in a calligraphy class. "That's your dirty hand," admonished the teacher. The American did as she was told and then later related the incident with a laugh, as though it were just another Japanese custom to try—like sleeping on the floor or making sure you were clean before getting into the bathtub.

But it bothered me, and I asked various people about it—parents, teachers, members of the Tokyo Board of Education. "*Can* a Japanese be left-handed?" It remains a mystery, one of those unanswered questions. Some people assured me that the rigidity of the past is yielding to a recognition of human differences. Others told me that the impossibility of writing Japanese characters with the left hand is the pragmatic reason for the restriction.

The left-hand question relates to a more serious issue: What happens if a child fails? Over and over I was assured that no child fails in Japanese schools. Every child moves ahead with the group. The forty children who start school together remain together until the end of sixth grade. "But what if a student doesn't seem to be learning as much as the others?" I persisted. The official answer is that the teacher gives that child extra help and the child's parents pay for the services of a private tutor. "But what if the parents complain that the books are too hard or not interesting enough or too controversial?" I asked. I told members of the board of education in Tokyo about Phyllis Schlafly. This met with stunned silence. Finally, a man explained, "Such a situation could not arise in Japan. The schoolbooks are issued by the Ministry of Education. No parent or other private citizen would be qualified to disapprove."

Everyone with whom I spoke assured me that children help each other and that no child falls behind.

When I asked why teachers didn't agitate for smaller classes, I was told that forty is the "ideal" number for instruction. "A small class size cannot promote the good relationships that will be expected of students in society," a principal asserted. His tone convinced me that Confucius must have left behind a tablet of ideal numbers for school administrators. But later I learned that the ever-pragmatic Japanese go to a variety of sources to obtain their sacred numbers. I asked about faculty meetings and was told each school has fifteen faculty representatives who meet to discuss curriculum and other matters (Andrew Carnegie having established that fifteen is the ideal number for productive meetings).

Nonetheless, not everybody is so sanguine about forty youngsters progressing through the grades in a pack. A decade ago Japan's National Assessment of Education Research Institutes asked elementary and junior high teachers how many of their students were not keeping up with the curriculum. They acknowledged that 50 percent of their students were not keeping up with the curriculum issued by the Ministry of Education.

I did not pick up that figure in a conversation with a Japanese teacher. I read it in a book. Visitors to Japan must always be alert to the fact that many Japanese censor what they say to foreigners. Even among themselves, they often describe things as they would like them to be, not as they really are. For example, the Japanese are proud that they have never been invaded. They term the American occupation as "visiting" or "staying." Also, it is common practice to avoid answering a question, particularly if the information might wound the feelings of the foreign visitor who asked it.

When I was visiting a Buddhist shrine with a Japanese schoolteacher and an American exchange student, I noticed some little white papers tied to the shrine and asked, "What are those?"

The schoolteacher was obviously discomfited. He didn't say a word but stood there chewing on his lip. Finally, he turned to the American student and said, "I'm not sure of the translation. Why don't you explain?" She told me that the folded papers were cranes.

"Oh," I exclaimed, "prayers for peace!"

"You know about them? You know the story?" The Japanese teacher was astounded. I assured him that many American teachers had read the story of Sadako and the thousand paper cranes to their students and that we, too, wanted no more Hiroshimas or Nagasakis.

Almost anyone who visits Japanese schools will come back applauding the quality of the artwork produced by the children. Certainly they do produce lovely objects. But again, things aren't quite as they seem. Just because the children's art on display in the schools is lovely does not necessarily mean that the Japanese children are, in the words of a prominent commentator on U. S. education and recent enthusiast for things Japanese, "encouraged to express their ideas and feelings."

Free expression of feeling and creative blockbusting are very American notions and are quite antithetical to what the Japanese are trying to achieve in their schools. Japanese children are taught the very precise rules of a given structure — be it haiku or fan making or flower arranging or mathematics. The relationship between formula and feeling may be something for philosophers to argue over, but anyone who observes Japanese art classes in action will have no doubt that form is what counts and feelings must take care of themselves. There isn't much time for feelings — even after school. Students are too busy with cram classes, memorizing set answers for that high school exam that looms large in the lives of young Japanese children.

The differences between painstakingly mastering a few traditional forms and the American practice of learning a little bit about a lot and then "doing your own thing" became strikingly clear to me during our visit to a junior high art class. A very talented and enthusiastic teacher had organized her class into six groups, with six or so students per group. Individual members of each group were given a blank fan and told to decorate it. The teacher assigned a different decorative style to each group.

All of us American teachers in the room were impressed by how well the students shared the tools — no fuss, no noise, *and* no mess. One glue brush was sufficient for each group, and the glue ended up only where it was supposed to go. (This may not seem remarkable to all readers, but remember, we are talking about twelve- and thirteen-year-olds.) As individual students needed special supplies — a special kind of paper, a knife — they helped themselves from an array on the teacher's desk. "X-Acto knives!" gasped an American teacher. "I wouldn't dare hand them out in a group this size."

A Japanese boy drew "coolness" in Japanese characters on his fan. Then he drew a hanging bell, the symbol of beautiful noise. "Traditional decorations for Japanese fans," explained a translator in approving tones. So the boy had decorated his fan correctly, according to accepted tradition. (I could hear an American teacher saying to her class, "Think of all the sounds *you* think are beautiful." And there wouldn't be a right or wrong answer because beauty is in the eye — and the ear — of the beholder and everybody has a right to his or her own opinion and so on.) When an American sitting at that table carefully copied "coolness" from the Japanese, everybody smiled and clapped. The television crew filming our visit rushed over to record this event. Everybody was delighted that the American had gotten it right. When one student copies another's work in an American school, there is accusation and acrimony, not applause.

38

This is not to suggest that all the Japanese students produced the same thing. Each group was assigned a traditional form within which to work, and within these limits a variety of quite lovely fans were produced. Some results, then, were wonderful. But it is crucial that the casual American observer understand and appreciate the limitations.

And some students, both American and Japanese, did not so readily fit into this routine. A Japanese boy sat fanning himself, not putting any decoration at all on his fan. The teacher was very busy helping the large number of students with the many different techniques going on simultaneously. I couldn't tell whether she didn't notice this boy doing nothing or whether she was carefully seeming not to notice. Every so often the recalcitrant boy got up and took a tool from her desk. By the end of the period he had four tools but no work on his fan.

I asked a young translator (himself a product of similar schools), "If this were a regular class—one without visitors—would a boy like that be allowed to do nothing? Would he be punished, made to do the work after school, or what?"

The translator was unnerved that I focused on the atypical student. (I could imagine his thoughts: "Just like an American. Here's this large class tidily working at the assigned task, and this troublesome visitor insists on noticing the exception.") The translator told me, "Just a minute," and walked to the other side of the room—to watch the boy more closely and, no doubt, to gather his own thoughts. Finally, he came back and replied with what I came to recognize, at least by American expectations, as a Japanese non-answer: "He is a good boy. He just likes to pretend that he is a juvenile delinquent." The translator had never set eyes on that boy before, and I wasn't asking about that particular boy anyway. I wanted to know how the schools work, what happens to kids who don't cooperate, kids who don't learn on schedule, kids who fall between the cracks.

This was a question I asked over and over in as many ways as I could muster during my two weeks of visiting Japanese schools. I never got an answer. What I got were piles of timetables—slickly produced schedules of what the Japanese student learns and when he or she learns it. Japan is so inundated with visiting members of educational commissions and committees that these schedules are printed in English. A visitor can know what every eight-year-old in Japan is doing at 10:03 on Tuesday. But it is far more difficult, if not impossible, to find out how an eight-year-old might grow up to be that man I saw on his hands and knees scrubbing the steps at the railroad station.

One of our American students did not follow directions in the fan-making class either. He was quickly intimidated by the way his fellow group members were able to form bits of bright paper into intriguing collages, so he decided to draw a picture on his fan instead. The vice principal of the school was in the room, walking around, genially commenting on the students' progress. Seeing the American drawing a scene of kimono-clad women and temples on his fan, the vice principal shook his head. He pointed to the Japanese students at the same table, all busily working on collages, as directed by the teacher. A few minutes later he returned. "Time passing," he cautioned the American, who grinned and cheerfully continued his picture. The administrator was visibly distressed but refrained from more direct intervention.

I have read that the Japanese find our penchant for asking questions to be embarrassing and rude. In fact, once I was being interviewed by a Tokyo reporter, and, after he asked me a tough question about American kids who don't succeed in school, I tried to turn the tables, asking him the same thing about Japanese schools. He replied, "I'm the one who is supposed to be asking the questions." At first I thought he was kidding, and I laughed. But then I realized that he was very serious. I had violated the proper interview structure. Needless to say, he didn't answer my question but continued with more of his own. I was interviewed three times, and the same question was always prominent: "What about all the race riots in your schools?" Like Americans, the Japanese are prey to their own stereotypes.

I was frustrated by the Japanese eagerness to provide stock answers to my questions. They were prepared to discuss broad social issues, such as the one they call "bullying in the schools," but they were unwilling to focus on one bad boy. I talked to an American who had taught at a Japanese vocational high school, not a school that produces students for first-rate colleges or white-collar jobs. It is, in fact, a school where students admit that they hate school, that they are only interested in fashions, rock music, and fast cars. "Ask about the 'hitting teacher'," she advised me. She explained that in each school one teacher is selected as the "hitting teacher," and it is the job of this teacher to make a public example of unruly or disrespectful students. A common ploy is to pull one student to the side during the first school assembly, slam him against the wall, and actually beat him hard enough to leave marks. This serves as a warning to all the others of what will happen if they don't toe the line.

And so, when I met with the principals, with members of boards of education, and with other teachers, I asked about this hitting teacher. Their answers were resounding and unanimous. "Impossible!" they said. When I tried to press a junior high school teacher on this point, she said it is her job to talk to a recalcitrant student, to reason with him until he "is persuaded" to behave. A principal listed appropriate punishments: standing in the corner, missing lunch, extra assignments, a longer cleaning period. They assured me that nobody would dream of hitting a student.

"What do you think of our children cleaning the schools?" beamed Mr. B. Watanabe, head of the influential parent-teacher organization and himself a principal for thirteen years. The Japanese enjoy the astonishment American visitors exhibit when they learn that there are no janitors in Japanese schools, that the students clean the schools. Watanabe explained that Christian countries hire specialists to clean their schools but Japan follows the Chinese tradition that makes it the duty of the schools to impart the importance of cleanliness to children. The parent-teacher organization is preparing a booklet urging parents to give their children more cleaning and other chores at home, though Watanabe acknowledged that crowded apartment conditions and the fact that students are too busy studying for high school exams may prevent this from happening. Watanabe wanted to be sure that I understood that the importance of student cleaning is not for them to *help* but to *share*. Such sharing, he emphasized, teaches children to become valuable members of the group — be it family, school, community, or nation.

Americans who might be quick to jump on this cleaning idea as a device for building student responsibility while saving tax dollars should realize the deep roots and significance of the practice in Japan. I have heard of a Zen community in which members rise at 3:00 A.M. to wipe their floors until they shine — at the same time, so the theory goes, making their spirits very bright. Principals also inject something of a mystical note into their explanations of students' "sweeping clean their minds" as they clean the school corridors.

American enthusiasts should recognize, however, that such cleaning is not limited to schoolchildren and practitioners of Zen. Teachers take turns cleaning the swimming pool — even during vacations. In some businesses employees are expected to take turns coming in early and cleaning the place — including the toilets. As one principal remarked, "There is satisfaction in knowing you can depend on a group and they on you."

The Japanese passion for doing things in the prescribed way can take Americans by surprise. A small group of us signed up to take a watercolor lesson. A translator relayed the directions of the master teacher to us. Before each student was a small fruit arrangement to be painted in accordance with the technique demonstrated by the master. Some of the combinations were provocative: peach, pepper, and kiwi cut in half; small bunch of grapes, peach, and two plums; and so on. My eyes riveted on a bunch of huge, dark purple grapes grouped with a lemon. I'd priced a similar assortment of fruit in the basement of a large department store and then hurried back to the hotel to check with translators whether I was mixed up about money conversion. *Could* one bunch of grapes cost twelve dollars and one melon thirty dollars? Yes, indeed, the translator assured me, explaining the Japanese custom for presenting perfectly formed fruits as special gifts. Now I was learning that they also used the perfectly formed fruits for still-life models.

Since the group I was traveling with was made up of art teachers and their students, there was no hesitation in picking up the paintbrushes. After watching the master quickly paint his fruit, the Americans started on their own productions. Though they were proud of their work, they were in for a shock. The master teacher sat with each student and quickly painted over his or her work, deftly shading each piece of fruit in the "acceptable" manner. The American art teachers were outraged. "What kind of instruction is this?" they wondered. The students were hurt. One girl looked at her redone painting. "It's nice," she acknowledged, "but it isn't mine."

The Americans did not appreciate the fact that the master saw his job not as encouraging the expression of individual style but as teaching a revered pattern or form. Ian Burma points out that, unlike French, Italian, and American cooks, a Japanese cook does not usually invent recipes. Rather, an apprentice spends years imitating the movements of a master, learning the *kata*, the form, of the trade. "A Japanese master never explains anything," says Burma. "The question of why one does something is irrelevant. It is the form that counts."

I can think of all sorts of justification for the master's technique of showing the Americans where their creations did not measure up to the standards of the traditional style he was demonstrating. But before we try to transplant Japanese educational methods into American schools, it is crucial that we examine the reactions of these Americans to some of those methods. And we must take these reactions seriously. We don't need to claim that our teaching strategies and goals are better than those of the Japanese, but we do need to understand how very *different* they are. The American teachers and students who were enjoying other aspects of Japanese tradition—chopsticks, communal bathing, and kimonos—were suddenly up against a tradition they found repugnant. The teacher who had ecstatically declared that "chopsticks make food taste better" was the most outraged of all when the master painter tinkered with *her* painting. Of course the American strategy of instruction often leads to superficiality and occasionally breeds chaos. Today's critics like to point out that we offer a smattering of many things but guarantee expertise in none. Yet I saw some evidence that indicates that Japanese training does not produce the uniform level of expertise some American enthusiasts would claim for it.

For example, we read that all Japanese youngsters learn to play two musical instruments. Since band was my own great love from fourth grade on (I learned to play a number of instruments and pursued music theory), I watched a sixth-grade music class with great interest. The forty-member recorder group played "You Are My Sunshine" and some

Japanese folk songs. Since the melody produced was recognizable, I have to assume that some students in that class had indeed become minimally proficient on the recorder, but it was hardly a performance one would label as sparkling. At least half a dozen students didn't play a note during our hour-long visit. They held the recorders to their lips—and giggled—but they did not blow a note. And those who did blow produced a plodding sort of sound.

I observed a similar lack of enthusiastic participation in a high school math class. The students had worksheets filled with agonizingly long columns of addition. They were using abacuses. I sat at a table with four students and watched their flying fingers. Everyone at that table had the same problems. Two girls noticed they had come up with different answers but neither cared enough to recheck the addition. They just shrugged and went on.

A lesson in ikebana, the Japanese art of flower arranging, exposed the East/West differences once again. A master teacher demonstrated a basic ikebana technique. The Americans watched closely, some even taking notes. Then they took their own flowers and branches and tried to copy what the teacher had done. Since she was accustomed to giving demonstration lessons to large groups of foreigners, this teacher was gentler in suggesting where individual Americans had gone wrong. And since few Americans knew a thing about Japanese flower arranging, they were more receptive to her suggestions.

At the same time, an assistant teacher moved around the room, helping people get their flowers moving in the right directions. When a cameraman from a Tokyo TV station started to film an American's arrangement, the assistant teacher rushed in to give it one final poke. After all, many Japanese viewing the show would know the way things were supposed to be. Throughout all our lessons, our Japanese hosts made every effort to help us do things the right way. They wanted us to look good.

When I told an American thirteen-year-old that the assistant teacher had been studying ikebana for fifteen years and was still taking lessons regularly, she was astonished. "Why would anybody need to study it for so long?"

"Then you think you will be able to do ikebana when you get home?" I prodded.

"Sure," she said. "It might be hard to find some of the branches—I don't think our florists sell branches the way the Japanese do—but I can arrange them the way I want. You just do it the way it looks good to you."

Out of the mouths of babes. She might have asked why an apprentice cook spends three years learning "the perfect way" to slop a bunch of rice from his right hand to his left, forming the perfect ball, or why a karate apprentice spends so much time sweeping the gym. The thirteen-year-old's question is not just an expression of juvenile arrogance or insensitivity; it also springs from exuberance and self-confidence. Her question is something that proponents of transplanting Japanese methods into American soil must reckon with. We do, after all, encourage our youngsters to believe that they can do anything, to believe that their opinions and feelings count. We do set them many problems for which we provide no model, no explanation, no answer. We expect our students to figure things out for themselves.

One of our educational buzzphrases of the sixties is now resurfacing: divergent thinking. Japanese educators concede that they might not be training or even encouraging their students to think. I heard this concern expressed at every level of Japanese education—boards of education, principals, teachers, and parents. But for us American teachers plain old thinking isn't even enough. For us, thinking must be divergent, off-the-wall—the more original, the better. We hold competitions for gifted children in which we ask them to solve problems that require creativity, to figure out different uses for such common objects as a paper clip, a newspaper, a brick. In these competitions, the children whose answers are the most unlike everybody else's score the most points. Those who do things the "accepted" way, the same way as everybody else, need not apply. So much for teamwork.

I mentioned to the Japanese educational leaders that American elementary students are encouraged to think about controversial topics. They learn about acid rain, nuclear weapons, and so on; they discuss politics and hold mock presidential elections. The officials acknowledged that such opportunities are rare in Japanese schools. "We give knowledge, based on taught information," explained a principal. "We can't encourage creativity until we have taught information. There will be opportunity in college for students to develop their own thoughts and form opinions," he continued. I could not help but wonder how this reliance on college fit in with Prime Minister Nakasone's description of the academic atmosphere of Japanese colleges as "Disneyland."

A member of the board of education said that students need what the Japanese call *judging capability* and *coordinating capability*. I asked the educational leaders sitting at the table with me how one teaches judging capability. There was a long silence—followed by giggling. Finally one of them said, "Ah, that is difficult." Mishima said that in the Japanese language exactness of expression is purposely avoided. I wasn't sure whether my companions were avoiding precision or avoiding controversy, but in either case I have no notion of how they produce judging capability. I do have a notion of how they produce letter writers. Students learn a textbook format: inquire about the well-being of the recipient and then remark about the weather. There are set phrases for each season, even for each month.

Most critics of Japan's educational system (including the Japanese themselves) point to the fact that it is driven by the examination system and that the exams measure students' willingness to memorize rather than their ability to solve problems. Japanese teachers are ever cognizant of the proverb, "A nail that sticks out must be hammered in." They are duty-bound to produce a standardized product.

In contrast, the folklore of American education reveres those school misfits who grew up to be Teddy Roosevelt or Thomas Edison or Albert Einstein. We are ever worried (we say) about making a potential genius sit in the corner, crushing the instinct to follow a different drummer. Japan's Confucian roots argue against catering to the individual, against encouraging the exceptional. In Japan one must always consider the good of the group. When Japanese parents were asked what they expected the schools to teach their children, 98.3 percent replied: the discipline of group life.

Even exceptions to the rule are orchestrated. I remarked to a principal how impressed I was when our American students played against a Japanese team in a version of dodgeball. The gym was packed with bystanders, and every time the foreign students scored a hit, they received resounding cheers. "Sportsmanship is emphasized," the principal smiled. "Except when a school has a reputation for excelling in a certain sport. Then victory may be the goal." Presumably, such a school's opponents would not be cheered.

We must be ever wary of stereotypes, of course. Even when talking of a school system with such a centralized, regimented curriculum, it is dangerous to refer to *the* Japanese schools as though they all fit into one mold. Clichés are especially troublesome in Japan because the Japanese seem to enjoy the same ones we do. "The Japanese are very good at copying," three different translators assured me. "Americans are very democratic people," smiled a business executive when I commented that the Japanese are much better about buckling up in their cars than are Americans. And American students are very quick to pick up some overworked Japanese abstractions. As we sat looking at the fifteen rocks in the famed Roan-ji Garden, one bewildered eighth grader asked, "What *is* this?" His friend quickly supplied the answer in very solemn tones, "We are observing the basic elements of life." They both laughed.

When I ordered rice and my Japanese companion rolls, the waiter, knowing the way things are supposed to be, brought the rolls to me. In another restaurant, when our entire group of Americans ordered rice, the waiter was stunned. He brought someone out from the kitchen to explain that they could provide us with bread instead. After all, everybody knows that Americans insist on bread with their meals. We stood firm for rice, however, and the waiters and the cook stood around to watch us eat it. Perhaps they thought we might get sick.

Over and over, the Japanese asked me the same question: "*Can* you eat sushi?"—as though consuming raw fish were an inherent trait or a special talent. When I told my very amiable questioners that I can and do eat sushi, I don't think they believed me. They preferred to believe that a foreigner wouldn't even try such an odd thing and that, if she did, she'd find it indigestible. They prefer to believe that sushi is uniquely Japanese.

But we shouldn't make too much of the popularity of sushi bars in the U. S. or of McDonald's in Japan. Such superficial familiarity in no way indicates that the nations are coming closer to understanding each other. We must be especially wary of a cultural arrogance (and naïveté) that presumes that since Disneyland has come to Tokyo, Japan is ready to sign on as the fifty-first state.

In addition to being extremely proud of their cultural traditions, many Japanese are convinced (and this conviction is centuries old) that they are a fundamentally different people, different not just from Americans but from all other peoples. Bookstores carry scores of best-selling volumes attesting to the fact that Japanese is the most difficult language in the world, that Japanese blood is a different temperature from the blood of other races, that the Japanese have a different type of brain. When I was sitting with a group of Japanese educators, one of them observed, "We all studied English for twelve years, but we still need a translator." He smiled deprecatingly and then explained, "The Japanese find it almost impossible to learn English." Basil Chamberlain, among others, has pointed out that English is taught in Japan "as an academic exercise with so much attention to memorizing fine points of grammar . . . that it ceases to be a means of communication." But educational leaders find it more convenient to blame their genes than their teaching methods.

I was puzzled when members of the parent-teacher organization and the Tokyo Board of Education kept insisting, "You are a brave and courageous woman." They thought it phenomenal that I would journey to their shores all by myself—without husband, relatives, neighbors, or colleagues from work. I misunderstood the source of their awe and replied, "But Japan isn't dangerous." They were, of course, referring not to physical danger but to a kind of psychic trauma. They found it incredible that a woman would venture forth all by herself to a land as foreign as theirs, a land, after all, in which the people eat raw fish and speak an impossible language.

I mentioned that I had decided to change professions after having been a teacher for more than sixteen years. The change meant moving across the country and taking on an entirely new set of responsibilities. (I left out the part about leaving my husband behind.) I pointed out that, though my vocational change was dramatic, it was by no means unique.

Americans are constantly on the move—physically and professionally. So our educators have to help students become self-reliant, able to stand alone—anywhere. I asked if they thought that their educational system prepared its students to make such changes when they were forty years old. They replied as one with an emphatic, "Impossible!"

Japanese teachers prepare their students to function as members of a group, as people who can be relied on to fill their assigned role. This group identity seems to prepare the well-educated, hardworking citizens of Japan for the paucity of creature comforts they face. The beauty of the traditional Japanese home is little more than elusive abstraction for people who face the overwhelming population density of the urban areas. I found it incongruous that, in a nation so fond of technical gadgetry, only one-third of the people in Tokyo have access to a flush toilet. Roughly one-third of Japanese communities have modern sewer systems (compared with 85 percent in the U. S.), and the pollution in Osaka is monumental. In a nation with an overabundance of color televisions and video games, there are few dishwashers or clothes dryers. Perhaps the electronic gadgets are only for men. Because of the terrible housing crunch, one-third of the people who work in Tokyo must commute more than three hours to work. But point to these facts and the man on the street will respond with statistics about the nation's affluence, the balance of trade, the bullet train, even Disneyland. The Japanese seem to assume that what is good for the nation—the group—must be good for them individually.

Members of blue-ribbon education commissions rush out of our universities exclaiming that in Japanese schools *nothing is left to chance*. They point to a curriculum that is sequential: every first grader in the land learns the same thing, so that the second-grade teacher can carry on from where the first-grade teacher left off.

And, on the surface at least, this is how the Japanese system of education works. The government assigns the required texts, the teachers teach the prescribed material, and the students pass from rung to rung on the carefully constructed pedagogical ladder—right on up to lifetime employment at a large corporation. Male, white-collar workers do anyway. Nobody talks much about how the Japanese educational system works for women or for blue-collar workers and laborers. Women make up 40 percent of the work force in Japan, but they are seldom promoted to higher positions than answering the phone and brewing the ubiquitous green tea. "Honor the man, despise the woman," teaches an ancient proverb, and one gets the feeling that education is vital for Japanese boys but still only ornamental for girls.

I kept asking, Where does that woman weeding the median strip along the highway fit into the educational and social system? Or the man removing the scuff marks from the stairs at the train station (using something that looked like a toothbrush)? Such people certainly do not fit our image of Japan as a combination of Madame Butterfly and industrial whiz kid. I asked everyone I met—from junior high school students and teachers to translators to a priest in a Zen temple—how the clerk at McDonald's fits into the educational plan that leaves nothing to chance. Are menial laborers considered failures? Do teachers worry that they have failed them? Does the Ministry of Education worry that the books have failed them?

I never got an answer. Indeed, people seemed puzzled by the question. Of course, nobody fails in Japanese schools—at least not for six years or so. The class of forty youngsters that starts out together in first grade will still be together in sixth grade. A group identity is carefully nurtured through these years. And it is quite wonderful to see those cheerful youngsters helping one another. But something quite unsettling is rumbling beneath this carefully controlled surface in which students wear uniforms even to school picnics and girls are not permitted to perm their hair. Somewhere beneath this calm and comforting surface there are the cram schools, the pushy education-mamas, a brutal sorting-out for a wide array of high schools, punk rockers in Yoyogi Park, teen suicide, and so on. But that's another story. Those fifth graders do score extremely well on math tests, and the Japanese do sell a lot of cars and cameras. And this is what the expert American commentators seem to care about.

An educational bandwagon seems to be gathering momentum for bringing the methods and materials of Japanese education to the United States. But I wonder if the experts riding this bandwagon aren't distorting the Japanese system by zeroing in on the test results and the carefully arranged sequences of skills. Would it not be equally valid to concentrate instead on the Japanese penchant for collaborative learning or group copying from a master model?

Numerous American observers have claimed that the Japanese do so well because they leave nothing to chance. But nobody explains how a chance-free system could be transplanted to America. Nobody asks teachers why they might prefer philosopher/educator David Hawkins' image of good teaching. Hawkins tells us that the good teacher must be ready for the unexpected appearance of the bird in the window. I will concede that the American willingness to "go with" the serendipitous and the novel is our weakness. We often wander off track, follow frivolous fads, and forget to keep in touch with a central core. But our flexibility, our willingness to try new things, to let children explore on their own, is also our very real strength. And it cannot be handed out by a ministry of education.

World traveler and social commentator Paul Theroux cautions that things can be too orderly. He is troubled by the sight of a mob of people waiting on a sidewalk in Osaka for the light to change: "A society without jaywalkers might indicate a society without artists." American educators should stop and ponder what an elementary school without divergent thinkers, without nails sticking out in all directions, might indicate. Japan is a wonderful place to visit, but would we really want to go to school there?

LEARNING

RECEIVING NCTE's OFFICIAL kudos—the *English Journal* award of "Best Article by a Classroom Teacher" for "Reading for What?" and later for "Question of the Day"—gave me the courage to explore in a larger public forum the issue of children who don't fit into neat-and-tidy curriculums. After the NCTE pieces, I wrote several rather cautious, pull-at-the-heartstrings pieces about somewhat whacky, out-of-kilter kids: "Will You Recognize the Ready Moment?," "Okay to Be Different," and "To 'Pete,' Who's Lost in the Mainstream." These pieces walk a thin line, admitting that some children are very different without descending into the despicable domain of "kids say the darnedest things." If the administrators in my own district had a fifteen-year history of ignoring my published words, then an assistant superintendent in Michigan made up for it. He wrote, offering me a job. He said Pete and I would both find a welcoming place in his district. I was more surprised to learn that some superintendents read *Education Week* than I was by the job offer.

Finally, I was ready to go public with "P. L. 94–142: Mainstream or Quicksand?" It's a piece I'd been writing and rewriting for more than a decade, first for my local union newsletter and later for a since-defunct curriculum newsletter for administrators. Where "Question of the Day" and the other pieces venture out cautiously into dangerous territory, hinting that all students are not now nor ever will be equal in their intellectual attainments, "94–142" pulls no punches, insisting that it is insane not to teach different students differently. A hardheaded piece, it is written from the heart of my classroom. I quote no experts, relying instead on the stories of my students.

The editors at *Phi Delta Kappan* tell me this is the kind of piece they like to publish. They know they will get lots of mail. Ninety-nine percent of that mail denounces me as malevolent, incompetent, and worse. After "94–142" was published, *Kappan* ran four pages of bile from professors of education plus a positive letter from a teacher in Alaska and one from the head of the Special Olympics. I found it fascinating that the only two letter-writers having direct experience with special children supported my views. Two professors insisted that I'd be a better person if I took their college courses. Then, a year later, *Kappan* ran a piece by several

51

professors who received funds from the U. S. Department of Education to respond to my assertions. I see my pieces reprinted in college texts, and I hear by the grapevine that there are photocopies of it circulating in college classrooms, but my experience has been that bile, not delight, provokes the professors to write letters. Maybe I'll ask the U. S. Department of Education for funds to report on the phenomenon of professors who write letters-to-editors and professors who don't.

P. L. 94–142: Mainstream or Quicksand?

Recently I have traveled the country telling stories about students who have touched my life in the past twenty years. Without fail, audiences shed tears when I share heartwarming anecdotes about Charles, the odd-ball eleven-year-old I welcomed into my third-grade classroom.

Although these upbeat stories about Charles are true, they are far from the whole truth. You just can't tell the whole story in a forty-five-minute talk in a crowded room. As John Updike has observed, the larger the audience, the simpler is its range of response. A packed room is the place for black-and-white sketches — mostly white. One roughs in a few bureau-cratic enemies and lots of victories, and the audience responds warmly. There is no duplicity here. I savor my triumphs and am eager to give teachers the uplift that such shared victories bring. The auditorium is not the place for the gray ambiguity of unanswered questions, not the place for soul-searching, not the place for a heart-on-the-sleeve teacher to con-fess her fear that maybe a lot of youngsters like Charles are drowning in the mainstream.

It is devastating for someone like me to be forced to acknowledge that my dealings with Charles had a dark side. After all, we teach because we are convinced that we can make a difference, a lasting difference. Our job is to push back the darkness, to light a candle. And for someone like me, who had taught oddball seventh graders for so many years, "getting one young" was a dream come true. If seventh grade sometimes proved too late to save a child, surely a third-grade teacher could intervene soon enough.

Even on my gloomy days I still believe that, though my colleagues who refused to mainstream Charles turned out to be right, it was for all the wrong reasons. In his own quirky, idiosyncratic fashion, Charles did learn; in a harum-scarum sort of way he even made a few prodigious leaps. He learned an impressive amount of dinosaur lore; he became an avid note writer; to his classmates' amazement and delight, this boy, who could neither add nor subtract, could shout out the answer to 9 × 7. Ini-tially so high-strung that he vomited when he thought other students were looking at him, Charles became the boy who stood in front of an audience of ninety and narrated our class production of *The Frog Prince*. He went from the boy who circled the room making weird chirping

53

noises whenever his classmates squeezed close together around me for story time, to the boy who sat in the middle of the squeeze and begged me to read more.

But even Charles recognized that all of this was not enough. He was reluctant to go on to fourth grade with the rest of the class and asked me if he could return to my third grade for a second year. "I know where things are," he said. "I could be your aide." I was charmed by his suggestion. "Why not?" I asked his resource teacher. "He did so well this year, just think what he could do with one more year."

She liked the idea too—until a phone call forced us to face reality. Charles' mother informed us that Charles needed quite specific information about sex.

Charles' life passed rapidly before my eyes. He wasn't a winsome little eight-year-old. He was now a gangly twelve-year-old who couldn't add or subtract with any reliability, couldn't tell time, and couldn't pass a spelling test even when all the words were three-letter rhyming words, such as *pan, man, fan.* This twelve-year-old on the brink of puberty simply could not come back to my third grade enough times. No matter how much affection, acceptance, and information I offered him, he wasn't going to "catch up"—not even with third graders.

A boy like Charles is so difficult and so "delayed" that it is natural for a teacher to cling to the positive moments—the time he actually discussed dinosaurs with another student, the time he marched down to the principal's office and read him a story. Can I be blamed for letting my nurturing instincts hold sway? For avoiding the larger question of whether spending half the day or more in a "regular" third-grade classroom was truly appropriate to the needs of a boy approaching puberty?

Michael Dorris says that children like Charles inspire wishful thinking; we optimists are convinced that, with lots of love and just one more little push, the child will be okay. In *The Broken Cord,* Dorris tells Adam's story. Dorris adopted Adam at age three, knowing that the boy had serious problems but armed with the conviction that love and a good environment could overcome all obstacles. Over the years Adam's full-scale WISC IQ score remained constant in the 64–76 range, and his performance in other areas fell below even what might be expected of a child in that range. Dorris remained constant in his belief that Adam teetered "so close to the edge of 'okay' that there was no way he would not succeed."

Adam's teachers seemed to agree. Year after year a string of report cards proclaimed Adam's progress in reading, math, and map skills. One report announced that Adam had "demonstrated good ability and understanding with regard to our unit on geometry." But Dorris finally realized that, although they spent long hours on homework every night, Adam just wasn't managing.

In retrospect Dorris sees that Adam "learned" the same low-level skills year after year. Progress reports to the contrary, Adam at eighteen cannot tell time or read a map; he has no notion of money and will cheerfully pay ten dollars for a doughnut. Never mind any principles of geometry.

For those who insist that the primary purposes of mainstreaming are better socialization and the enhancement of self-esteem, Dorris describes a heartbreaking collision with reality. Despite yearly report cards that proclaimed Adam's great progress in making friends, Dorris notes that, in all his school days, Adam "never once received so much as a telephone call or an invitation from a 'friend.'" When I read that, I cried. For all the satisfaction I took in helping my third graders learn to be tolerant and even kind to Charles, I have to admit that I never saw any evidence of friendship. Those third graders tolerated Charles because I was there. I would wager a large sum that Charles has never received a phone call from a classmate, either. Yes, he made charming breakthroughs, giving us occasional, tantalizing glimpses of a more normal boy—but even on his best days, Charles was still an uncomfortable, oddball child.

Long before I met Charles, I had known Lucille. Immediately after the passage of P. L. 94–142, the Education for All Handicapped Children Act, my school district put all "educable" children entering seventh and eighth grades into a regular academic program. So none of Lucille's teachers knew that she had spent her entire elementary career in special classes. I suspected that something was amiss the first week of school and asked to see her record. The guidance counselor told me Lucille was one of six siblings in special education; she had never been in a regular program until she hit seventh grade. He reminded me of the new federal law.

When I asked why we teachers hadn't been alerted to the special difficulties of Lucille and similar students, he told me that such information was confidential—that it might prejudice teachers and prevent them from treating "educable" children "equally" with other children in the class. So youngsters dumped willy-nilly into the mainstream were left to suffer embarrassment in front of their peers when they couldn't read aloud or solve math problems at the board or locate rivers on a map.

Lucille was kind, cheerful, cooperative, and always anxious to please. She was very proud of her high marks in spelling as she progressed from third-grade to fourth-grade words. She had good decoding skills and liked using the typewriter and listening to poetry tapes. She seemed to comprehend nothing.

When Lucille first told me she was having a terrible time in science, I tried to avoid the issue. The course was rigorous, modeled on the teacher's own college biology course. But Lucille was so anxious to pass a test—any test—that I went to the teacher, got the questions for an upcoming exam, and began to coach her. Lucille and I worked during the lunch break for three weeks. We labored over the structure of the cell. She drew cells on the chalkboard and cut cells out of construction paper; she made flash cards; we drilled; we invented acronyms to help her remember. Lucille would learn the material one day and forget it by the next, and so every day we started over. She never gave up. She desperately wanted to pass that test.

Lucille appeared in my doorway right after the biology test. "I didn't do too good," she confided, adding in a whisper, "I think I'm going to be sick." I tried to rush her to the lavatory, but we didn't quite make it. Evidence of Lucille's "failure" lay visible in the hallway. The poor child told me that she was sorry she had let me down. But in truth, I'd failed her. I vowed then never again to drill children on such inappropriate material.

I read in texts advocating mainstreaming that disabled students need "a chance to shine," that they "will learn from nondisabled students," that students with disabilities must be "seen as peers of nondisabled students." But nobody can make a disabled student equal, and nobody can promise a disabled student a phone call from a friend.

When following the mandates of P. L. 94–142, we need to figure out just what it means to mainstream children "to the maximum extent appropriate to their needs." Many school districts lump all children with learning problems together in a sort of academic twilight zone. The educable mentally retarded, the low normal, the learning disabled (whatever that means this week), and the emotionally disturbed are all sent off to regular English, science, social studies, and mathematics classes—until the situation becomes too traumatic either for the child or for the teacher. I always figured my district had to see blood before it would *de*-mainstream a child.

Tommy was amazing proof of a system run amok. His name appeared on my official class list the first day of school. I asked why he wasn't there, and the students replied, "Oh, Tommy never comes to school. Not even in first grade." He was a legend in his own time. I checked the records: Tommy had shown up eight times in sixth grade. He was sent on to seventh grade because he had already been held back three times, and teachers don't like to have tough, streetwise fourteen- and fifteen-year-olds in the same classroom with naïve ten- and eleven-year-olds. Hardliners who insist on the elimination of social promotion don't seem to be stepping forward with much advice on how to make mainstreaming work harmoniously for the little girl who keeps a teddy bear in her school locker and the randy hulk who should keep condoms in his.

I began agitating for the district to take Tommy's mother to court and get him into school. And for some reason, somebody did something. The departments in charge of social services and probation got together and sent a trainee to pick up Tommy at his front door every morning and escort him to the front door of the school. Predictably, Tommy came in the front door, raced through the building, and disappeared out the back door.

I heard about all this after the fact. Had I known about the plan to escort Tommy to school, I would at least have stood at the back door. But, as with most bureaucratic schemes, teachers are the last to know. And then we know only because the students tell us.

So the social service folks changed their strategy. A woman appeared in my doorway with Tommy and announced, "I'm with *him.*" When Tommy sat down, so did she. She pulled out a thick textbook—a psychology text, no less—and read all period, carefully underlining selected portions with yellow highlighter. Tommy did a bit of work when I crouched by his chair. As soon as I moved to someone else, he unleashed his repertoire of obnoxious tricks. When the bell sounded the end of the period, Tommy dashed out of the room; his companion grabbed her book and ran after him.

I phoned the main office and asked what was going on. I was informed that Tommy now had a court-appointed aide to keep tabs on him. "Good," I thought. Tommy needed one-on-one tutoring. The two or three times I'd worked with him had convinced me he could learn. He was, in fact, very cooperative when I worked alone with him. He liked that individual attention. But I had a classful of students, and Tommy was no good at waiting, at taking turns, at working by himself. He had never been in school long enough to learn these necessary rituals. If he could not have the teacher's immediate and total attention, he became indifferent at first, then hostile, and finally destructive. But with his own aide—maybe we had a chance. I immediately began to dream about Tommy getting some of the individual attention he craved, getting used to school, maybe even succeeding in school.

Fat chance. Tommy's aide quickly let me know how mistaken I was. She informed me that she was in our school solely to see that Tommy made it to class. She was not there to teach him, to talk to him, or to respond to him in any way once he was inside a classroom. She was taking graduate courses at night and had her own books to worry about; she certainly wasn't going to be bothered with Tommy's books. That was my job.

Tommy began racing out of his classes faster and faster. For a few days he just ran around the locker areas, letting the pursuing aide keep him in sight. Other students stood and watched and cheered him on. I suspect a few teachers were silently cheering too. Certainly none of us intervened. The aide had set the ground rules: our job was to teach; hers, to chase. The game soon lost its charm for Tommy, and he began dashing out of the building, losing his aide in the city streets, and returning to his life of petty crime. The last I heard, he'd been declared incorrigible and "sent away."

Another child in the mainstream for the first time, Joey, was taking a full academic curriculum when he wrote me this note:

Dear Mrs. O.,

For Christmas Santa brought me skates, coloring books, and shaving cream.

Your friend,
Joey

I didn't know whether to laugh or cry. Certainly the gifts were appropriate. Joey was a lovable child-man: fifteen years old, 5'8" tall, 150 pounds. Who could believe that Joey's teachers could possibly follow mainstream mandates and present him the academic curriculum at his appropriate level? And how could Joey's classmates provide something called "socialization" for a boy who needed both coloring books and shaving cream?

Joey's social studies teacher gave him a lot of special attention. But giving a student like Joey only a fraction of the study packet doesn't help him. Behaviorists can insist until the chalk turns to cheese that "all students can learn the school tasks expected of them if the tasks are rigorously programmed and the students are given enough time." Michael Dorris knows it ain't so, and Joey's teachers know it ain't so. Sad to say, youngsters like Joey don't know it. They have the faith of the innocent. They think that if they just work hard enough, they'll get it. While I was trying to teach Joey the difference between a city and a state, he begged me to coach him for a social studies test on the U. S. Constitution. While I was trying to teach him to address an envelope, he worried about writing a term paper on James Madison.

Even the most optimistic of us must admit that, given all the time in the world, Joey is not going to catch up. The school need not accept blame for the fact that he is not going to be a chemist or a cashier—or probably even a member of Congress or a vice president. But the school must shoulder heavy blame for failing to help Joey learn the things he *could have* learned, things he needed to know. Maybe his teachers should have spent less time helping him participate in some small way in lessons on Washington's battle plan, the three branches of government, or the causes of World War I; maybe someone should have helped him learn to tie his shoes and make change for a dollar.

When a seventh-grade teacher of social studies confronts her supervisor with some of the academic dilemmas posed by mainstreaming a boy like Joey, the supervisor insists that the child is in regular classes primarily for social reasons—"to learn how to get along with others, to make friends." The teacher is advised, "Be nice to Joey. Don't pressure him. Don't expect too much." So Joey's curriculum consists of the benign smile, the reassuring word, and the encouraging pat on the head. Social skills are the goal; cognitive development is seldom mentioned.

It is easy to be nice to Joey. He is a lovely boy. But just how "socializing" is it for him to sit in class after class not understanding the material—and being ignored by the "regular" students? The sad fact is that proclaiming equality, legislating equality, and even funding equality have never raised anybody's I.Q. And I'd like to see evidence that these actions ever improved a "poor perceptual-motor development of the body schema" either—or inspired a phone call from a friend.

Proponents of mainstreaming claim that all children can work on the same subject but at different levels. In effect, they say: give every child *A Tale of Two Cities* or *Foundations of Democracy* or *Modern Biology*. The Robins can read the whole book; the Blue Jays need read only half; the Pigeons can copy the table of contents five times. The Robins can dissect a frog; the Blue Jays can watch a movie about a frog; the Pigeons can play leapfrog. So the Robins go to the university, the Blue Jays might make it to a community college, and the Pigeons are cheated from learning what they can learn—what they need to know.

Then there was Arnold. He had an I.Q. of 68 and a history of abuse and neglect. He hated changing classes. I had to push him out of my room and down the hall to his next class, but he would run around and sneak in the back door of my room. He was terrified of eating in the cafeteria. He said that the other children stared at him and made fun of him. "Why can't I stay with you?" he would plead. "I'll just sit and read a book—I promise."

So I'd weaken and let him in, and then the litany would begin. "I bet you hate me too. Yeah, you really hate me. Everybody hates me. Everybody in this whole school hates me." Arnold would start listing the 1,126 people in our building, all of whom hated him. On and on he'd go, whining and wheedling for attention and approval. I soon realized I couldn't give Arnold enough. He sucked up approval with the power of an industrial vacuum cleaner, and all it did was make him whine for more.

But I wasn't a saint. After two weeks of keeping him with me during lunch, I locked my door. I figured if I didn't break up my day with at least fifteen minutes of peace and quiet, I'd soon be making bizarre noises too.

Arnold set his own course. Lots of days he did nothing but pester everybody in the room. The whole school got a blessed respite when he settled in on his spelling agenda. Always a good speller, Arnold spied the official departmental list for the eighth grade on my desk and decided to learn every word. For him, this was the pinnacle of academic achievement: a seventh grader learning eighth-grade spelling words.

For two months Arnold studied the list all day—in social studies, math, science, and physical education. He was never without the list. He ignored all other subjects, insisting, "I've got to learn my words." Arnold's other academic teachers were grateful. Studying spelling words gave him something to do. When he was huddled in a corner poring over his words, he wasn't running around the room making frog noises or pinching other students.

Every week or so Arnold would let me know that he was ready to be tested on another section of the list. He never scored less than 80, and he proudly showed off his 100s to the principal, the school nurse, and anyone else who would look. He tried to show his classmates, but no student would let Arnold near enough.

When it came time to do research for oral reports in our class, Arnold's social studies teacher—anxious for something to enter in her grade book—agreed that, if he reported on a famous American, she would give him credit too. For about a month Arnold carried around a boyhood biography of George Washington, frequently interrupting the class with anecdotes about George.

"When George was born," Arnold began his oral report, "his father looked at the dollar bill and said, 'I think I'll call him George Washington,' and that's how the baby got his name." I must have looked startled, because Arnold addressed his next remarks directly to me. "You have seen his picture right there on the dollar bill, haven't you?" He reached into his pocket, pulled out a dollar, and held it up. "That's how he got his name. Right off the money." On the departmental final exam, this boy was expected to explain the difference between communism and democracy.

If students and teachers are disoriented by mainstreaming, it also sends confusing messages to parents. Bobby's foster father wanted him removed from my class because he "keeps bringing home first-grade homework and first-grade spelling words." The man felt that such baby work was an insult to a seventh grader. He pointed out that Bobby was passing biology and social studies. So why the problem in language arts? Why didn't I give him seventh-grade work?

It is not easy to tell a parent that mainstreamed students *don't* fail, that his child can't read that biology book, or that a lot of teachers—not knowing how to handle the mainstreaming dilemma—give all mainstreamed students passing marks and give higher marks to the docile ones who cause no problems. How do you explain to a parent that this is called socialization?

Mainstreamed students get 90s on essays copied out of the encyclopedia—essays that stop in the middle of a sentence. "The teacher asked for two pages, so I wrote the two pages," Sophie says without a hint of irony. If the encyclopedia passage she's copying on Pocahontas runs out before the requisite two pages are filled, she just carries on with James

Polk. It is all the same to her—all equally meaningless. This is the curriculum of keeping them quiet, the curriculum of copying; it is also the curriculum of coping for the teachers trying to follow as best they can the rules of mainstreaming.

Every year Billy's teachers reported that he was "making good progress with decoding skills," but by the time he reached seventh grade he was in a constant rage because he couldn't read. I don't think anybody lied about that "good progress." He did make progress: every September he started from initial consonants, and by every June he had reached the *cr* blend.

As academic pressures mounted in the middle school, Billy's rages grew more frequent, and his mother was often called to school for his disciplinary hearings. She confided to me that she read only with great difficulty and that Billy's father couldn't read at all. She enrolled Billy in the nearby university reading clinic. Billy was thrilled that his professor was interested in him and was convinced that the professor would perform miracles. After every session, I'd get a blow-by-blow account of what the professor had said, what lesson the professor had taught. Billy was making rapid progress on the same decoding skills he'd "mastered" every year in school. And I hoped that maybe his new optimism could work miracles.

When Billy proudly showed me the "new book" he was reading for the professor, chills went down my spine. Like everyone else in Billy's old school, I'd known about him when he was a hyperactive third grader: I'd seen him race around the corridors. I'd also seen the vice principal sit and read with him every day—out of that very same book. A lot of earnest, caring teachers had tried very hard with Billy, but, like Michael Dorris' son, Adam, Billy seemed to have had one year of elementary school repeated eight times over.

After half a dozen or so trips to the university lab, when Billy realized that there was no miracle in the good professor's bag of tricks, his enthusiasm evaporated. He became surly and, according to the professor's report, "exhibited acting-out behavior of an antisocial nature." Since the university reading lab did not operate under the same constraints as a public school classroom, the professor kicked him out.

Billy found a life outside the mainstream. He dropped out of school as soon as he legally could and became a petty criminal. He has been in and out of jail ever since. I don't think it had to be that way. I wish we teachers could have acknowledged that Billy wasn't a mainstream child and offered him a different curriculum. Why did he get the same decoding skills year after year in elementary school and then an academic curriculum in middle school? What would have happened if, when Billy hit seventh grade, we'd said, "Okay, there are a few children who aren't going to learn to read—particularly if they are obnoxious, refuse to cooperate, and refuse to work at it"—and tried something else? We never gave Billy any chance to show what he *could* do, so he got even by making everyone around him suffer. But the sad part is, nobody suffered as much as Billy.

So-called liberal doctrine holds that "special classes"—a relic of education's dark ages—produce demoralization, low self-esteem, and inferior education. And I have seen plenty of evidence that they do. In the worst cases, the special education room is just a holding tank with a curriculum of movies and M & M's: even in the best cases, the curriculum has never taken a direction very different from mainstream academics. We never offer true alternatives but are lured time and again by the people who claim that everybody should learn the classics. We are very reluctant to admit that some people should be allowed—even encouraged—to be different.

We are good at accumulating labels: minimal brain dysfunction, perceptual-motor aberration, impaired learning efficiency, sensory deficit, delayed interpretation of input, and so on. Maybe we should spend less time on labels and more time providing meaningful alternatives for all students who don't flourish in the mainstream. As moved and challenged as I was by Dorris' book, I think little good will be served if it only inspires bureaucrats to look for children who qualify for the label "fetal alcohol syndrome." Of what use is any label to child or teacher if the school system can't come to grips with how to educate the child who is different?

Michael Dorris points out that in the media it is chic to portray the learning disabled as "invariably conscientious, anxious to please, desirous to make a good impression." But Adam taught Dorris to face hard facts: "Adam was not like that. Though I knew him to be sweet, gentle-hearted, and generous, the face he showed to the world was sullen. He avoided work whenever possible, refused to pay attention to his appearance, was slow to motivate, and only occasionally told the truth. His attitude discouraged even those who began their association with him enthusiastically. . . ."

For years Dorris was blinded by his dreams for Adam and not able to see him whole. Now that he has recognized the boy's shortcomings, it doesn't mean that he loves Adam less. Recognizing the shortcomings of special children doesn't mean that I care about them less. It just means that I am finally ready to move beyond slogans and to admit to some dark disappointments. I won't give up lighting candles, but I'm ready to admit the limits of candlelight. I'm ready to stop letting dreams of a more equitable society blind me to the very real and very different educational needs of special children.

To 'Pete,' Who's Lost in the Mainstream

September

Dear Pete,
Welcome to the Middle School. I hope you have a good year. I will write you a note every day, and I hope you will answer.
I went sailing a lot this summer. Did you do any fun thing?

Your friend,
Mrs. O

DeaR Miss
Mrs. O. I DieD Niet Have a NiCe SumRe The eND

Dear Pete,
You got a haircut! I like it! I cut my husband's hair. I'm very quick. And he is very nervous. He says "Be careful!" a lot.

DeaR Miss MRs O
iM Going To See nay ukce thats iN PRiSeiN Thaes WKaNDe

October

Dear Pete,
Answer this, OK? I miss hearing from you.

Dear Pete,
You did good work yesterday. Keep it up!

THAnK yOu. ThE ENd

November

Dear Pete,
What do you like to do when you are not in school?

SeliPe

Dear Pete,

Sleep? That does not sound very exciting. How many hours a day can you sleep?

Did you eat a lot on Thanksgiving? We are still eating turkey. Even my cats are getting tired of turkey.

geT OFF mY BaKe

Dear Pete,

No, I won't get off your back. Sorry. I am here to teach you to read, and I will do it.

geT oFF mY bak. OLeny Kidye

Pete Smith

Dear Pete,

I know. You are quite a kidder. But even if you're only kidding I'll be on your case every day. That's the way teachers are.

WRITE me every day. No kidding.

December

Dear Pete,

I hope you have a good Christmas. I'm getting my cats some catnip. They will be happy. I'm getting my husband a book I want to read. That's the way it goes.

YEs I will HaVe a gooD ChriStmaS yR por HUsbN

March

I dont winte to do the note to day

Smith. p.

Dear Pete,

That's OK. I have days like that too. And you have never heard anybody complain about writing letters the way my husband does. Good thing he's not in this class. He'd have a fit if somebody told him to write a letter EVERY DAY.

You are doing pretty well. Look at all these notes. It would take me six weeks to count them all. I'm proud of you.

May

Dear Pete,

My cat sits on top of the refrigerator, and it makes my husband MAD. He yells at the cat, but the cat doesn't care. He just does it again.

Sam thaing wetha my dog But He sits on the kioscue [couch]

Dear Pete,

Pets are tricky. They like to get their own way. Do you know any kids like that?

Yaw me and my barther

June

Dear Pete,

I hope you are not too sad. There is no school Friday and no school Monday. Be brave, Pete. Don't cry!

I'm too happ

Dear Pete,

Happy? Well, I know you will be sad soon. Just think—all summer I won't be around to bug you.

Mrs. O

I hop you ar her nathyer [next year] becase iT wont Be no Fane Weth out you PLes com bake

freNd Pete

[Note: Pete could not read any of the teacher's notes. They were read to him and then he wrote the replies.]

Dear Pete,

I'm not sending this letter to you, because I don't know how to say goodbye, and I don't know if you would understand me when I say I'm sorry.

I reported on the very first day of school last September that you were in critical trouble. The people who heard me asked, "How can you tell so soon?" Apparently, a teacher is not supposed to notice until the third month of school that a seventh grader doesn't even know the alphabet. I kept insisting that you needed special attention, though, and after a month or so your name was put on a list.

Every time your name was mentioned, school officials moaned, "Why wasn't something done about that kid in elementary school? How can a child get all the way to seventh grade without being able to read?" People checked into your background. Your mother's prenatal emotions are crucial in the evaluation process. I kept asking, "Why don't we do something about Pete's problem now?" But one cannot rush the bureaucratic process or leapfrog any step.

In November, an administrator announced to the Committee on the Handicapped that, like Rockefeller and Einstein, you are dyslexic and will never learn to read and that I should get a tape recorder. That administrator has never met you, Pete. And that's no solution anyway. I announced that someday when your parents got wind of this pronouncement and sued the district, I would testify on their behalf. So then I received an administrative memo ordering me to teach you to read. I also received a tape recorder. It's called administrative privilege. And cover your ass.

There was talk by some administrators that the problem would be solved if we could just get you labeled emotionally disturbed. After all, nobody expects those kids to read. And you did get in a lot of fights, Pete. You were always in the office. But you know it's better for people to think you're mean than dumb, right?

I kept telling people that you aren't psycho, aren't loony, aren't even mean. You are a big, tough kid who is desperate about not being able to read. I begged people to get you some individual help, to take you out of so many academic classes. By the time you got to me — the last period of the day — you were exhausted, mostly from playing the tough guy all day (so nobody would notice you can't do the work).

Administrators insisted nothing could be done about your academic schedule until we heard from Community Services. I wonder who those guys are and why we think they should solve our problems.

Every week on my lesson plans I stated that I was not meeting your needs and would like an administrator — any administrator — to come to our class and help me organize a program for you. Of course, I knew they didn't know the first thing about meeting your needs, but it was a way to keep putting on the record that you needed help. And nobody came — not even for an official observation. I think they were scared of both of us, Pete.

In April we finally heard from Community Services. They had misplaced your file in November but found it again around February after we bugged them daily for three weeks. But in February the neurosurgeon quit and nobody could find the E.E.G. he had done. So you had to be wired up again, and you weren't thrilled. I remember you joked about how people thought you were nuts, and I didn't know how to deal with your pain and frustration.

After your second E.E.G., a nice lady from Community Services finally told us that three physicians, a psychologist, and a social worker had examined you and reached the careful diagnosis that you don't read so well and have never liked school. Now that was news worth waiting for, wasn't it, Pete? Their prescription was that we should be kind to you and work with you individually. Now, I've been pretty darned nice to you, Pete, except for that time when you threatened to punch my face in. That day I yelled a little, but you didn't throw the chair at me after all and we both calmed down. And we really haven't had much difficulty since. Except you still can't read. And you're angry all the time.

School officials are happy because now you are labeled "special ed." and they won't be held responsible if you don't learn to read. They can insist that teachers give you a passing mark. This year I've refused. That seems ironic, doesn't it? The teacher who wore her heart on her sleeve for you all year is the only teacher who gave you a failing grade. The authorities asked me to give you a 65. Well, Pete, they came pretty close to making that an order. But I refused. I said it would send a false message to your parents. Worse, it would be giving you a false message. If I said you passed language arts, I'd be saying you had done adequate work.

But I know and you know, Pete, that it just ain't so. You enjoyed the books I recorded and you enjoyed our notes, but you refused to do anything else. I can think of all sorts of complex psychological explanations for your refusal to cooperate. I can understand your curses and your threats, but I care enough about you to say, "No way, kid." The buck stops here. It's not easy, but I can't just look the other way.

This class is about as individual a program as is possible: two teachers and fourteen students each period. And it's the only class you failed. You passed every other academic class, regular classes with thirty students. I wish that meant you did well in those classes, but I know the truth: some teachers would rather not rock the boat.

I asked for permission to give you an Incomplete, but the principal said the computer can't deal with that. The computer can't deal with that and we can't deal with you, Pete, so what's next?

I admit I was tough on you, Pete. My toughness was an expression of my hope and faith in you. I don't give up easily on kids, and you are definitely an okay kid. I figured we had one more year to work (and fight) together. But I have just been informed by an administrator who has a way with words that my program has been "liquidated." Two teachers for fourteen students is not cost-effective. So you can't come back here next year.

The people in charge assure me you will do fine in a regular language-arts class now that you have the special-ed. label. You won't fail, Pete. You are guaranteed to graduate on schedule. You can look at the pictures in the book, participate in class discussions, or put your head down and go to sleep. Nobody hassles mainstreamed kids just so long as they are quiet and don't cause trouble. Mainstreamed kids don't have to pass tests. They can go to the library and watch filmstrips.

People tell me I worry too much about teaching you to read. I know: Rockefeller and Einstein and Edison and Da Vinci. Even if I could believe 10 percent of the claims, I don't see that it has much to do with you. People keep telling me that if their own kids were "special," they'd want them in all the regular classes. That's what mainstreaming is all about. It's called "least restrictive environment," Pete. Mainstreamed kids aren't in academic classes to learn content or skills; they are there for something called socialization. I've never quite figured out just what that is. I wonder how sociable it is for a kid to be faced all day with work he cannot do, surrounded by classmates who can.

I brought your name to the Committee on the Handicapped because I wanted you to get relief from a heavy academic schedule. I had hoped you'd get an alternative program, one that would build on your strengths and provide you with more specialized help in reading. I thought a special-ed. label would do that for you, Pete. I was wrong. These days, a special-ed. label invites the people in charge to wash their hands of your special needs. They can shove a twelve-year-old boy into the mainstream, tell him to socialize, and give up entirely on teaching him to read.

Your friend,
Mrs. O.

Question of the Day

THE LIBRARIAN AND I both felt it was a shame that my remedial seventh and eighth graders couldn't read her books, so we decided to do something about it. We couldn't just say, "Read!" because the library had been stocked before school opened, stocked by someone buying from a grade level list, by someone who believed, no doubt, in the notion of gifted readers. Our library had three copies of Anatonia Fraser's *Cromwell*, four novels by Faulkner, and two copies of *Crime and Punishment*. One of the advantages of the good old K–8 building became apparent as soon as we tried to use our new library in our new middle school: all those great fairy tales, Dr. Seuss, and Easy-Read books were missing: no picture books, no Carle, Spier, Lobel, or Sendak. A lot of the "universal" books were missing, those books everybody can enjoy. Unfortunately, E. B. White, Hoberman, Cole, Ciardi, and Prelutsky are listed only in primary catalogues. Inexplicably, authors like Koningsburg, Patterson, L'Engle, Hinton, and Hunter were also missing.

Rotten readers are always eager to go to the library and hang around. They thumb through magazines or look at filmstrips if the librarian insists they must "do" something besides take the screws out of shelves. Both the librarian and I felt it was important to wean kids away from the ubiquituous screen. Filmstrips may have some benefit as yet unrevealed to me, but like their stepparent, television, they make for passivity, requiring nothing from the viewer. As educators, as people committed to books, we felt it was hypocritical to discredit TV and then plug those squirmy, bored nonreaders into the sound-filmstrip machines. Sometimes peace and quiet come at too high a price.

So we invented the Question of the Day. The best way to describe the need for the Question of the Day is to introduce Michael. Michael was one of the most turned-off kids I knew. He was a bright boy from a concerned, loving family. He liked cars and model planes and hot air balloons. As an eighth grader, he was beginning to discover that he also liked girls. Michael was popular with his peers and was good enough in sports to be on the high school freshman football team.

Michael's only problem seemed to be his inability to read. He approached the printed page first with evasion, next with bluff, and finally with panic. He had the classic signs of learning disability and frequently drove me to distraction with his complaining. When his ever-ready charm wore thin, I suspected that Michael was just a bit lazy. His favorite phrase was, "Well I can't help it." He'd heard so often from teachers that his dysfunction wasn't his fault that he used it like a real pro. Once when I told Michael his spelling list for the coming week would be the days of the week, he whined, "All of them?" But then he laughed. Michael's humor and very real charm often saved the day—for him and for me.

Michael had experienced nine years of failure in school, so he approached most new projects with "I don't think I can do that." When I told him about a "What would you do if you were Superman?" contest (one hundred words or less) sponsored by the local newspaper, he asked me if everyone who entered would get a prize. I had to say, "No." I had to explain that the harsh world out there isn't like the remedial reading cocoon: everyone doesn't win. So Michael lost interest in the Superman contest. He knew that kids in remedial reading were sure to be losers in the real world.

The Question of the Day was invented for kids like Michael, but the librarian and I knew better than to approach him directly with, "Michael, we have a question for you to research" because we knew Michael would shut us out with, "I don't think I can," or "Do I have to?"

So we told Laurie about the Question of the Day. Laurie was the kind of student every teacher needs to keep her sanity. Laurie had very poor abstract reasoning abilities, decoded at a third-grade level, often didn't comprehend 10 percent of what she decoded, and was eager to do any work suggested. I don't think Laurie learned a lot, but she worked hard. It is a sad reflection on reading programs, and school in general, but the Lauries of the world keep things running smoothly. One can deal with just so many Michaels at a time.

We gave out a monthly prize for "most homework handed in." We had to give two prizes—one to Laurie, who always did three or four times as much as anyone else—and a second prize to the leader of the rest of the pack. Laurie would demand eight pages of dictionary drill before a holiday weekend. "So I will have something to do," she explained. I was reluctant to give in to such requests because even though Laurie loved looking up long words and copying out reams of definitions, she couldn't read any of it. Even when I read her definitions aloud to her, she didn't understand them. Laurie never asked that something make sense; she only wanted to keep busy. I tried to get her to read books over the holidays, but she wanted to *produce* things; reading seemed far too passive.

On a Monday morning I told my students that the librarian was starting a contest. Few kids paid any attention. *Contest* is not an enticing word for kids who have themselves pegged as losers. From a mile off, rotten readers can spot a trick to get them to read. Laurie was the only one to express interest. "What kind of contest?" Laurie decoded on the same level as Michael, understood about one-tenth of what he did, but saw herself as a winner and accepted new challenges eagerly.

"Every day the librarian will ask a question. At the end of the week the person who has answered the most questions will win a prize," I explained.

Laurie was out of her chair and off to the library before I finished the explanation. Laurie had not been to the library all year. It was the one thing I hadn't been able to persuade her to do. Her favorite position in the room was at my elbow. I suspected she was afraid I'd hand out extra homework if she left the room.

Laurie was back in five minutes, a very serious expression on her face. "The librarian needs to know what mammal has webbed feet and lays eggs." Laurie got the *E* encyclopedia off the shelf. "*E* for *eggs*," she explained.

This is why rotten readers have so much trouble doing work in their academic classes. Just a week before Laurie was trying to research famous battles for her social studies class and she got the *F* encyclopedia. "Do you know what a mammal is?" I asked. The bell ending the period rang as Laurie was making a list of mammal characteristics from the dictionary definition. I had to shove her out of the room to go to her next class. A frequent complaint of poor readers is that just as they get interested in anything, a bell rings and they have to go to a different class and start something else. We insist on the Harvard model for everybody: if you're twelve years old (or eight or nine in some "innovative" grade schools), then you have to "grow up" and get ready for high school. If you're fourteen, then you've got to accept responsibility and get ready for college. Growing up and accepting responsibility means changing teachers and classes every forty-five minutes. Reading, willing, and able . . . or not.

Kevin had heard about the contest from Laurie when she was down in the library. He asked me, "Do you know the answer to the question?"

"I have no idea," I admitted. "I didn't even know any mammal laid eggs."

Michael wanted to know what we were talking about, so Kevin explained the Question of the Day to him. Michael was immediately intrigued. "Dolphins are mammals — no webbed feet though." When he was in seventh grade I tried to tap into some of his interests and had taped part of Livy's book on dolphins for him. "How about ducks?" Michael looked at me, hoping my expression would reveal the answer.

Ten years of working with poor readers had taught me how good they are at waiting for the teacher to give the answer, even when she isn't aware of giving it. "Where might you find out the general characteristics of mammals?" I asked.

"The dictionary," Michael smiled. He couldn't resist the little dig. "But I'll never find it, since I can't spell it. There are a lot of *m*'s in here, Mrs. O." I didn't give him a phonics lesson; I just spelled the word. He and Kevin read the definition together: mammals have a backbone, body hair, are warm-blooded, and nurse their young.

"I think it's a frog," said Michael. Kevin agreed. They got the *F* encyclopedia and found frog. Sure enough, there were the webbed feet and the eggs. All three of us were excited. Then they read, "Frogs are cold-blooded."

Michael could see the futility of wild guessing. "Maybe I'd better get a book on mammals." Michael didn't like the library; he was always complaining they didn't have "any good books down there." What he meant, of course, was they didn't have any books he could read.

Michael returned in fifteen minutes with a huge book on birds. I was stunned. I mean, Michael was smart; he had common sense. "Why did you choose that particular book?" I asked, keeping my voice as noncommittal as possible.

"Well," he said, "I looked in the card catalogue [Good boy! One of my most persistent themes is insisting they find things for themselves] and they had so many 599 books. . . ." He sighed. Michael's sighs as indicators of intellectual exhaustion were monumental. He had turned the sigh into an art form.

"Too many mammal books so you chose a bird book instead?" I couldn't help it; I started to laugh. Michael laughed too.

"Not really," he said. "Birds are mammals, too." He paused. "Aren't they?" Another pause. "Well, they lay eggs."

"Look at your list," I suggested. "Do they nurse their young?"

"Sure. They bring them worms and stuff."

"Nursing means something very specific," I explained. "Do you know what it means when a mother nurses or suckles her baby?"

"Oh," Michael blushed, but then he laughed. "Well, I just got a little mixed up. I guess I got the wrong book." But he still was interested. He didn't become defensive. He didn't give up. He was even fairly cheerful about going back and facing the monumental shelf of 599 books.

My students were very familiar with the layout of the library. I'd made a lot of laminated cards with tasks to help students become independent: find a book about mountain climbing, a recipe using chocolate, a picture of the Taj Mahal. The tasks weren't entirely arbitrary; I chose things I hoped would intrigue the kids enough to browse in the books. My notion was that even if kids couldn't read very well, they could be trained to use a library, to locate specific information when they needed to. My hope was that once they possessed these skills they might learn to

72

enjoy books a little. I was continually exhorting the very kind library aides, "Don't do it for them; make them use the card catalogue; make them learn to distinguish between an atlas and an almanac, a dictionary, and an encyclopedia." My students liked the library assignments mainly because they felt like real students when they were doing them. Other kids saw them working with real books for a change, not just filling in blanks in workbooks.

The librarian had "planted" a mammal book written on a third-grade level. When we heard of an elementary school closing down, she and I begged for their picture books and easy readers. People expressed amazement that a middle school library needed *Rumplestiltskin* and *Madeline*. No one who has taught seventh and eighth grade would question our need. Even good readers like to pore over old favorites occasionally, and children who have never experienced fairy tales, or not enough of them, have more than a casual interest. Their need is real.

Michael checked out the mammal book and it didn't take him more than ten minutes to discover a picture of a duck-billed platypus, complete with webbed feet. He read the text and found that it also laid eggs. Kevin, a much better reader, didn't participate, but he had kept half an eye and ear on the whole process, so now he knew the answer too, without lifting a finger.

Laurie came back later in the day and found the answer in pretty much the same way Michael did. Other kids in the room were interested — mostly in making wild guesses. Laurie and Michael were the only ones to write down the answer and turn it in to the librarian.

Tuesday morning Laurie rushed into the library before school began for the new question. She came to our room to announce it before going to her other classes: "What two birds can't fly?" Michael groaned when he heard it, "See? I did need that bird book after all." He tried the encyclopedia in our classroom and found *ostrich* mainly by luck. Kevin suggested that penguins don't fly, so Michael looked up *penguin* and had the answer. I asked Kevin why he didn't enter the contest. He just shrugged and said maybe he'd try the following week.

Meanwhile, all this sounded interesting to Arnold, so he started looking up mammals. He found the answer and went on to birds. With birds, however, he took a different approach: wild guesses. "Chickens. I bet it's chickens." He watched my face as he continued to make wild guesses, again the standard ploy of rotten readers: rely on the teacher's body language to know when you've hit on a right answer. Finally Arnold looked up *birds* in the encyclopedia, but he didn't read the text. He looked at the pictures, jabbed his finger at the page, and shouted, "These! They don't fly. I don't see any wings." When he didn't get any reaction from me, he yelled,

"Peacocks! That's what it is, peacocks." "Swans! I bet it's swans." This went on for half an hour. "Flamingos!" "Parrots!" "Turkeys! That's it—turkeys!" I began to wish the Question of the Day would self-destruct.

Finally I suggested to Arnold that he needed some sort of system. I helped him set up a chart of the birds he wanted to investigate. He decided to add columns of characteristics that had nothing to do with the contest: color of eggs, habitat, and so on. He liked checking off columns on his chart. He took it with him and cut two other classes to continue his work in the library, the locker room, wherever he could hide out. Arnold eventually found the answer, but he didn't write it down. He didn't care at all about the contest; he just found the question appealing. He entertained us with bird trivia for many weeks. He kept pestering the librarian, "When are you going to ask another bird question?"

I threatened her privately, "Don't you dare." If Arnold had gotten a fixation on birds again that term, it would have driven the rest of us crazy.

Laurie, having found the answer to the bird question in the morning, was afraid she would have nothing to do in the afternoon, so she went down and begged the librarian for another question: "What people discovered glass?" Two of the researchers went for the *C* encyclopedia. When I pointed out to Dick that he'd looked up *class*, he insisted, "I know. I'm just looking in here for what it says. This is interesting. I'll get to the other one later." All his school life people had been telling Dick that he mixed up letters. He was in seventh grade and still had a hard time admitting that he couldn't always make the proper distinctions.

This question was the easiest for them to answer independently—except they didn't know what they had when they located it. No one could pronounce *Egyptian*. Laurie had an extra problem. Thinking *people* meant family name, she went down the chronological listing of the development of glass until she came to a listing of a man's first and last name. I tried to explain to her that *people* could have the general meaning of nationality as well as the specific meaning of Bob Jones. I soon found it was too abstract a concept for her to grasp.

Once students hit middle school, the textbook writers, curriculum developers, and far too many teachers take it for granted that kids are able to categorize and deal with abstractions. Our social studies curriculum is a good example. After much complaint that the text was too difficult, a book written on the fifth-grade level was purchased. But we soon discovered it wasn't the "readability" that was giving us fits; it was the concept. The new book still expected students to answer questions about the Spanish influence in the New World, checks and balances in government, the westward expansion, the causes of World War I, the differences between communism and democracy. James Joyce posed the question:

"Who gave us this numb?" Students in social studies classes have the 4½-pound answer sitting on their desks.

I wish the guys who wrote that book—and the guys who insist that every kid can learn from it—could have heard Arnold's oral report on George Washington. We required oral reports from all the students in reading class. Students were expected to get up in front of their peers (ten other kids) and talk about information they'd found in the library. Such "reports" usually lasted about one minute.

Students used our laminated research cards to get started. The cards came complete with questions: How much does a newborn elephant weigh? What does it eat? How long does it live? Favorite topics included turtles, snakes, butterflies, lions. Surprisingly, other favorites were foreign architectural landmarks, especially if they looked "different": The Leaning Tower, the Eiffel Tower, the Taj Mahal. Each card had a picture on it, so the student knew what it was about before trying to read the questions. Later on, they used cards with pictures only. They had to think of their questions. Finally, there were no cards. We called it "independent research" and insisted that students choose topics on their own.

When we started the oral reports, Arnold was refusing to go to the library, so I suggested he choose a famous American and read a biography. His social studies teacher agreed to give him badly needed credit if he did a report in our class. Arnold chose George Washington and for about a month, whenever I tried to steer him toward any other work, he claimed he was reading about George. He frequently interrupted other students with anecdotes from George's boyhood.

Finally the big day arrived and, after much prodding (and threatening), Arnold stood up in front of the group. For a kid who was always pestering everybody else, trying to get attention by taunting, calling names, poking, and kicking, Arnold was suddenly very quiet. He stood in front of eight other kids and grinned, blushed, twisted his legs. Then he sat down and said he couldn't do it. The other kids coaxed and told him it wasn't so bad. Finally he stood up again and started talking. "When George was born," he began, "his father looked at the dollar bill and said, 'I think I'll call him George Washington,' and that's how the baby got his name."

I must have looked startled because Arnold addressed his next remarks directly to me. "You *have* seen his picture right there on the dollar bill, haven't you?" He reached in his pocket, pulled out a dollar and held it up. "That's how he got his name. Right off the money."

At the end of the report, one of the students asked Arnold if he'd ever met George Washington. "No," replied Arnold. "But I've seen him on TV lots of times." Nobody disputed this, and it wasn't out of politeness that nobody challenged Arnold's claim. They'd probably seen George on

TV too. Many seventh and eighth graders have no notion of "history" or "time"; they find it perfectly reasonable that their parents voted George into office. George is no more distant to them than is Kennedy or Nixon. But when I try to help them study for final exams, I'm supposed to explain time lines; they are expected to place in chronological order: Columbus, Magellan, Daniel Boone, Woodrow Wilson, FDR, the cotton gin, Hiroshima, and Sputnik. Teachers get upset when students think Vietnam was the war where Americans dressed up like Indians and dumped tea into the harbor. During all the Bicentennial hoopla, not one of my students could tell me what event we were celebrating. Ask them what country they live in, and they will reply New York, if not Troy. Piaget tells us that 25 percent of twelve-year-olds are abstract thinkers. We plan our curricula as though 90 percent were.

The library contest was good for me. It provided a very clear reminder about individual learning styles, things I was too apt to forget in the day-to-day routine in our class. First of all, only about one-third of my students participated. I see no reason to make everybody do the same thing. I don't see my primary function as teacher preparing my students for assembly line regimentation. I don't like plugging them all into the same sequences. Maybe this would be more efficient; certainly it would be easier to correct *a, b, c, d*. But it would also be deadening, dispiriting, and wrong.

The Question of the Day reminded me that sometimes I reacted too much to Dick's obnoxious attitude, forgetting that he'd go to any lengths to cover up or avoid admitting a mistake — even a straightforward perception mistake, something about which I'd thought I'd been able to relieve their anxieties. Michael could shrug off reversed letters with an "oh well." Dick couldn't.

Of course, I knew Arnold was "scattered," but the Question of the Day revealed how little structure he was able to bring to a problem. It forced me to seek out ways to further structure his day, to provide more links to his other classes. Arnold once decided he would be spelling champ of the eighth grade. He demanded a spelling test every day. Other teachers complained that all he did in their classes was write his spelling lists. He went through all the words on the department's official lists for seventh and eighth grades, and he seldom scored below 80.

The Question of the Day helped me make great inroads with Michael. I had tried to talk to him about his defeatist attitudes many times, but he'd shrugged it off. After his great success with duck-billed platypus — the whole class tried to say it quickly ten times (unsuccessfully but with much laughter) — I brought up the old issue. "Michael, do you realize you conducted independent research, and not once did I hear an 'I can't' or a 'Do I have to?' And, Michael, *I* learned a lot besides. I didn't know half that stuff you researched. I certainly didn't know a thing about duck-billed platypuses." He grinned. Then he grinned some more. "I know," he said quietly.

Michael did not win that first Question of the Day contest. Laurie did. She kept getting extra questions. I soon put a stop to that. Laurie would have turned it into a sixty-eight-Questions-a-Day contest. I sometimes wondered how Laurie could get out of her other classes so easily. By all known measure, she was one of the least academically able kids in the school, but she seemed to spend most of her time out of class: she ran errands, got "free time" in the library. Whenever we wanted to know why the fire alarm went off, why Arnold was in the office, where the custodian kept the mop, we asked Laurie. She was always on top of what was happening in the building.

I suspect one reason Laurie was released from class so often was because it is tough being faced with a child who can't read. Since reading instruction has become institutionalized and specialized, science and social studies teachers are convinced their mission is to teach "content matter" and leave reading instruction to the reading teacher. Once a student hits middle school, even language arts teachers don't teach reading: they teach literature and grammar. At a joint meeting with the social studies department, some language arts teachers suggested that their social studies colleagues might concern themselves with student writing. There was nearly a riot. The general feeling was that the language arts people were trying to get away with something. "We don't ask you to teach World War I. We aren't going to teach verbs."

Much to my surprise, Michael persevered, and he won the second week's contest. Michael, the boy whose mother read all his texts aloud because he "couldn't do it," found a way to answer the questions. He found a way to use materials in the library. He found a way to cope.

Michael's mother revealed a nice spin-off from the contest when she came in for conferences. "He comes home with the most intriguing information. Every night at dinner he stumps his older brothers with questions like 'I bet you don't know two birds that can't fly.'" She looked at me, "Michael has always been able to remember things he's been told, but he insists no one is telling him these things. He says he's finding this information in the *library*, in *books*." I told her it was true. She cried a little, and so did I.

I had been hinting to Michael's mother that she stop reading all of his texts to him. I decided it was a good time to push that issue. "Let him do some of the work. Michael can cope much better than either of you think he can." I suggested, "Why don't you just leave the house some evening, telling him you expect the homework to be done when you get back?" It was a radical suggestion to make to the devoted mother who had patiently read every science chapter, suffered through every social studies assignment since second grade. "Michael is not going to have you sitting at his side all his life," I insisted. "You must help him to become more independent."

She did it. The Question of the Day provided the breakthrough, the evidence that Michael could cope. All three of us then had to live with the decision. Michael told me he'd probably fail science if nobody read those chapters to him. "Maybe so," I said, "but you'll never know what you can do until you try." He started bringing his books to class, started assuming responsibility for asking for help when he really needed it instead of claiming he couldn't do any of it by himself. Michael began to learn to throw away the adult crutches he'd relied on for so many years. His grade in science did drop, but he passed.

I suggested that Michael's mother continue reading to him but that they read together for pleasure. I sent home books they could enjoy together. This plan did not work. It seemed too frivolous to both of them. Reading had been too deadly serious for too many years for them to envision it as a pleasurable activity. Schools have a lot to answer for.

Reading will undoubtedly never be a real pleasure for Michael, but I am happy to report that it is something he has learned to value. He occasionally drops by our class. "Do the kids here still read? Do you still get all those newspapers? Do they do library research? Do you read stories to them? Do they read jokes to you?" I nod. Michael adds, "I never liked reading. You made me do it. I should be reading now, but we don't read in my English class at the high school. Filling out workbook pages isn't the same thing."

No, it isn't. Michael is no dummy. He understands what the perpetrators of so many skill programs do not: reading must have a purpose, and ultimately, that purpose must be linked to our curiosity, our need for beauty, humor, order. Drilling for the CAT or the state competency exam is too small a purpose to satisfy the Michaels of the world. It isn't good enough for the Lauries or the Arnolds either. They need—and deserve—more.

Michael wouldn't be surprised—as I fear his "skills" teacher might—to know that researchers Leinhardt, Zigmund, and Cooley found (*Educational Research Journal* 1981) that the amount of silent reading was far more important to reading growth than the amount of time spent on skill sheets or workbooks. The students in my remedial classes have proven to me again and again that we all need poetry, humor, mystery, and tragedy from words. Words tell us about the world and about ourselves. My students know that even reading an encyclopedia passage to find out if penguins can fly is of infinitely more value than filling in eighty-three blanks in a cloze passage.

The materials we use reveal the values we hold. I am continually amazed, and disheartened, by the low esteem in which my reading colleagues hold books. They tell me they can't find the time to read to their students. They can't take the time away from drill and "content" practice (now there's a term to try my soul). They regard my adherence to books as somewhat charming ("Sue sure does love books") but essentially frivolous. ("Sue, your program has been cancelled. The EDL system is much more efficient.")

Not long before Michael graduated from eighth grade, his mother wrote me, "I like to think I would have written to thank you on my own, but I am writing this letter because Michael asked me to. We both want to thank you. Michael was very emphatic that our thanks should be in a *letter*, in words that would last."

I couldn't tell you Michael's score on the CAT, and maybe that's why my program was cancelled. But I do know he learned something important from me. Michael learned that he could find out about duck-billed platypuses on his own. He learned that words count, that words can give joy, that carefully chosen words will last. I think these are far finer gifts than the ability to circle consonant blends.

Will You Recognize the Ready Moment?

AFTER TWELVE YEARS as a secondary teacher, I voluntarily transferred to primary. As a third-grade teacher, I looked forward to getting kids at an early age, capitalizing on their freshness, their curiosity, their willingness to explore and experiment. Just into my second week, I received the spine-chilling news that students in third grade learn Cursive. Cursive is always referred to that way in third grade—with a capital *C*. Cursive, I learned with foreboding, is a hot topic in third grade.

I was anxious to do whatever a third-grade teacher does. So, in the fourth week, I dug through the closet and found a dusty manual that showed all the letters in big, magnificent Palmer swirls. I propped it in the chalk tray and tried to copy the swirls on the chalkboard while the children tried to copy them at their desks. They moaned and groaned and complained it was too hard. Leslie pouted. Then she wept, wailing that it wasn't fair. She'd been in special classes for the handicapped up until this year and had never been taught cursive. I explained that nobody had, and it was my job to teach it. She sobbed, "I don't know how. It's too hard. I can't." Then she crumpled up her paper and put her head down. "I hate cursive."

Finally, after three weeks of torture, I quit. I stuck the manual back in the closet and told the kids to keep on printing. For half the day the three third grades were split up into low, middle, and high reading groups, and I had the bottom one—the kids who either couldn't or wouldn't read, the kids who told me they hated reading. Did we have time for cursive? No, we needed to spend our time learning the drama, the humor, the mystery, the boisterous laughter, and the silent pleasures of reading.

Upon Student Request

The middle and high reading groups did learn cursive, however, and they enjoyed showing off their new skill. Occasionally there were snide comments in the hallways about kids who still printed. I continued to ignore the Palmer manual. But in mid-March an interesting change began to occur in the low reading group. Every so often when a student asked me to spell a word on the board, she'd add, "Write it in cursive." Children began to ask me how to form individual letters. Then one day Leslie demanded, "How come we aren't learning cursive?"

By that time I'd been around third graders long enough to suspect that within the kids lie certain pedagogical truths that need to be heard. So I told Leslie, "As a matter of fact, we're starting cursive today. Right this minute." I promptly wrote their spelling words on the board in cursive. "Try it for yourselves," I suggested. I didn't get out the manual, didn't insist on proper swirls. Instead, I just walked around and gave advice where it seemed needed. Two kids had trouble copying all ten words. Leslie filled her entire page, writing the list over and over.

After that, every Monday I wrote their spelling words in cursive so they learned the letters in a somewhat haphazard fashion. Occasionally someone would ask for a specific letter, and I'd demonstrate. Everybody could do his own name very well so each became an expert on those letters: Leslie held workshops on the capital *L*, Gina on the troublesome *G*. Then they began to ask for cursive renditions of the poems I printed on the board each day. I felt like a translator at the United Nations, putting everything on the board in two versions—manuscript and cursive.

Just three weeks after this reintroduction of cursive, Leslie, with great fanfare, presented me with a note that was entirely in cursive: "Dear Mrs. O., I love lemon ice cream, vanilla ice cream, butterscotch-swirl ice cream. . . ." Leslie had listed all thirty-one flavors from an ice-cream list.

"Where did you learn all that cursive?" I asked in a note responding to hers.

"You taught me," she wrote. "Don't you remember?"

I began comparing the cursive production of my low reading group with that of other children who had been painstakingly practicing Palmer method all year. There didn't seem to be all that much difference. It was clear that a few children in all reading groups had not made a good transition to cursive yet. But insofar as my low group had made it, they had made it painlessly.

The Child's Timetable

Children aren't lazy. They like challenges, but they know when they can't handle something. In the fall my reading group knew that cursive was high-prestige stuff. But they also knew that it was too tough for them at the moment. When they were ready for it they let me know, and then a lot of them picked it up overnight.

We must stop pretending that we can be train conductors programmed to keep kids operating on someone else's ideal schedule. Why not take, instead, a learning-to-ride-a-bicycle approach. Nobody would try to establish an optimum grade level for bicycle riding. No one knows just how a kid first does it or how many times he has to fall before he will succeed. But we can agree that for all our help, encouragement, and wiping of tears, he has to ride that bike by himself.

Of course, children don't always know what's best for them in all matters. But we teachers need not always assume the worst, need not operate on the principle that kids are inherently lazy and that they must be forced to learn according to someone else's prescribed schedule. I don't deny that it would have been possible to teach cursive in September. I am aware of learning theories claiming that children with reading problems benefit from cursive. But there are research dogmatists promoting just about everything, and the classroom teacher must look at her own students and decide what is best for them. Not forever and ever, but for this hour, this moment. Instead of filling in my intentions for each block of time in my weekly lesson book, I always thought it would be more to the point to scrawl across all five columns, "What do I plan to do this week? My best."

It always seemed to me more important to get my class to like writing—that is, the creation of ideas—than to spend a lot of time on handwriting drills. When Chris, who had the messiest penmanship I had ever seen, and whose parents diligently made him practice writing every night, growled, "I hate writing," I replied, "But you really get upset if I haven't written you a note to answer."

"But that's not writing," Chris insisted. "That's talking. I talk and you answer me."

I can't imagine why any child would want to write only to repeat meaningless lists, or learn to read if the only prospect is more workbook pages. But it is easy to forget that education isn't just an accumulation of 6,548 skills. As poet-farmer-teacher Wendell Berry points out, "Good teaching is an investment in the minds of the young, as obscure in result, as remote from immediate proof as planting a chestnut seedling."

Standing Up to the Curriculum Coordinators

The educationists would have us produce an assembly-line model at the end of each lesson and each year—a product that has mastered a precise number of calculable matters and in the correct order. But we must resist. We must not abdicate our authority; we must stop relinquishing to the theorists, the state mandators, and the curriculum coordinators the decision of what is fit and right to teach. Maybe now that minimum-competency bookkeeping has revealed itself as the dispiriting tedium it really is, we can gather up our courage and set aside 143 basic skills, keeping faith in our own intuitions for recognizing the teachable moment.

I once had the privilege of watching Daryll discover that 16 bottle caps on one side of a balance weigh the same as 16 bottle caps on the other side. It took him 3½ hours of hard work to convince himself of this fact. Then and only then did he quickly confirm his suspicion that 6 wooden cubes would balance 6 wooden cubes; 12 marbles, 12 marbles, and so on. I had desperately itchy fingers watching Daryll make his discovery because he'd be on the verge of it, and then he'd mess it up by putting the bottle caps and a block on one side and four marbles on the other side. Scientific method can be as messy for six-year-olds as it is for Nobel Prize winners. Teachers can't provide shortcuts to discovery. What they can — and must — do is provide time and space for the child who is ready to make his own discoveries.

Instead, an "ideal" timetable created by textbook writers, state credentialists, school boards, and an epidemic of advisors is pressed upon the classroom teacher. This pressure breeds the proliferation of the purple plague of the classroom: skill sheets. Everybody feels comfortable knowing the child has done a certain number of these sheets. The skills can be marked; competency levels for individuals and groups can be charted and sent off to the administrator who tabulates such things.

But children themselves find out very early what is regarded as authentic work in school — workbooks and skillbooks and apostrophes are authentic. Reading with joy and sorrow isn't. Chris, a reader in my low group, suddenly started peppering his writing with those nasty little marks, apostrophes. Just about every time a word ended in *s*, Chris threw in an apostrophe near it, sometimes on one side, sometimes on the other. Even with his name, which he began writing as *Chri's*. "What gave you this idea?" I asked him. "My friend showed me," he beamed. "That's what they are doing in the top reading group."

Chris, author of fifteen fan letters to Jack Prelutsky ("I have read 20ty of your poems. I may read them all"), probably figured that once he knew cursive, the lack of the apostrophe was the only thing keeping him in low reading. After his fifth letter to Prelutsky, I confessed to Chris that I'd only mailed the first one. "That's all right," he said, "I just like writing him. I love his poems." It is hard to explain to Chris that time spent loving Prelutsky's poems is time infinitely better spent than that devoted to drill on the apostrophe. There is no storybook ending for Chris and the apostrophe. He did not learn it. To have insisted that he always knows best would have been naive, although not as destructive as saying that he never did know best. That is why teachers are needed. They can make decisions about the apostrophe and everything else based on their knowledge, intuition, and sensitivity.

Maybe the reason curriculum coordinators and teachers like apostrophes and plural endings so much is that it's apparent by the end of the lesson whether the kid can do it. Never mind that he probably won't remember where the funny little marks go tomorrow or next week. You can give a test and document it. Fifteen letters to Jack Prelutsky is not adequate documentation. With reading—real reading—you are never quite sure. Essentially the child's involvement and interaction with a book are a contract that must be struck anew with each book he reads.

I tell myself that I can't expect Chris to appreciate that I taught him to read—and enjoy—lots of poems. But then I realize that I didn't, not really. I provided the books, the time, and the encouragement, and then Chris began to read. Exactly how he did it remains a mystery to me, one that I can't reconstruct in three—or forty-three—steps, one that I can't duplicate for another child.

Setting the Stage for Discovery

All of this is not to say you can't "prime the pump" by continually providing kids with learning opportunities that you think are important for them. Just that you can't make learning happen when—and how—you want it to.

I work with rhyme a lot with children because I've found that, somehow, it holds a clue that enables children to cross the bridge to reading. Basal committees have an idea of this and stick in a few poems and supplement them with workbook drills and so-called activity sheets of the *fan-man-can* variety. But by mid-second grade the basals are done with rhyme and the child is expected to move on to more sophisticated stuff. However, I had a whole classful of third graders who had no notion of rhyme, so I gave them a rhyming spelling list every week. They memorized the lists but still didn't seem to "get" that if *might* and *sight* and *fight* all ended the same way, so probably did *light*. Never was that axiom "You can teach and teach and teach but that doesn't mean the kids will learn" brought home more forcefully. But I didn't give up on rhyme.

I had a pet theory that kids who don't like books will probably never like them if they don't respond to rhyme. So when a child refused to choose a book during our daily silent reading period, I always handed her a rhyming book—with no comment. Cindy growled her usual growl about hating reading and tried to avoid even touching the book, but my scowls were as fierce as hers, and finally she began turning pages—maintaining her mean, mad look for twenty minutes. Then I saw the light of learning. She reread the page she was on and then quickly turned back and reread previous pages. She went back over each page, touching words, carefully checking her newly discovered theory.

She brought the book over to my desk. "Guess what? This book rhymes!" That was it. The next day I handed her another book. This time it only took ten minutes before she was at my elbow, exclaiming,

"You know what? This one rhymes too!" This time she added, "You know how I can tell? All the words end in the same letters. That makes them sound alike." Every week for two months, as I put the spelling list on the board, I'd said, "Look how all these words end in the same letters." But kids have to ride their own bicycles when they are ready. Cindy ferreted out every book in the room that contained even a single rhyme. Then she moved out to the library, telling the librarian, "I like any book, just as long as it rhymes."

Three months later, Cathy made the same discovery in pretty much the same way. A severe stutterer, Cathy said she liked rhymes because she could read them aloud without stuttering. That gave someone the idea that maybe they could memorize poems and recite them. It was fun reciting these poems among ourselves, but the kids wanted to show off their talents to the rest of the school. Cathy worried that her stuttering might reappear at an embarrassing moment, and so her friends came up with the idea of choral recitation. Soon we had troops of kids from the third grade low reading group traveling throughout the school reciting verse. Had anyone asked me in a theoretical way where I stood on the evils of memorization, I wouldn't have hesitated in my reply—until the children showed me differently.

We teachers never learn. The next year, recalling the lovely moments of insight with rhyming books, moments that paved the way for a rush to the narrative books *Amelia Bedelia, Nate the Great,* and *Peter Rabbit,* I decided to create a rhyming curriculum—not a repeat of the dreaded spelling lists but something enchanting and engaging. But I had a new group of students. They had different abilities, different needs. Their teachable moments would be something we had to discover together, not a rehash of last year's, not something I could structure or even anticipate.

John Holt tells of the little boy who "finds it mysterious and exciting that the label that said 'fruit cocktail' yesterday still says it today." Such moments must not be taken for granted. Nor can they be prescribed. It does no good to announce to the class that the label will always say "fruit cocktail."

The Kids Will Guide You

When Leslie complained that she couldn't do something because she was handicapped and it was her first time in public school, I reminded her that it was my first time in third grade, and we'd better just struggle along together. Leslie was spoiled, overprotected; she cried a lot. She was also brave, determined, exuberant, strong-willed, filled with humor. Severely hearing impaired, she was one of the most expressive children I have ever known. During the first semester I spent a lot of time hugging her, wiping her tears, writing her notes, finding special books to delight her. I also tried to toughen her up, gently teasing her, helping her learn to laugh a bit at herself.

Then one dismal day during my annual February panic, when bureaucratic nonsense combined with the conviction that churlish winter would never end and I hadn't taught the kids a thing, Leslie hugged me as she left the room. She looked up and said very earnestly, "Now don't you worry. It's OK. We are going to learn it. You are doing a good job." She also left a note on my desk, telling me about a new adventure with her cat. She added, "P.S. A lot of people love you."

No, we aren't always aware of just what we are teaching. I didn't know my February desperation was so obvious to the children. I hadn't guessed my love for Leslie would be returned tenfold. I am not proposing that children are possessed of Original Virtue; I don't support the notion that Kids Always Know Best. What I am saying is, What's the rush? We must be very careful that in following some preordained timetable we don't miss significant sights along the way. If we reflect on our own days in school, we realize that what is memorable are those side trips.

In *Earthly Pleasures* science writer and maple-syrup maker Roger Swain tells us that even where the sap flows best "the drops form one at a time." They also fall one at a time. Even in our present circumstance of instant everything, you can't hurry maple syrup—or third graders. Neither is a project for the impatient. Swain goes on to say that in boiling the sap as well, "the change from colorless sap to a light amber syrup is impressively slow." So, too, the change from an intransigent reluctant reader, the child who only scowls at books, to the boy who insists on copying *Peter Rabbit* in longhand because he liked reading it so much. It doesn't happen overnight or even upon completion of 1,682 workbook pages. We must recognize that children make great intuitive leaps but in-between times things often seem impressively slow.

While he is waiting for the sap to become syrup, Swain meditates on why he does this, recounting the tedious minutiae of getting everything ready, the physical exertion and discomfort, the frustration of the endless wait for results. Then he concludes, "There's a satisfaction to being involved in something so justified." One can only hope that teachers take a few minutes to meditate on their activities and come to the same conclusion.

References

Swain, Roger. 1981. *Earthly Pleasures.* New York: Scribner's.

Okay to Be Different

"CHARLES CAN BE a little strange," his special education teacher warned me. Charles was being mainstreamed into my third-grade reading group for the morning. In the afternoon he would return to his special education class.

At age eleven, Charles was three years older than the average third grader. Conferences with his social worker, psychologist, and mother revealed a history of abuse, emotional upheaval, and retarded development. But we hoped he would find a place in my group of "low" readers.

For the first week, Charles was on his best behavior. He was so determined to be "normal," to fit into a regular class, that he sat like a statue. Each day started with a fifteen-minute silent reading period, and during that time Charles' eyes remained frozen on his book. Whenever I asked him about his book, he assured me it was "very, very interesting."

The child who insists he likes all books usually likes none but can't admit it. As long as Charles played the role of model student, I couldn't discover his interests and help him become involved in books. But after about two weeks of watching the other children talk and tease and complain, Charles began to loosen up. I considered it a triumph the day he muttered that he hated reading, too.

Charles also told me what was wrong with my book collection: "No dinosaur books." The next day I brought in a large dinosaur book. I hoped the colorful illustrations would help him get through some of the difficult text while I searched for an easier, more suitable book.

Charles stuck with the large book. He would page through easy-reading dinosaur books that I found, but he always returned to the more difficult volume. He insisted it was a "real" book. As our silent reading period increased to half an hour, then to forty-five minutes, I urged Charles to try other books. He would obligingly glance at fairy tales, riddle books, mysteries, adventures. But he didn't read them. Instead he would return to his dinosaur book.

Charles hated for me to read aloud. Whenever I sat down with a new book, the other children happily crowded around, taking turns snuggling up close. Not Charles. He would sit far off in another corner, scowling and twisting his body into strange shapes. To make doubly sure that I understood his discontent, he would make strange chirping noises as I read.

A Weirdo

One day Charles vomited. After the mess was cleaned up, he started crying and moaned, "I'm a weirdo and a retard. I never can do anything right."

I was devastated, not knowing how to comfort this child who was indeed a bit odd. His classmates—who'd never really warmed up to him but never bothered him either—came to the rescue. "Everybody vomits sometimes," they reassured Charles. Then each had a vomit story to tell as proof that Charles was behaving normally. Finally I began to feel queasy and announced, "Enough sharing." But as I pushed ahead with the lesson, the children worried over Charles and continued to sneak to his desk with another whispered "My Most Embarrassing Vomit."

Charles stopped sobbing but he kept his head down on his folded arms. I couldn't tell whether his classmates' messages were getting through to him. But the next day he came to class carrying a bright yellow sign. "Would you put this up on the bulletin board?" he asked me.

It was a note to the class, listing each child's name and concluding with "I love this class very much." Opposite the message was a large smiling face that I recognized as myself—the red hair was the giveaway. Charles' special education teacher later said he had told her the names of all the children; he asked her to help him spell them correctly, insisting that it was very important to get them "just right."

Charles wasn't the only child who had problems other than difficulty with reading. The group included a deaf child, a severe stutterer, an asthmatic, and a child who was alternately hyperactive and zonked out by medication. Several children had failed a grade, some couldn't make their letters go in the right direction, and one excellent reader couldn't make letters at all. For all that, these children were normal third graders; they laughed, they pestered, they complained, they rejoiced, and they cried. But when someone had a personal crisis, they gathered round as one and offered consolation.

Of Compassion and Cocoons

Because of the school's emphasis on reading, these kids were with me for half the day, and I grew to know them well. I was impressed by their sensitivity to each other's needs and, as it turned out, to my needs as well.

Cathy was energetic, sociable, enthusiastic, cheerful, and loved to share jokes and stories. But she was a stutterer. Seldom could she utter a sentence without halting, repeating, struggling to get the right sounds out. No one ever commented about her difficulty or expressed impatience that we had to wait so long for the punch line.

One day the usually ebullient Cathy seemed strangely reserved, and her friend mentioned that someone in the cafeteria had teased her about her stutter. Before I could say a thing, the class was up in arms, making speeches about how no one is perfect, how everyone has problems. "Besides," said Joe, "Cathy doesn't stutter that much." "And she tells good stories," added Jennifer. "Some people are ignorant," offered Bobby as he patted Cathy's arm. "Just ignore them."

Leslie was in public school for the first time, having spent her early schooling in a special class for the deaf. She wore an elaborate microphone set so she could hear much of what was said, but her speech was hard to understand at first.

The children formed a cocoon around her, treating her like a china doll, bringing her presents like new pencils and erasers. If teachers couldn't make out what Leslie was saying, she had a score of ever-ready interpreters hovering around. When we needed a heroine for a class play, the children chose Leslie; when she didn't understand knock-knock jokes, kids took turns reading them with her, patiently explaining and helping her to "hear" the pun. When she cried, they comforted her; when she was selfish or obnoxious, they pretended not to notice. Leslie was allowed and even encouraged to be queen of our class for about three months.

Then, as she settled into school routines, the class decided by some unspoken consensus that it was time for Leslie to begin learning to be a regular student. They made her wait for her turn. She was no longer always first in line; and if she pushed, she got pushed back. The first time they let her cry, pretending to go on with their work, they were obviously nervous. But nobody gave in. I followed the kids' lead, ignoring Leslie's tears, fighting back the same urge the kids were fighting. Together, we helped Leslie toughen up, helped her become a normal third grader.

I had my own moments of consolation from these children. I'd been going through a rough period; work was piling up and administrative directives were coming down — nothing unusual. But I let it get to me, and one day I yelled at somebody for a minor infraction. It was a real bellow. It was also sort of funny because we all froze after I did it. I broke the stunned silence with an apology: "I'm sorry. What you did was wrong, but it wasn't worth all that. I feel bad when I yell at you."

The kids crowded around, assuring me, "You don't yell. Not really." They wanted to give me explicit stories about real yelling that they had known in classrooms. I was touched that they responded to my vulnerability so quickly, so compassionately.

Fat Cats to Flies

Charles kept chirping when I read aloud. This behavior went on for months. One of the children asked me, "Why does he do that?" I could only reply, "I don't know." Charles was the only child I had ever encountered who could resist read-aloud time. The first breakthrough came when I read *The 300-Pound Cat*. The children were enthusiastic about the outrageous humor and the wonderful illustrations. Charles, of course, was too far away to see the pictures. He maintained his scowl, accompanied by weird body contortions. But he began inching his chair across the room. By the time I had finished the story, Charles was behind me, whispering in my ear, "That's like *The Fat Cat*."

"What's that?" I asked him. How would Charles know? I thought. He only looks at that dinosaur book.

"Fat Cat is like that 300-pound cat," Charles explained patiently. "Fat Cat eats a lot. He gets bigger and bigger." Charles got up and went to the table, quickly unearthing the small paperback, a Danish folktale. Following Charles' lead, I read the book to the children. Then we all read it together, each child taking a page. Charles indicated he wanted a turn too. That was the first time he'd read aloud in front of the group.

When we finished the book, Charles said, "It's like the boy in *Mother, Mother I Feel Sick, Send for the Doctor Quick Quick Quick* and the old woman who swallowed a fly in *I Know an Old Lady*."

I was stunned. Not only was Charles reading, he was making connections.

After that, hardly a day went by that Charles didn't make some connection between books or between books and events in his own life. He discovered *Clown of God* and *The Last Leaf* on his own and began to write stories about the death of his father, intermingling them with observations from the books.

Charles had come a long way from those early days when he wouldn't say a word in class or read aloud or take part in any group activity for fear of sounding weird. Now he took another step: Charles volunteered to be narrator for a class puppet production of *The Frog Prince* that would be presented to all 70 third graders. The puppeteers were concealed behind a screen, but the narrator—Charles—had to stand out in front all by himself, the only member of the troupe visible to the audience. Charles was so enthusiastic about his performance that he suggested presenting the play on the auditorium stage for the entire school.

Charles taught me a lot about not underestimating kids. Although I saw him making great strides in social interaction and came to know that he was reading and appreciating many books, I still worried about the dinosaur book. I wondered how I could justify the fact that Charles spent an hour or two a day poring over a book that I was convinced he couldn't understand. I worried, but I held my peace. I reminded myself that kids want to be regular; when they persist for days and months at what looks like an irregular activity, they aren't doing "nothing," they're not "wasting time." They're responding to needs that the teacher isn't able to recognize at the moment. Charles kept on with the dinosaur book.

In March, the homeroom science class began working on projects for the science fair. Fred, a top-notch student, decided to make a dinosaur diorama. Charles offered to lend his book. He also offered some advice. "Everybody knows about *Tyrannosaurus rex*," he said. "Why don't you make some of the others?" He leafed through the book. "Like this one. He's called *Therizinosaurus*. He has arms eight feet long with great big claws." Charles continued turning pages rapidly as two or three other students came over. "Or this one—*Cetiosaurus*. He swallows stones to help him digest his food."

And so it went. Charles could pronounce the long names; he could also offer specific information about how one dinosaur differed from another. His repertoire of dinosaur facts was truly stunning. (Still, he had basic misconceptions. One day while slowly turning the globe, he commented, "I guess dinosaurs never will come back. Some of them were thirty feet long, so they would never fit. Look, here's Africa." He spread his palm over the continent.)

Try, Sam

That spring we faced the regularly scheduled standardized tests, an event that made everyone nervous. What could be worse than isolated questions about structure, and comprehension questions about ugly paragraphs? On the first day, Charles had marked all four of the possible answers for the first three questions before I caught him. I made him erase it all and then pleaded, "Try, Charles, please try! I know you're nervous, but I also know you can do it. Just think of all the books you've read this year. Okay, so this test isn't nice to read, but how about showing the people who made this test that you *can* read?" Try he did, and he showed those people that he could read on what they call a 3.8 grade level.

After the tests, I read the kids a story and urged them to relax, mess around, and unwind. Charles started talking to Sam, the brightly colored papier-mâché parrot that hung over the book table. He showed Sam all the pictures in a book, then started reading to him. Then he began chanting, "Fly, Sam, fly! I know you can do it. Please try, Sam! You may be nervous, but you can fly." Then he whispered, "Would you teach me to fly, Sam?"

As I got to know Charles, as he endeared himself in many ways, I found it harder and harder to face up to his very real limitations. I wanted to say to the authorities, "Look how far he has come. Give him some more time." But I had to acknowledge that he was now almost twelve and his behavior still hadn't reached the level of an eight-year-old. He was running out of catch-up time.

During the last week of school I asked the children to choose their favorite book of the year and to do a project about it. Charles was immediately enthusiastic. "I know which one I want!" he exclaimed. I thought to myself, "Yep, I know too."

But Charles surprised me. He didn't reach for the omnipresent dinosaur book but went to the bookcase and dug out a book he had hidden behind several others. It was *The Ugly Duckling*.

Charles, who had never written more than six sentences about any topic all year, wrote nine pages. This was the first sentence: "The ugly duckling found out it is okay to be different."

CURRICULUM CHOICES
TOUGH AND EASY
· ·

STARTING WITH "To Hell with Rip Van Winkle," published in 1969, I've been writing about *standards*. The pen-pushers have come up with new terminology; the issues have remained constant. But standards are more about political agendas than they are about classrooms. "To Hell with Rip Van Winkle," "Reading for What?," "Who's Afraid of Old Mother Hubbard?," and "Literature Has No Uses," deal with the same issue: how a classroom can foster and celebrate literacy.

In one sense, "Smuggling Reading into the Reading Program" may seem a bit dated now, but the point of the article, using real books instead of textbooks, is not. Little more than a decade ago this piece was rejected by *Language Arts* and *Reading Teacher*. Being more of a pro at editorial rejection, I cut my moping period in half before sending the piece to *Learning*. Less than a week after I mailed it the editor phoned, informing me they were revamping their November reading issue so my piece could run as the cover article. After that they called me often, asking me to write on a variety of topics. It was the beginning of a fruitful writing period for me. (It is no surprise that I held on to my loyalty to the very idea of *Learning* long after the magazine as I'd known it yielded to the lure of focus groups and ceased to exist.)

The computer software reviews, "Beware the Rosy View!" and "How Today's Software Can Zap Kids' Desire to Read," still have plenty to say for today's market because schools have taken the low road with regard to computer-assisted instruction. Actually, the view of computerized reading instruction is less rosy today than it was ten years ago. These days when you find a student receiving his reading instruction on-line, you will find a child labeled Chapter 1 who is slogging through electronic workbook pages of kill-drill. When a school takes this low road, lining up behind the naked emperor of computer literacy, computers are a waste and children are the losers.

By the time I sent "Ruffles and Flourishes" to *Atlantic Monthly*, I knew quite a bit about how editorial offices operate. Nonetheless, I was naïve enough to suppose the *Atlantic* would be different. I sat on pins and needles for one whole year, waiting for their response. In the meantime, Bob

Boynton (who was always asking me what I was up to) had shown the piece to Mary K. Healy and Gordon Pradl, and they wanted to publish my entire fifty-four-page research piece in *English Education*. But I stubbornly clung to the idea of having my tombstone read "Published in *Atlantic Monthly*."

Finally, I wrote to the *Atlantic* office, asking, "What's happening?" The editor phoned, "I'm so glad to hear from you. We want to publish part of your piece, but we've misplaced your address." I picked up on "publish," ignoring completely the "part." *Atlantic Monthly* squashed my fifty-four pages down to two columns. So I'm left with the guilt that I should have gone with Gordon and Mary K. in *English Education* and the lingering satisfaction of contemplating my tombstone.

I have to add that, unlike educationists, *Atlantic* readers do write wonderful letters. One man jumped off a transcontinental train in Denver to mail me a letter. A mother promised never never never to allow her children near a basal. Jeff Brown, author of *Flat Stanley*, and I had an extended correspondence about what the basal thugs did to his story. He hadn't known about it until I wrote the article.

Some people have told me that "Ruffles and Flourishes" is dated, that basals now contain whole, original text. Some do. Some don't. Anyway, editorial meddling is not the whole issue. The real point is that the teacher should never trust any publishing conglomerate to choose the literature she brings to children. The real point is that children should have a choice about what they read.

Bob Boynton, being an honorable editor, has asked me if "When the Reading Experts Gather, What's Their Real Agenda?" is dated, if conventioneering hasn't improved in the last ten years. I will concede that publishers now bring beautiful trade books to the exhibit hall, but in a deep sense this doesn't matter much. More and more, the beautiful books are accompanied by ugly little activity guides. Ironically, these guides are more shoddy than the guides the basal folks produce. I don't see much evidence in the exhibit halls or the lecture halls supporting my abiding conviction that putting wonderful books in the hands of individual children, that encouraging children to choose their own books, must be the core element in a reading program. Ten years ago, in response to my criticism of the circus atmosphere of the convention, a California reading teacher wrote an angry letter-to-the-editor. She said having her picture taken with the basal promotional character Mr. Fig was a highlight of her life. I want that teacher to take heart: there is still plenty of fun for her at any big convention. For starters, basals still rule the show, and she can have her picture taken with any number of loud and colorful basal tagalongs. I am convinced that any teacher who has been to a large convention recently will find a shock of recognition in my article.

Rereading "Reading for What?," I am reminded of one story I haven't told about the assistant superintendent in charge of curriculum. In the article I talk about some of the joys and frustrations of setting up a school from scratch: the teacher and the students get to choose everything from a red velvet sofa to the curriculum. In our early days the assistant superintendent in charge of curriculum sent us a pickup truck full of curriculum. She had ordered central office personnel to photocopy fourth- and fifth-grade mathematics and grammar books for every student in our school. That is a lot of paper. Unfortunately, it was photocopied on both sides so we couldn't even use it as scrap paper. What struck me, more than the illegality and insane expense of her curricula, was the typical bureaucratic attitude about disaffected students: assuming that students who hated school were *behind* in something called basic skills. Those students didn't hate school because they couldn't do it; they hated school because it was conducted in a language that excluded them. My job was to work with those students to find a curriculum with meaning, intrigue, and consequence.

Everything I know about teaching tells me that curriculum choices are the most important choices we make. We can't let anybody send in our choices in a pickup truck. As it turned out, I found our math text in the M.I.T. bookstore. The students were both surprised and delighted to discover they could tackle problems in probability, linear functions, Fibonacci sequences, topology, and more.

One more footnote to the story. Jack went into the Marines. He was pleased to be accepted and asked me to be one of his sponsors. Recommending a boy to the Marines went against everything I believed in, but being a teacher means making choices; it means choosing when to hold firm to your own convictions and when to yield to the needs of your students. Jack was clearly our most obnoxious student, also the one I was proudest of. I'd been through a lot with him, including incurring the wrath of the county district attorney when I testified in Jack's behalf when he appeared in court to plead guilty to a breaking and entering charge. Jack needed the Marines. When he showed up at my house with the papers, I signed them.

To Hell with Rip Van Winkle

Now it's called an urban school, but I've taught through its various metamorphoses: tough school, racially mixed school, culturally deprived school, culturally disadvantaged school, culturally different school, underachieving school, inner-city school. The sociologists get more innocuous, but the building and the curriculum remain the same. I wonder if it's mere naiveté or perhaps something more ominous that causes bureaucrats to pretend they have changed anyone's life-style when they strike "slum" from their official lexicon and speak instead of "multiproblem neighborhood." As Jules Feiffer once pointed out in a poignant cartoon, "I'm still poor, but I've got a great vocabulary."

Sociologists, psychologists, urbanologists, and parents who wonder why kids turn on to pot, banana peels, LSD, amphetamines, glue, and worse should spend a couple of nights with elementary school textbooks. Take the basal reader, for example. Designed by publishers who, one suspects, must be moonlighting from their regular jobs as scriptwriters for John Wayne films, these readers ostensibly inculcate the essential cultural heritage to which every American child has a right, if not a need. In reality, these readers show a world we never knew, a world our parents and *their* parents never knew. The basal readers contain nothing relevant to the present-day world of pollution, political and industrial rip-off, technological innovation, consumerism, urban decay. James Joyce posed the question: "Who gave us this numb?" Schoolchildren across the nation have the 4½-pound answers in their desks.

Interspersed with the stories and poems in basal readers are aphorisms bracketed in blue or red boxes. These are intended to inspire the reader to greater aspiration, if not achievement: "The fearless man is his own salvation"; "To do nothing is the way to be nothing"; "Faith can move mountains"; "Speak to the earth and it shall teach thee"; "Knowledge is more than equivalent to force"; "God helps them who help themselves." Although these and similar heady expressions are subscribed to, if not practiced by, the Silent Majority, one wonders about their significance for the adolescent in an inner-city school. It is doubtful if faith moves mountains even in suburbia. Certainly it doesn't get the streets plowed or the garbage collected in the central city.

The ghetto youngster knows about being nothing if you don't have a job. He looks at his unemployed father every day. He hears his teachers complaining about the good-for-nothing lazy bums on welfare. He sees his mother cleaning toilets at Howard Johnson's and can't see that for all her *doing* she's any better than nothing.

As unemployment rises and becomes a middle-class phenomenon, more people (perhaps even textbook publishers) will be forced to take another look at some of the aphorisms taken for granted for the last 150 years and made hallow in basal readers. Note the recent breast-beating in the mass media over the plight of the unemployed elite, the out-of-work engineers and Ph.D. physicists. They are recognized as victims of a changing society, and no one calls them bums as they stand in line for the dole. But textbook publishers supply what the market demands, and the school market exhibits what McLuhan calls the rearview syndrome: eyes always to the past, they can't deal with the present or anticipate the future.

If textbooks reflect the values of nineteenth-century America, they are only providing what the teachers expect. Basal readers and social studies texts are defended by the educational Establishment on the grounds that every American child should share in a common heritage. Ostensibly, the standardized texts enable the teacher to know the child. If a teacher knows that no matter where Sammy went to school last year, from Anchorage to Anaheim to Atlanta to Albany, he was exposed to Dick and Jane in first grade, Hilda Heron and Flossie Flamingo in third grade, South America in fifth, Rip Van Winkle in eighth, she is confident she knows something vital about Sammy. So if the basal reader gives Sammy culture, it gives his teacher security. Security is *Rip Van Winkle*.

But no one actually reads *Rip Van Winkle*. The only way the reading teacher can be certain her charges are at least exposed to this cornerstone of American education is to read aloud to them. Most of the kids can't— or won't—struggle through such multisyllabic convolutions as:

> The great error in Rip's composition was an insuperable aversion to all kinds of profitable labor. It could not be from the want of assiduity or perseverance for he would sit on a wet rock, with a rod as long and heavy as a Tartar's lance, even though he should not be encouraged by a single nibble.

After reading the passage aloud, the teacher must translate: "Rip liked to fish." The kids wonder why the author couldn't have said so. Rip just doesn't reach contemporary kids. Trudging up hill and over dale, fowling-piece on his shoulder, Rip, I venture to guess, doesn't reach many contemporary adults. But Rip belongs to a part of Americana that the Establishment, though itself not willing to read, is still reluctant to relinquish. The Establishment is sure it knows what is good for other people to read. They themselves can read Harold Robbins or Erich Segal or Jac-queline Susann or Arthur Hailey, but kids must read the classics.

Although I do not advocate Arthur Hailey for second graders—or any other age—I do feel that children might be able to handle something a bit more meaty than Lucy losing a tooth. Children who cut school to keep up with their afternoon soap operas and who come to school discussing the excitement of the Boston Strangler or the humor of Flip Wilson must take out their textbooks and read about Lucy's hamster. A case might well be made that the execrable reading taste of the middle class is a direct result of the artificiality, sentimentality, and just plain bad writing of basal readers.

Students in the eighth grade, whose reading abilities range from first to twelfth, boys interested in football, girls interested in boys, all are forced to pretend to read the same book. All must struggle through thirty pages of Longfellow's immortal *Evangeline*, rendered immortal, it seems, only through the insistence of editors of basal readers who refuse to let it sink into the oblivion it so richly deserves. The adult should ask himself if he could stand thirty pages of:

This is the forest primeval. The murmuring pines and the hemlocks,
Bearded with moss, and in garments green, indistinct in the twilight,
Stand like Druids of eld, with voices sad and prophetic,
Stand like harpers hoar, with beards that rest on their bosoms.

There are six footnotes to a page, and as with footnotes in most weighty tomes, they do little to clarify the stagnant waters.

For those who are still coming to school after the finish of *Evangeline* there is the old chestnut *The Man Without a Country*. Again we find six footnotes to a page, explaining such essentials as *non mi ricordo*, canebrake, fortnight, border chivalry, cotillions, Winfield Scott, Vallandigham, Stephen Fuller Austin, Fernando Po. What reader of best-sellers would stand for six footnotes per page interrupting the excitement of the story?

Publishers explain in the weighty teacher's manuals accompanying their weighty basal readers that "Reading is decoding." "Reading is crit-ical evaluation." "Reading is using ideas." Nowhere do they hint that reading just might be interesting, exciting, or even fun. Decoding is some-thing we must take very seriously; reading itself is becoming passé. When I complained recently to a representative from a prominent publishing house that if one passed out all the ditto sheets on dictionary skills, decoding skills, phonics, inferential skills, etc., recommended in the teach-er's manual, the kids would have time to read only once every three weeks, he informed me that "in this new linguistic approach, reading isn't so important as it used to be. Decoding's the thing." No matter textbook-sare dull; we aren't supposed to encourage the kids to read anyway. It's no wonder slum kids quit school, feeling they can learn more from the streets. The wonder is that more middle-class kids out there in suburbia don't also give up in despair. Such noted poets as Karl Shapiro and Laurence Ferlinghetti and May Swenson and Gwendolyn Brooks, to name a few, have written meaty poems that appeal to urban youth. Kenneth Koch, himself a poet and urban teacher, has written a book on how to teach *real* poems to urban elementary youth. But basal readers specialize in inspirational lyrics by unknown ladies with three names. Abbie Farwell Brown, for example writes:

No matter what my birth may be,
   No matter where my lot is cast,
I am the heir in equity
   Of all the precious past. . .

Most ladies with three names, it seems, have never heard of inequity. One can only ponder why the past of the black youngster or the Irish or Jewish youngster is so precious that no one dares mention it in the so carefully innocuous basal readers or why social studies texts pass over Black Heritage in a hurried, embarrassed paragraph. School districts purchase a few reference works such as *The Negro Almanac* or *Biographies of Black Leaders*, and then, feeling safe from any possible criticisms from "radical" groups such as the NAACP or the League of Women Voters, continue to use the same old whitewashed texts. Children may do a book report on a famous black man for extra credit, but they know the *real* thing is in the textbook because on the final exam no one ever asks about Martin Luther King, Jr. or Crispus Attucks.

Fearing that the child may not learn his lesson well in social studies, editors of basal readers make certain he gets a double dose; his literature text is filled with bright rays of democratic inspiration. In a unit titled "Heritage," students are required to join exuberant voices in a choral reading, "Four Faces on a Mountain." Here they read that:

Lincoln's face . . . typifies the birthright
of every man—
To rise by hard work and study from the
depths of poverty
   to the highest office in the land.
His calm and solemn face shows America's
love of its fellowmen
   and its deep sense of unity of purpose.

Children read about love of fellowman and unity of purpose while outside the school walls their parents and neighbors scream about busing and welfare and abortion and amnesty and impeachment and gasoline. It might be well if reading teachers concentrated their efforts on encouraging children to *like* reading and left the inspirational rhetoric to William Buckley and Julie Eisenhower.

In social students class city kids learn that "New York State offers more opportunities for jobs at good wages than any other region in the world" and "The Empire State enjoys excellent railroad services. Railroads serve all sections of the state" and "In New York there is one passenger automobile for every four persons. This shows New York is a wealthy state." The ghetto kid can figure out this arithmetic: "We got nine people in our family, and we ain't got no car. Where's our car? We should have two f----n' cars!" Claude Brown asks the question which these textbooks so blithely ignore: *"Where do you run to when you're already in the promised land?"*

Publishing houses point with pride to their newly integrated readers, but coloring Dick and Jane brown doesn't make them inner-city. Or give them Soul. In the Ginn 360 Series, for example, Pat is a nice brown color but definitely middle-class. The teacher's manual goes so far as to instruct the teacher to be sure and point out to the children that Pat's father is a *doctor.* No way could just any old black kid creep into the basal reader; he had to be the son of a doctor.

Some recent texts make a real attempt to provide "ethnic appeal." They include one or two biographical pieces on blacks. The kids hate it. "Every year George Washington Carver," complained one seventh grader. "I been reading about him and his peanuts since third grade. If I have to read about him one more time, I'll vomit!" Carver is the publishers' favorite Negro. Along with Booker T. Washington. Avant garde publishers include a story about Jackie Robinson.

Although there has been a superficial attempt to vary the skin tones in recent basal readers, nothing has been done about the text itself: the flavor can best be described as unsalted pablum. In one series Mama actually puts on gloves to go to town; she dons pedal pushers when she's feeling really racy. Parents always smile at their children; children always smile at their parents. Cleanliness ranks second only to Politeness. No little boy in a basal reader gets sent to school without breakfast; no father is out of work. No basal reader admits that people are acquainted with those powerful emotions: rage, hate, love.

Basal readers are filled with the grand achievers exercising their privileges in a nation of opportunities, Cinderellas trading their rags for riches, paupers working hard and becoming princes or shareholders in ITT.

"Those who deserve, get" is the hallmark of these weighty tomes. One expects to turn the page and find a story by Ayn Rand.

Poor boys are mentioned in a story about Father Flanagan's home, but not a single boy who lived there ever again got in trouble with the law. Not a single one. This is undoubtedly offered as inspiration for boys like Roosevelt Jones, the wiry sixth grader who says he "wouldn't want to live at no home with them priests and penguins." One suspects he doesn't believe such a place really exists. He knows about homes for wayward boys. He's been there. Waiting to go "away" for the third time, he claims this time he's going to a detention home in Rome, Italy. "I been to Rome, New York, man. This time it's It'ly."

One reads of wonderful demonstration programs in Brooklyn or Seattle, where students are actually treated as living, breathing people of the latter part of the twentieth century, and one is happy, forgetting that these programs couldn't be more atypical. One forgets that those warm, humanistic, dedicated teachers—George Dennison, John Holt, Herbert Kohl, and Jonathan Kozol—don't teach in public school. At least not for long. One forgets the vast majority of students in typical towns across the nation who are bored to tears—or pot; one forgets the ordinary city school, ruled by a board of education culled from a well-meaning Silent Majority with a message to spread and money to save.

Teachers occasionally admit that the existing textbooks don't work, but they blame the failure not on textbooks but on the kids. "If I only had the right kind of kid ..." Show them Daniel Fader's *Hooked on Books* and they mumble, "How can I test them if they don't all read the same stories?" or "It sounds good, but my supervisor ... accountability ... the regents ... college boards ..." Some deserving researcher should get a Ford Foundation or Carnegie grant to determine at what age children really fail the College Boards. Pre-K classes can't justify their existence as "socialization groups" or "creative play centers." They must train children for the serious business of being successful in kindergarten. Success in kindergarten is measured by the score on the Reading Readiness Test, which asks urban kindergartners to identify such esoterica as pine trees, ferns, and bamboo.

I am enough of an optimist to believe that boards of education would accept curriculum changes; they would like to see exciting, creative programs, providing they don't cost too much money. But most teachers, being themselves products of stultifying school systems, are, by nature, passive; they are followers; they do what has been done to them, so they see nothing amiss in teaching the inspirational drivel written by those unknown ladies with three names. They see their province as passing out facts the syllabus said should be passed out; few feel that they themselves can "discover knowledge." After all, what are textbooks for if not to pass on knowledge already gathered by experts?

What every school system needs is a few revolutionary spirits. The only problem is that although such spirits manage to enliven their immediate surroundings and even instill a spirit of exuberance and curiosity, revolutionaries generally lack staying power. Here today and gone tomorrow, few manage to stick at the same dreary school, teaching those same difficult kids year after year. The people who do stick it out are the rather dull little ladies who are so scorned by the intellectuals. We may deplore them, but what would we do without them?

We could, as Paul Goodman suggested years ago and Ivan Illich more recently, shut down the schools, but I don't see that our present society has anything better to offer. It is unrealistic to propose some idyll in the country as a solution to the city kid's woes; it is also unrealistic to suppose that learners can, as Illich suggests, gain access to the persons who can teach him the tricks of their trade. The thought of the Teamster's Union members showing black kids from the slums how to drive a rig boggles the mind.

Bad as our city schools are, they really are no better than the society demands—or deserves. The starting salary in the typical city system is $7,500; the maximum after twenty-eight years and thirty hours of graduate work beyond the master's degree is $15,150. We live in a society that honors money; if you make a lot of money you are somebody; if you make little money, you're nobody. Teachers rank far down on the valued occupations list. Somehow we expect more from teachers, and when they disappoint us, we're bitter. How many creative lawyers are there? Talented, dedicated doctors? Even the mediocre ones don't work for $7,500. The teaching profession does attract a few martyrs, a few idealists, a few intellectuals, a few people who really love working with kids and who don't give a damn about salary. But let's be realistic: most of these noble souls are women whose husbands bring home healthy paychecks.

I began my teaching career in a high school in Queens, New York. After pretending to teach *Silas Marner* and *Johnny Tremain* to ninth- and tenth-grade urban youth, I dropped out of the scene when I was told my next duty would be Tennyson. Outside the building kids were commandeering the subways, terrorizing passengers just for the hell of it, buying and selling dope, prostituting themselves, having babies, running numbers; inside the school I was supposed to teach Tennyson.

After teaching college courses for several years, I developed a strong interest in the education of the young child. Since I was officially certified, complete with a fancy seal of bureaucratic approval, I anticipated no difficulty. Nevertheless, I had a tough time finding a job. School administrators seem to like what they know; they hire graduates of local teachers colleges, sons and daughters of local residents. The first point against me was the fact that I was coming directly from college teaching: "You'd be too intellectual for us." Second point against me was that my graduate degree is not in education: "You'd be too intellectual for us." Third point against me was that my degree is from Berkeley: "You'd be too intellectual *and* too radical for us."

I was persistent, however, and after several interviews I was hired as a remedial reading teacher in the acknowledged "tough school" in the city. Also illustrative of the way city school systems often function, I did not meet the principal of my school, the director of the experimental program in which I'd work, any of the teachers, or any of the students before the first day of school. None of the people with whom I had to establish a close working relationship had any voice in the hiring procedure.

Now, as I hand out hammers and nails and saws to my second grade "problem readers," I wonder if anyone in the bureaucratic maze still worries about intellectualism in my classroom. Certainly my fellow teachers wonder and worry about my hammers and saws, but interestingly enough, the neighborhood parents send in scrap lumber and nails. They understand that if a kid is uptight about not knowing his vowels and blends, it just might be more valuable to let him pound a few nails than to make him do six ditto sheets on vowels and blends.

This is not to say that kids don't read in my room. If the textbooks and the teachers are horrifying, the kids are something else. Amazing. Despite the 4½-pound books, despite years of Dick and Jane and *Evangeline* and Sir Walter Scott, most of the kids still read. They don't carry home the basal readers; they try to avoid opening these even in class. They certainly don't do homework or pass tests. But they do read: magazines, newspapers, paperbacks, biographies, jokes, stories and plays written by the kids, songs, slogans, graffiti. We are starting a new reading project where kids learn to 'read' paintings, sculpture, and photographs. Another popular project is called Propaganda; kids learn to analyze magazine ads and TV commercials. As one bright young fourth grader put it, "I don't believe it. Why isn't there a law against it? They aren't selling cigarettes; they're selling flowers and springtime and people in love!" She asked to stay during lunchtime to examine more ads. "We need to know this . . . I don't want to be tricked." She and other kids made their own ads on videotape, mocking television commercials.

If the educational bureaucracy likes what it knows, kids know what they like. They read Ciardi's "Why Nobody Pets the Lion at the Zoo" and Hughes' "Go Slow" with enthusiasm while failing literature exams on Wordsworth's "Daffodils" and Guiterman's "Alamo." First graders take home books on optical illusions and snakes; second graders take books on foreign languages; third graders learn about writing secret codes; the library has trouble meeting the demand for books on dinosaurs and cooking and judo. But teachers won't believe that all this is legitimate reading. Teachers not only like what they know, they distrust what they don't know. Basal readers offer the security of a teacher's edition, complete with questions and answers. Education courses don't prepare one to make up a lesson plan on Ferlinghetti or optical illusions. And every administrator knows that a good lesson is preceded by a lesson plan. There are exceptions, however. Roland S. Barth, himself a principal, tells a marvelous story in his book, *Open Education and the American School,* about his first visit to Elementary Science Study, then still under the aegis of the National Science Foundation. He asked a lot of questions and seemed to get few answers. Only years later did their approach begin to make sense to him. I repeat it here because I see it as a simple explanation of the way I attempt to run my classroom:

"Can I see lesson plans for a unit?"
—We have none.
"How does a teacher teach without plans?"
—You put the materials out and see what the children do with them. When children ask a question or need something, you help them.

It's easy to see that such a philosophy would drive most administrators nuts. Most teachers too. The hardest thing in the world for a traditionally oriented teacher to learn is how to keep her hands off the kid's learning process. She should work long and hard at preparing the environment, but she can't do the kid's learning for him.

As I said, we do a lot of reading. One of the most popular units is Physics. Yes, physics. I don't hand out some monstrous test and demand a written report. I don't give examinations. Therefore, the kids don't consider me a teacher or what we do schoolwork. Everybody knows that real schoolwork means writing the spelling words ten times and being tested on them. Nevertheless, I hand out a chapter entitled "The Physics of Sound," taken from a real book and typed on index cards in the form of experiments. The kids have to read the cards in order to do the experiments. They are anxious to do the experiments because they are fun and because after a kid writes up his observation of eight experiments, he gets to make a musical instrument out of a Clorox bottle, lumber, fish line, eye screws, garden hose, a funnel, and whatever other "good junk" he can find on the shelves.

Another popular unit is Structures. Kids have contests to determine who can build the strongest clay bridge, the highest tower of straws. To do this, they research in the media center, watching filmstrips about bridges, reading books, looking at photographs. One of our most popular "events" was the showing of a movie from the Physics Department at

Rensselaer Polytechnic Institute, Troy, New York. This movie shows the collapse of a bridge because of resonance with the wind. One sweet young thing from the Sound Experiments project watched the bridge and said, "Isn't that like the rice experiment?" She had taken a Quaker Oats carton, cut a hole in the side, stretched tissue paper over the top, and put rice on the paper. Then she observed that when some children shouted into the hole, the rice jumped. The experiment card provided her with some technical information about the frequency in some children's voices matching the natural frequency at which the air in the box liked to vibrate, the matching frequencies producing resonance and causing the rice to jump. She must have had fifty-three kids shout in her box before she wrote up the experiment. *Then* she was prepared to make the intellectual jump to associate the convoluting bridge with the jumping rice. It was a crystal moment that every teacher dreams of experiencing.

Another aspect of this story is worth nothing: kids love repetition. They often do the same experiment over and over again. Is it fair for the teacher to insist, "No, Johnny, you've already done page 16; now you must go on to 17"? I like to think that if I hadn't let Jeannie repeat her rice experiment 8 or 12 or 23 times, she might never have made the impressive intellectual leap. More important, given the initial impetus of the experiment card, Jeannie did the entire project herself. No carefully staged teacher-demonstrations in my classroom. As an old Chinese proverb put it:

I hear and I forget;
I see, and I remember;
I do, and I understand.

Needless to say, a lot of test tubes get broken, a lot of glue is spilled; luckily, not too many fingers get cut. I keep peace with the custodians by saying, "Just walk on past my door. I'll be responsible for the cleaning up."

My colleagues may carp, "But if you let one kid repeat the same experiment over and over, other children are deprived of the opportunity of doing it." First of all, every child Jeannie rounded up to shout in her Quaker Oats box learned about the experiment. Secondly, there is no minimum body of knowledge which is essential for everyone to know. While Jeannie was doing sound experiments kids in other parts of the room were engaged in needlework, color chemistry, typing, magnets, playwriting and scene design, bones, bridges, optical illusions, maps, consumer awareness.

Most schools are better organized to serve the needs of adults than those of kids. I believe that my first duty to children is to make them happy. I don't believe that anyone can teach a hostile seven-year-old. Oh, the teacher can teach and teach and teach; but that kid just ain't gonna learn.

One of the greatest weaknesses of American education is that the student is never given the opportunity for self-discovery. This weakness is even more telling in urban schools where the structure is even more rigid than in suburbia: we're dealing with "tough" kids so we have to keep them in line, right? We forget that discipline and liberty go together. We're quite efficient at imposing discipline; we're scared to death of liberty. So we set up rituals: in the first grade the child must learn to read, ready or not; in second grade he learns to subtract; multiplication in third. If he doesn't perform these rituals on schedule, we have labels for him: failure, underachiever, slow learner. At nine o'clock he does spelling, from which nothing follows; at ten o'clock math, from which nothing follows, at eleven o'clock science, from which nothing follows. It's a convenient system for the teacher, but such rigid classification does little for the student; it may well be a hindrance. When a kid observes an optical illusion, makes a careful drawing of it, measuring distances and angles, writes up his explanation of the cause of the phenomenon—is he doing math, science, or language arts? Does it matter?

The urban teacher who passes out reams of dittoed lessons manufactured on Madison Avenue and who feels proud when her class is two lessons ahead of the teacher across the hall is like the pilot who reported in from somewhere over the Pacific: "I'm lost, but I'm making record time!" We buy fancy hardware to jazz up the trivia: ditto-sheet teacher manuals in three colors, overhead projection sheets of Washington's battle plan with forty-three overlays in sixteen colors, talking typewriters, electronic multiplication systems, talking globes. But we never ask what is the child learning numbers for? So he can grow up and make accurate body counts in a Vietnam of the 1980s? It seems to me to be more important to do the right thing than to do the thing right. I remember a saying from my own school days: "Fifty million Frenchmen must be right." I didn't have the slightest idea what it meant, but it seemed to mean there's safety and complacency in numbers. Schools seem to operate on this theory. I prefer Bertrand Russell's version, "If fifty million people say a foolish thing, it is still a foolish thing."

Bruce arrived in my room at 2:30 every afternoon to do chemistry experiments. Sometimes he had trouble reading the cards, but he always found another kid to help him. He wrote up each of his experiments, often asking for help with his spelling. He was so careful about writing up his results that other kids began to rely on him to do their writing. Finally, one day I asked him who his classroom teacher was; I wanted to write her a note, commending his work. Imagine my surprise to learn that he was in Special Class. Everybody knows about those kids: they are either dumb or emotional cases. Either way, they cause havoc in a normal classroom, so they are lumped together in a room and *they are not supposed to bother other kids or teachers.* So what was Bruce doing in my room? He'd heard other kids talking about it and when he was supposed to go home at 2:30 he sneaked back into the building and came for chemistry.

I got on the phone to the administrator in charge of Special Classes. My colleagues warned me I was crazy to call her and "rock the boat." She came right down to my school with Bruce's folder. I told her my story and said I felt that if an experienced teacher couldn't pick him out as dumb or "emotional," then he should be given a chance at regular education. And he was given the chance. It wasn't easy. When a kid is treated as dumb for five years, it takes a while to convince him he can succeed in school.

The day the *New York Times* published a number of feature articles on the birth of quintuplets, the female "problem readers" couldn't get enough of it. Nobody had to devise some phony drills to get them to use the dictionary. They were looking up ovaries, fertility, gynecologist, gestation, hormones. Of course, by edict of the board of education, I was not supposed to give sex information, but that was a legitimate reading lesson so I showed them the picture of a newborn baby in *The Family of Man*. Astonishment. Disbelief. No one knew about the cord. News travels fast in a school, however. Before the day was out, eighty-four students trooped into the room and asked to see the cord. Kids grouped in the corridors to discuss the phenomenon.

Sylvia, dubbed the "Zulu Chief" by her teachers and regarded as the toughest, nastiest kid in school, read her copy of Ethel Waters to six girls gathered around the table. She stopped at one point and whispering started. One girl hissed, "You ask her." "No, you."

Finally I couldn't stand it any longer and said, "Go ahead, somebody ask me. There's not a word in that book that I'm afraid of. So ask me."

"What's a bastard?" asked Sylvia.

One of the milder terms in Sylvia's everyday vocabulary and she was anxious to know what it really means. I explained and the girls were vastly relieved to learn it's so simple. They had feared much worse. That opened the door to other words and we trooped to the library to check *THE* words in the *American Heritage Dictionary*. How can a kid have any respect for castrated classroom dictionaries, the ones that don't have any of the good words?

When she wasn't reading about Ethel Waters, Sylvia would sneak to my room to listen to a tape of John Ciardi reading poetry with his children. The tough girl, universally feared by her teachers, clutched the book in one hand and sucked the thumb on the other, rocking back and forth. She played her favorite poems over and over.

Roosevelt Jones, scheduled for his third trip to reform school, nearly went crazy when one of the kids read "The Idiot" by Dudley Randall.

That cop was powerful mean.
First he called me, "Black boy."
Then he punched me in the face
and drug me by the collar to a wall
and made me lean against it with my hands
spread
while he searched me
he kicked me and cuffed me and cussed me . . .

Roosevelt, enrolled in remedial reading for five years, veteran of years of drill on initial consonants and blends, the tough black kid who wore one gold earring and who could barely stumble through a preprimer, decided if books have things like that poem, he'd better learn to read properly before he got sent away again. He was scheduled for my room three times a week; he appeared as many as five periods a day. When I protested, he screamed, "I want to *read*!" No classroom teacher ever missed Roosevelt and came looking for him. Grateful for the peace and quiet their absence brought, no teacher ever sought out either Roosevelt or Sylvia.

By the end of the year Roosevelt was reading fifth-grade work. He read the local paper every morning, filling me in on the latest auto wrecks and murders. He checked the *New York Times* for a good sports story, especially if it happened to be about boxing. He liked to read out loud, in a big, dramatic voice, something like a Baptist preacher at a crowded revival meeting. Roosevelt could make the New York Mets box score sound like Samson bringing the temple down upon the multitudes.

Mildred was sixteen and in the eighth grade. She told me she was "a little slow in reading." On standardized tests she scored on a second-grade level. She had never been in remedial reading because her recorded I.Q. of 76 makes her ineligible for special help designed for "underachievers." The choice is simple. Do you pretend that Mildred is going to read *Evangeline?* Do you make her feel inferior because she can't? Or do you help her find something she can read and enjoy? Mildred was a basketball fan, able to quote all the rebound, free-throw, and other data about the Celtics, the Lakers, the Knicks. She took home a book of basketball biographies, each chapter dealing with a current pro. The book was written on a fourth- to fifth-grade level. Mildred kept the book for three weeks, bringing it in every few days to assure me she was taking good care of it. She put a cover on it, wanting to keep the book bright and shiny. Many of the children deface the basic readers with one hand and patch the paperbacks with the other. During the three weeks Mildred gave me a running commentary on each player in the book. Finally she handed it back with tears in her eyes. "The best book I ever read," she affirmed. "And I read it. I really did. The whole thing."

Sylvia, the tough "Zulu Chief," gained eighteen months in her reading scores, finishing the year above grade level. But she failed all her courses. Already a head taller than anyone her age, she was forced to repeat the grade. Sylvia wasn't much good at repeating. She hit teachers, threw chairs at them, cursed them. And she hid out in the library, sucking her thumb and listening to John Ciardi read poetry with his children. She refused to learn Washington's battle plan, interest rates on mortgages, the name of the author of "The Midnight Ride of Paul Revere," the names of the first men on the moon, the difference between a phrase and a clause. The coup de grace came when Sylvia stole ice cream from a delivery truck near the school. She carried cartons in all flavors to the school and distributed free treats to everyone, even teachers. The authorities insisted she was incorrigible and could never learn a thing. At fourteen years of age she was permanently excluded from the city school system.

Sylvia was not so certain of her teachers' judgment. During her final week at school she gathered up some of the books she had read: *His Eye is on the Sparrow, I Want to be Somebody, Nigger, Autobiography of Malcolm X, Manchild in the Promised Land.* Sylvia put her hands on those books and said, "You know, it just proves that people who start out bad can do okay for themselves."

Sylvia never reached eighth grade and therefore she didn't read Rudyard Kipling's inspirational chestnut, "If," standard fare for eighth graders across the nation, but, like it or not, middle-class America, she has a pretty good idea of what it takes to survive in the world we've given her.

Reading for What?

MANY HIGH SCHOOL English departments responded to the competency test mania and the back-to-basics drives by abandoning electives and returning to traditional courses. Although I am not sorry to see the comic book hero and the grammar of 8-mm filmmaking bite the dust, neither am I convinced that every student should be required to read *Julius Caesar* or pretend to write a term paper. Why don't we consider getting off the teeter-totter of pedagogical extremes and consider why we want students to read and write.

We offer college-bound students a watered-down college curriculum: a touch of Milton, as it were. This seems to have worked, after a fashion, for the past fifty years or so, and it seems inevitable that high school English teachers will continue looking to Harvard as their guiding light. The minor forays taken by some teachers off into *relevant* topics are merely temporary aberrations. Such courses lack the staying power of the hoola hoop. The majority of English teachers continue to do what they've always done: to prepare students for college even if they aren't going to college.

English for noncollege-bound students differs from college prep English in that the reading and writing assignments are shorter — not different, just shorter. It is as if some great Curriculum Planner in the sky spread wide his arms and said, "Let there be Milton for the millions!" College-bound kids read all of *Paradise Lost*; noncollege kids read only selected stanzas. Everybody gets the same old literature questions about theme and plot and genre and rising action and conflict.

Some noncollege students don't encounter Milton or sonnets or rising and falling action. These students are at the bottom of the barrel; they go to lab. In the lab, "reading" is choosing answer *a, b, c,* or *d* after each paragraph — without looking back. Nothing takes the joy, the interest, and even the sense out of reading like all those dumb questions at the end of the paragraph.

After a brief stint of teaching *Silas Marner* and *Julius Caesar*, I avoided high school teaching and all its concomitant worries about genre for eight years. Then I had the opportunity to set up my own English program in an alternative high school. Although officially part of the public school system, we were given a storefront in center-city and forty disaffected girls and boys no one else wanted. These students, emotional dropouts forced to attend school or be sent to jail or residential placement, came from every social and ethnic group. Many were involved in drugs, both selling and using. The police wanted them kept off the streets and the regular high school wanted them kept out of their hallways. The attitude of the official curriculum planners was, "Do what you want; just keep them away from us."

Two teachers and one counselor in our program were expected to provide a total program for the students. Ostensibly the academic program was built around a competency-based curriculum containing those social studies, health, and science concepts deemed necessary to be a productive citizen. To graduate from our program (and receive a high school diploma) students had to complete 120-plus competencies and read and compute on the eighth-grade level. They also had to have an approved job skill with several hundred hours "certified" on the job.

One might say we taught the "whole child," somewhat in the manner of elementary schools (at least those elementary schools that haven't tried to become like high schools by departmentalizing). Such a system is considered impractical in most monolithic city schools, where English teachers are expected to process 150 of the dreaded themes every time they have the nerve to make an assignment. But as more and more schools become accountable for their dropout rates, they will be forced to seek alternatives, ways of educating students that look to a source other than Harvard.

When they first came to us, students repeated over and over, "You know what I really hated about high school? Changing classes all the time. You'd just get started with something and then you'd have to move to another class and start something else. All those teachers—they drove me nuts!" Big, tough eighteen-year-olds told me they liked being able to do their work in one place with just one or two teachers. They liked being able to work at their own pace, neither slowed down nor pressured by other students. These students were expressing a need for continuity, integration of subjects, and scheduleless study. It does not seem like such an outrageous request to me. We've listened to the needs of Harvard for years. Why not try listening to some disaffected students for a change?

Such a program provides English teachers with a wonderful opportunity to help students become literate. It is their job to help students understand what they read in newspapers, to relate it to what they read in history books, to show active concern, perhaps, by writing their congressman or a "Letter to the Editor." Reading and writing thus become the foci of the entire curricula, not some set assignments frozen in time and petrified in insensibility.

The behavioral objectives, color-coded theme units, ditto masters of study questions, and all the other paraphernalia hawked by the ed-biz firms and the state ed bureaucrats really aren't of much use. I have twenty-eight review copies of short story and poetry anthologies, any number of texts on how to inspire (or coerce) Johnny to write, read, think, appreciate. I think it is time that educational policymakers acknowledge the existence of students for whom "None of the above" is the prevailing attitude about school.

Our classroom, outfitted with Salvation Army sofas and chairs, was filled with reading materials: daily copies of the local paper, the *New York Times* and the *New York Daily News*, paperbacks of every type—best-sellers, thrillers, mysteries, romances, joke books, science fiction, sports, comic books. We had a petty cash fund, so every so often I'd take a few students shopping for books at a local store. Usually the students and I just talked casually about what they were reading. I don't think I ever asked anyone the theme of a book. A number of the problem-centered Dell/Laurel Leaf teenage novels became the focus of minibibliotherapy sessions. Occasionally we'd get three or four kids reading the same book so we could discuss it as a group, but usually this was because of students' personal problems, not because we wanted to talk about literature.

We had a lot of single copies of traditional English classroom books. The students liked seeing the classics on the shelves. They wanted the place to have some semblance of a real school, even if they had no intention of reading *A Tale of Two Cities* or *Romeo and Juliet*. There were a few short stories and poems in high school anthologies I thought were especially provocative, so I assigned these works to most students at one time or another, complete with questions at the end. Sometimes I had the need to feel like it was a real school too. Because one student's three-hour stint in the classroom might start at 8:00, another at 8:45, and another at 1:00, we never had any of those typical English-class scenes where two or three students "discuss" a story with the teacher, i.e., give the "right" answers, while twenty-seven others watch the clock.

We had three rules in the Center: no drugs, no swearing, and read for half an hour. The first two rules were much easier to enforce than the third. Although all of our students could read at least on a fifth-grade level, and many were much better than that, few read willingly or with any pleasure. When we first opened the Center, I put many provocative books around the room. I don't think I ever saw a student pick up one. When I'd hand books to students, it became apparent that they were intimidated by the length. The first thing every student did was turn to the back to see how many pages there were. They'd spend half an hour complaining about the length rather than reading. So I started going through the papers every day, looking for sensational, weird, or intriguing stories to tempt students to the printed page. One student, aware of my technique, said, "Why don't you just bring in the *Enquirer* or *Star*? We'd read that and it would save you a lot of trouble." I told him there were levels beneath which I couldn't sink. I was, after all, still an English teacher.

We subscribed to *Time* for awhile, but that chatty sarcasm went right over their heads. Some students could read most of the words but couldn't understand the articles, or didn't care about the world pictured in those articles. The students preferred the gee-whiz, wham-bam of the *Daily News*. Should I be ashamed to admit that I encouraged them to read it? Sometimes English teachers must set aside their devotion to great literature and decide that their goal is to get kids reading, to use reading as a means of bringing them back into the world. There is a great barrier between the traditional English teacher and the teenager on drugs who is convinced that reading is old-fashioned. Ninety-nine percent of what goes on in the world is not relevant to these kids. They don't have hobbies, family ties, ambitions, or skills. Their primary concern is with feeling good.

What's the use of making students memorize the three parts of government, the Bill of Rights, the author of *Huckleberry Finn*, and the characteristics of the short story if they have no intention of becoming members of the community? I saw my job as English teacher as finding the "opener," the means of involving students in something in the world besides personal pleasure. Since I have a strong commitment to the printed word, I was constantly looking for that one item or article or book the student would actually read. By the time students are fifteen or seventeen, they are experts at faking reading so the challenge to jolt them out of their soporific state was a tough one.

I went through every publication imaginable. I don't know if Mark Hopkins and a log are enough to provide an education, but I do know that an English program for disaffected students must have access to a very wide variety of publications—and a teacher willing to read them. Every time I came across something startling or funny or maddening or awful, I'd cut it out and try it on somebody. If it worked, I'd laminate it so it would last being tried out on thirty-nine other people. We developed a "reading starter" box—stories about Siamese twins, stories about dolphins, stories about consumer rip-offs, headless bodies, runaways, the price of the vice president's bed. Often as soon as a student came into the Center another student would hold up a laminated card and say, "Wait until you read this one." Students began reading newspapers and magazines on their own, not waiting for me to clip stories for them. After a student had read the eye-openers for a couple of weeks, I'd suggest something longer and meatier, such as *Flowers for Algernon, The Outsiders, Temple of Gold,* or *Richie.*

Interestingly enough, the students seemed proud of the fact that I was a reader. I usually ate my lunch at the Center and read while I ate. Students always checked out what I was reading and sometimes asked to borrow it.

Carl took Bettelheim's *Truants from Life.* When he returned it he commented, "Some schools are worse than ours." He wanted to talk about the philosophy of "license" in schools. I gave him a book about Summerhill and he was stunned. Suddenly our school seemed quite conventional.

I heard two students talking, "I don't know why she works here, but it isn't because she's dumb." Students who are rejects from regular school programs fear their teachers might also be rejects. Who would *choose* to be in such a place? They don't see themselves as particularly desirable people to be around. It remains for the teacher to earn their confidence and admiration by being competent and professional as well as caring and compassionate. If one had to be emphasized over the other, I'd lean much farther to the side of competence. I've seen too many so-called alternatives that rip off the system and, even worse, rip off the students. A pulsating heart worn ostentatiously on the sleeve is definitely not enough. "Love" comes cheap these days; competence is harder to get.

When Jack first came to the Center, he wouldn't read. He wouldn't do anything but swear and wander around the room bothering people. He didn't have a job, and some days I thought he would drive me crazy. Even though he wouldn't do any academic work, he arrived at the Center at 8:00 and had to be kicked out at 4:00 so we could lock the doors. A couple of times he broke in and slept overnight. We found out that he was often kicked out of his home and then he'd sleep wherever he could—cars, vacant houses, and on our Salvation Army couch.

Jack was intrigued by Scrabble. Even though I beat the socks off him every time we played, it was the first thing I'd seen that interested him. I brought in an article about Scrabble hustlers in New York City. Jack was impressed by the money they made. The article mentioned that serious Scrabble players liked *Funk and Wagnall's Dictionary* because it had lots of extra word lists, words beginning with the same prefix, etc. I pointed out to Jack that I was sure our *American Heritage Dictionary* would be adequate for his needs but he managed to convince me to order *Funk and Wagnall's.* To tell the truth, I felt pretty good about telling my supervisor a student had requested a dictionary recommended in *Harper's.*

Jack then retired to a corner of the room with the Scrabble board and the dictionary—for six months. My supervisor deserves credit. Having hired his teachers after extensive interviewing, he then allowed them to be responsible for their students. He had faith in us and we all had faith in Jack. Supervisory judgment was present but casual. The supervisor would walk into the Center and say, "Jack still at the Scrabble?" I won't pretend that my smile didn't become forced by the third or fourth month and desperate by the fifth, but no one can *make* a high school student study anything. One can only provide an environment for possibilities— and then hope. Jack would occasionally challenge someone (never me) to a game, but usually he played against himself, muttering, cursing, leafing through the dictionary. Somewhere into this marathon, he agreed to start reading half an hour a day. Still he did no "work," that is, no assignments toward competency credit. He became an avid Dick Francis fan, however, and some days would read an hour or two before returning to his Scrabble training.

Finally Jack decided he was ready. He asked me to play him in Scrabble, and he won by three hundred points. My husband happened to walk into the Center just at the end of this match. "Your wife is OK as a teacher," said Jack, "but she sure ain't much of a Scrabble player."

After this triumph Jack agreed to some ground rules. One of us would play Scrabble with him only after he'd done the three hours of required academic work and only if he hadn't driven us to screaming fits with his frequently obnoxious horsing around. I don't think Jack could ever have agreed to these rules had he not first beaten me so badly. I'm sure Jack was a "reject" in school from the first day he entered kindergarten. I have never encountered a child who looked or smelled worse. A child so ill-cared for often has trouble learning to care for himself.

Jack decided to start his academic career with us by working on health competencies. They looked easy. Part of the studies involved reading about nutrition and planning personal menus. One assigned article was about American overconsumption of sugar. Jack was surprised at the amount of sugar in breakfast cereals. "No wonder my little brother's teeth are so rotten," he said. "Why do they put in so much sugar?"

"Why ask me? Do I look like Mrs. Kellogg?"

"You mean I should ask them?" he asked. "Yeah, why not," he answered himself. "It would be a business letter, too." One of the writing competency requirements was that students had to be able to write a business letter. It didn't make too much sense to me to devise phony little forms of pretend letters or fill-in exams with the proper terms: salutation, inside address, and so on. I required them to write real, honest-to-goodness letters, letters to real people, letters for which they received replies. *They* had to think of someone to write to.

Jack looked up the address of Kellogg's in my copy of *Consumer Complaint Guide*. He liked the idea of writing to the president of the company. Jack received an answer from Kellogg's, inviting him to visit their plant should he ever be in Battle Creek. Jack thought the reply was bullshit, but he tacked it up on the bulletin board and made sure whoever came into the Center noticed it. He liked the "Dear Mr. Wright" in their reply. All day he insisted we address him as "Mr. Wright."

In such writing projects there is no notion of "holistic grading," no trying to extract meaning from poor grammar and spelling. That will do, perhaps, for English themes, but not for real writing. Jack was anxious that he not "sound dumb." He used the dictionary; he used *The Harbrace Handbook;* he tried to con me into rewriting for him. Several drafts were necessary before he put the letter into the envelope.

Annie received an answer from Vice President Rockefeller. She'd read about the expensive bed he'd bought for his residence and was upset that the bed cost three times as much as her parents' home. So she wrote and asked him about it. The answer was strictly PR, all about his many gifts to charity. Students were interested in all the replies. We talked about voice, level of language, the purpose and politics of language. Annie's letter, too, went up on the bulletin board, as did Kathleen's letter from the White House. This tough girl who lived at a home for wayward girls wrote Amy Carter and wished her well in her new school. Mary, whose parents worried that she didn't care about anyone or anything, wrote the Quinlans a letter telling them she sympathized with their dilemma: "I thought it might make you feel better to know that people care about your trouble and maybe some teenagers might learn something from it."

When there were rumors the Center might be closed because of school district financial woes, the students wrote to the Board of Education and to their local congressmen. We typed all the letters with carbons and taped the copies up in the front window. Students loved watching passersby stopping to read the letters. "She's reading mine!" somebody would claim. "No, turkey, she's reading mine." Sometimes a few kids would go outside and propagandize for their letters. "See these letters? We'd like you to stop and read them. This is important to us." They all received replies from the congressmen; none came from the board of education. I was enraged by the thought that the people in charge of our schools couldn't bother to participate in this educational venture. Parents of one of our students were prominent in the community. They contacted a congressman personally. "That must be some place," he said. "I sure am getting a lot of mail about it." The Center didn't close. The students were convinced their letters saved the day. I have no way of knowing if this was true, but how many people ever have the experience of thinking something they wrote made a difference? It sure beats canned, behaviorized assignments.

I encouraged several students at the Center to keep journals. It all started because Iris wouldn't talk to us. She'd come to school looking sad but wouldn't tell us what was bothering her. I gave her a notebook and suggested she write down some feelings. If she wanted an answer she could leave the notebook in my desk drawer and I'd write back. I promised never to discuss what she'd written unless she gave permission.

That notebook appeared in my drawer regularly, usually with three or four pages filled. I learned that Iris was a street person; she had left home because she didn't like her mother's boyfriend. She stayed here and there with friends and when she didn't have a place to sleep she hung around an all-night hamburger joint.

Sometimes journals backfired. Doris liked the idea of a journal. She told us she was writing a lot at home and would bring it in some day. Then her mother phoned me, hysterical. She had discovered her daughter's journal. "I know I shouldn't have read it, but I did." The journal was a record of names, dates, and positions. Doris was a prostitute.

An alternative school English teacher has to face a lot of incidents like that. Specifically forbidden by the board of education to give sex information, we arranged for Planned Parenthood to do it for us. The day I took a girl to get birth control pills I thought, "I've never seen any articles about this in *English Journal*." I can't pretend liking the involvement in my students' drug, sex, and larceny activities. I *liked* working with words, convincing students to use words more effectively, to work at understanding other peoples' words better. But if my students were going to drop out of school because of pregnancy or drugs or burglary, then I had to learn how to deal with those problems too. You can't help a kid with words who isn't there to hear you.

In addition to reading and writing, we used films as part of the language arts curriculum in our school. Every Friday was film day. Our school was located in a discarded bank and an old vault made a great theatre. The projector could run all day without disturbing work elsewhere in the Center. I was just authoritarian and school-oriented enough to hand out evaluation sheets with most films. I didn't ever want students to think we were just "messing around," filling time and space. Students are quick to perceive make-work and no-work assignments. Our students, as much as they complained about work, seemed especially concerned that assignments be real. They wanted everything to count for something.

Some of the more memorable showings were *Unicorn in the Garden*, *Incident at Owl Creek Bridge*, *Welfare*, *Future Shock*, and *Night and Fog*. I tried to have books that either matched or complemented the film, so if a student thought *Unicorn* was pretty funny I could say, "How about trying some of Thurber's other fables?" I remember Carl commenting, "You have a book for everything, don't you?" I answered him, "Right. There *is* a book for everything."

Tom was incensed at the ending of a futuristic version of *Lady or the Tiger?* "Where's the book?" he asked. "I want to see how it is supposed to end." He went racing off to the city library to find the book. We showed *Tell-Tale Heart* and Annie was inspired to get a library card so she could check out some Poe.

Of course, Annie was often "inspired." I think she read the first five pages of nearly every book in the Center. She became interested in graffiti and I brought in Mailer's book and Herbert Kohl's. I had prepared a unit on names, both personal and public. Annie was intensely interested — for about two days. Most of our students had trouble sticking with any one topic very long. They liked to flutter from thing to thing. Finally I handed Annie a book and told her, "You are going to read this book, every single page of it. You aren't going to start any other 'fascinating' project until you finish this one book." She did it, and she turned a corner after that. She finished all sorts of things. Her mother phoned one day and said, "I don't know what you people have done, but Annie is a decent human being again. She even helps with the dishes." I think maybe our school gave kids time and room — to do nothing, to flit from topic to topic, to settle down to serious study at their own pace.

Night and Fog made more impression than we expected. The students vaguely knew about World War II. They'd heard of Hitler; most of them knew Jews had been killed. But none of them knew about the horrors of the concentration camps. No one watched *Night and Fog* only once. The film ran all day Friday and, by special request, again on Monday. Students left the Center and brought friends and relatives back to see the film. Then we read excerpts from Anne Frank's *Diary* and from *Hiroshima;* we examined the language of Hoess' testimony at Nuremberg and discussed the problem of responsibility at Mai Lai.

An inspector from the State Education Department visited our school. He saw students reading Dick Francis, Zindel, Hinton, Thompson, Goldman, Adam Hall, and he complained about the quality of our literature program. He liked the SRA kits, the McCall Crab readers, and all the other standard "Choose answers *a, b, c,* or *d*" fare customarily force-fed to "reluctant" readers. He decried as irresponsible our lack of class sets of certain standard classics. "What major work do your sophomores read?" he asked. I told him I wasn't sure if we had any sophomores but that I had taken a group of kids to see *Pajama Game* at the local community college. They went on their own time, outside school hours, and they liked it. One student joined a local theatre group. The inspector left the building muttering something about the state syllabus.

Ironically, although we were casual about many things in our school — dress, smoking, time, forms of address — reading was sacred right from the moment a student entered. More than one student commented that they'd read more in six months at our school than in six years in the traditional setup. As Jack put it, "Sue is nuts about reading."

I wrote a letter to the superintendent of schools, asking that educational jingoists be kept out of our building during working hours. "I'd rather explain our philosophy when the kids aren't around." No educational bureaucrat has ever explained to me what is so sacred about teenagers reading in a group. I wonder how many adults buy multiple copies of the same book and then sit around reading it together. I disagree with Sartre: hell isn't other people; hell is those multiple choice answers at the end of the story.

I may be consigned to hell—Dante's or Milton's or Sartre's—or at least stripped of my membership card in the NCTE for saying this, but I would rather get a single kid hooked on the newspaper habit than watch a whole class of students fake a group reading of *Julius Caesar* or *The Secret Sharer* or whatever. I'm not an advocate of the TV star curriculum: I don't order those awful biographies of the bosomy, throaty, or hairy celebrities. I think there exist reasonable and even exciting choices somewhere in between John Travolta and William Wordsworth. I think reading and writing can have meaning to turned-off kids, kids who smoke, snort, pop pills, kids who seldom know the world except as seen through the haze of their collection of so-called mind-expanding materials. The answers, however, are not in a teacher's guide sent out from some ed-whiz conglomerate. If teachers themselves are not passionately committed to the printed page, if they are not constantly reading and searching, then there is little hope they will be able to inspire their students to read. Teaching priorities have to change from one group of kids to another, but I don't think the real goals of our alternative school were so much different from those of more traditional English classrooms. Don't we all ask, at least occasionally, "Reading for what? Writing for what?" If we don't, we should.

Smuggling Reading into the Reading Program

I ONCE ASKED my students in remedial reading lab to fill in the blank in the sentence, "I would rather read than _____ ." Michael wrote in "die." I was saddened, but not surprised, by his response. For Michael and students like him in reading labs across the country, reading has been a kind of slow death throughout their eight or more years of public education. I fear the current life skills and competency mania is going to make their agony worse.

Administrators are currently anxious that I teach the cloze method and business letters. Why? Not because they have any inherent worth to my students but because they are what the state ed people are using to define competency these days. At the risk of sounding pretentious, I must insist that administrative bulletins on criterion-referenced skills and behavioral objectives and IPACs and computer-assisted instruction and getting back to basics may come and go, but my sacred calling remains amazingly constant: I am in the classroom to help kids learn the joy of words—both their own words and the words of others. I am waiting for the day when I receive an administrative directive demanding that I incorporate joke reading into my daily schedule, demanding that I exchange daily notes with my students, insisting that I prove a student found joy in words in my class.

Perhaps we folk in the reading business should step off the pedagogic merry-go-round for a moment and ask ourselves *why* we are trying to teach students to read and write better. Is it merely so they can pass state competency exams? Do we want children to decode only so they can decipher *TV Guide?* Can't we offer them anything more?

One year the "reluctant reader" is put in New Innovative Plastic Remedial Program A and in June his teacher certifies he has gained 1½ years in his reading skills; the next fall he is in Program B and he gains 1½ years by June; the next fall he is labeled learning disabled and put in Program C, where he gains another 1½ years by June. By the time he reaches seventh grade, the student has gained 1½ years in each of eight to ten reading programs but he has also lost from 3 to 6 years and is four grade levels behind the standardized norm. Remedial teachers shake their heads sadly and comment that there is no controlling what happens to children over the summer. Those summers sure produce one hell of a negative Hawthorne effect.

I wonder how often kids in reading labs hold real books in their hands. I get students who are better at circling short *a* sounds than I am, but who have never read a book. They have been labeled "reluctant readers" since their prekindergarten days, and as everyone knows, "those kids" can't handle books. They've been given diagrams to complete, beads to string, workbooks with letters to circle or underline. It seems to me that after seven or ten years in school, these kids have learned one thing about reading: they have to know whether to circle or underline.

Professor Richard Allington of the State University of New York in Albany, with refreshing candor, called these kids lousy readers. He's right. I go to reading conferences and hear ponderous talks about improving the psycho-socio-linguistic-motor-whatever skills of "reluctant readers," and I ask myself, "Reluctant to read what?" I've never found a child who could resist knock-knock jokes once he was taught to read them. I've never found a child who isn't delighted by Alvin Schwartz's anthologies of word fun. I've never found anyone of any age who could resist the charm of *Where the Sidewalk Ends.* My students listen to me read *The Acorn People* and *Incident at Hawk's Hill* and *Julie of the Wolves* and *The Great Gilly Hopkins,* and they beg for more.

Michael, the student who said the only thing worse than reading was dying, came back from high school to see me the day after *The Acorn People* was on television. "Did you watch it?" he asked. "I made my whole family watch. It was good on TV, but it was much better when you read it to the class two years ago. It meant more then. That book made us *feel* the challenge of the mountain."

Michael then suggested he come visit my junior high reading lab. "I'm not reading in my English class at the high school. We do a lot of workbook stuff, but we aren't really reading." Even reluctant readers know the difference between workbooks and real reading.

"Decoding's the Thing Now"

When I taught reading to fourth graders, I complained to the publisher's representative that if I handed out all the ditto worksheets the teacher's manual insisted I should, we'd have no time for reading. He told me that I must not invalidate the program by skipping worksheets and not to worry so much about reading. "In this new approach," he assured me, "the actual reading isn't as important as it used to be. Decoding's the thing now."

I think of the teacher who blindly passes out reams of standardized lessons and feels proud when her class is two lessons ahead of the teacher across the hall, and I am reminded of the pilot who reported from some-where over the Pacific, "I'm lost, but I'm making record time."

I also think of a teacher I knew who panicked when her projector broke and she couldn't show the filmstrips on dictionary use. I pointed out that our library had a class set of dictionaries, the real thing. She shook her head. Reluctant readers can't use dictionaries; they need film-strips about dictionaries.

I go to reading conferences and tell people that my students read all period every Thursday, and they wonder where I find the time away from vowel drill and blend recognition. "We have to spend so much time on skills," teachers sigh. I'd like to point out that reading *is* a skill, one sorely in need of practice by our lousy readers.

The students in my classroom don't do much decoding; instead, they read. They read a personal note from me every day; they read the news-paper a couple of times a week; they go to the library and find out what elephants eat or how long turtles live or how much blood is in the human body or who built the Taj Mahal. Once a week my students are forced to read for an entire fifty-minute period. I use the word *force* quite deliber-ately. Every Thursday each child is required to sit with a book for fifty minutes — no bathroom passes, no visits to the nurse, no phone calls home, no sharpening pencils. Every student is expected to participate, or at least to simulate participation, in something called sustained, silent reading. The teacher also reads — no surreptitious correcting of homework, no sneaking out for coffee. At first this amazed my students; most of them had never seen an adult read. They would want to know what I was reading, and they would check back later in the day to see how many pages I had finished.

I have to admit that these sessions are never easy in the beginning. Students twitch, turn, poke, fall out of chairs, fall asleep, cause shelves to fall. Kids are ingenious in their efforts to make silent reading time any-thing but silent. After a few weeks, however, they realize I'm serious, and most learn to sit quietly with a book. By the end of the year, everyone will have read several books. Some students will have read books of more than a hundred pages, something they didn't believe they could do.

Keith spent ten years in elementary school pretending to read. In my class he bluffed his way through a stack of *National Geographics* and a complete set of encyclopedias. He spent most of his time taking screws out of bookshelves, throwing spitwads, and insisting that he was bleeding internally. One day, after he claimed he had read every book and maga-zine in our classroom, I handed him *Hop on Pop* by Dr. Seuss. Keith started to turn the pages quickly, as he did with all books, but then he stopped and looked at a page. He stared at it for a few moments, and then went back to the beginning of the book and started mouthing words.

About half an hour later, Keith looked up with a puzzled expression on his face: "I did it. I *read* this book." He looked at me. "Seriously, Miz O, I read it. For real. I read the book. You wanna see?" He came over and started reading aloud. It wasn't fluent reading. Each word was struggled over, pointed at, sounded out. In one respect it was pitiful: Keith was fifteen years old. Who knows what reading level Grey or Fry or Spache would assign to *Hop on Pop*. But who could possibly care? For Keith and me that was a crystal moment.

Like readers who are grateful for *The Son of Monte Cristo* or *The Black Stallion Returns,* Keith knew what he liked. He ransacked the shelves for all the Dr. Seuss books he could find. I thought of the raised eyebrows in the faculty room when I mentioned that I, a teacher of eighth graders, belonged to the Dr. Seuss book club. I had to join on my own. The school district would readily purchase five-hundred-dollar reading kits and assorted mechanical wizardry — but not Dr. Seuss or a subscription to the local newspaper.

Hearing Words Sing

I picked up a copy of *Can You Sue Your Parents for Malpractice?* at a supermarket and read it during one of our silent Thursdays. A few days later, Nick, who had spent two years telling me how much he hated reading, asked me, "Can you?"

"Can you what?"

"Sue them?"

"Well, I guess you'll just have to read the book to find out," I said.

"I don't know," he said. "It's kind of long."

"Try it. Take it home."

"I might have it a long time. I'm not a very fast reader." I assured him I didn't care how long he kept the book.

"What happens if I don't finish it?"

Lousy readers don't start books because they're scared they'll be stuck with them forever. I told Nick I'd hate to have all the books I haven't finished lined up in front of me. "That book is written for fun, Nick. If you don't have fun with it, then give it back to me."

A week went by. Neither Nick nor I mentioned the book. Then one day he came in and said very casually, "That book isn't bad. I tried some of it." He looked at me for a few seconds and then said, "I'm not reading every word. I don't know some of the words." I told him I seldom read every word, and as long as he could make sense of the story, to keep going and skip as much as he liked.

A few days later Nick came in smiling. "Some kids in the cafeteria asked me if you could sue your parents." He pointed to the book stuffed in his back pocket. "I had it with me when I went to lunch. I read a little of one chapter in the cafeteria." It took every bit of control not to reveal my joy and amazement. "But you know," Nick went on, "the author doesn't really answer the question. Do you suppose she just put that in the title to get kids interested?"

"It worked, didn't it?" I laughed.

Nick laughed too. "It's a pretty good book anyway," he said.

Nick wasn't so different from Alphonse, whom I met when he was in second grade. I was supposed to teach one of those lockstep reading programs to him and other "disadvantaged reluctant readers." The publisher called all the little papers I handed out "stories," but Alphonse and Darlene and all the others knew they weren't stories; they were letters to sound out. I soon became so frustrated with this "complete reading system," which included no classroom library books, that I started making waves.

I made a few trips to the federal office funding the program and finally persuaded the staff that every reading class *must* have books; kits, cards, drill sheets, and filmstrips were definitely not enough. They came up with twenty-five dollars to fund a classroom library. The principal, impressed with my dedication to books, agreed that I could do anything I wished with my reluctant readers during the lunch break, just so long as we dutifully completed our little drill sheets during our official reading period.

The kids brought bag lunches and we ate together. They were apprehensive, wondering if they were going to be force-fed long vowels along with their peanut-butter sandwiches. I surprised them by teaching Darlene to tie her shoelaces. Another day I showed Alphonse how to use a screwdriver. All the kids learned to hammer a nail into a board, using a real hammer, real nails, and a real board. I wasn't sure what I was doing; I only knew I wanted those kids to stop worrying about all those long and short vowel sounds every time they saw me coming. So they hammered nails and I read aloud from the most attractive books I could find.

George Steiner once said, "That which you have not heard will not sing for you later. God help a culture where parents don't read aloud to their children." If our reluctant readers have not heard stories, how can we teachers expect the words on the programmed ditto sheets or the words in the carefully planned basal series or the words in the brightly colored reading kits to sing for them? And if words don't sing for them, how are these children ever to become amenable to the printed page?

After we'd used the tools and shared some good stories, I brought out some of my favorite books: *The Hat Book, The Foot Book, The Monster at the End of This Book, The Very Hungry Caterpillar.* Every child got a book. "You are going to read a book," I announced. They stared at me in astonishment.

I proceeded to teach them the relationship between the pictures and the words, so even if Alphonse couldn't recognize the phrase "too crooked," he could look at the crooked hat and then remember the right words.

During reading class we continued dutifully with our drills, my eyes and heart as glazed as the students'. During lunch we hammered nails and read books together. I make no claims about the actual reading done by those kids. I know they picture-read, memorized, or whatever. I left that school because I couldn't face another year of following a manual that told me when to stand, when to sit, when to breathe while I was "teaching" children. I don't know how Al and Darlene and the others did the next year. I only know that they occasionally heard words sing as they ate their peanut-butter sandwiches and hammered nails.

Newspapers and Elephant Jokes

I learned a lot from my brief time with Alphonse and Darlene and the others. My experience with them made me braver. I no longer sneak real reading into the lunch break while continuing dumb drills during the regular class period. Sure, I teach the business letter and the cloze system. My students have to achieve the state education department's notion of competency. But the core of our work centers on the possibilities of words, on my belief that children must experience the fun of reading.

I love bad jokes, and my students know it. They think they are doing me a favor when they read me an elephant joke — and they are. I never tire of hearing a child laugh over a Shel Silverstein poem he is reading. If a book is too difficult for my students, I tape-record it for them to listen to individually or I read it aloud to the entire class.

I scour the local newspaper for weird stories. The kids read about surgery performed on an elephant, bubble-gum-blowing contests, a cat who inherited a fortune. Sometimes I challenge a student to find the weirdest story in the day's paper. When I set Gennaro to this task, his eyes widened: "You aren't even going to tell me which section?" About ten minutes later, he shouted, "I found it! I found it!" and turned to his fellow reluctant readers and read them the story of a man who got so angry at his lawn mower that he shot it.

Roosevelt looks through the *New York Times* every Monday. He has discovered that's the day they run all the best sports pictures. (I didn't know that until he pointed it out.) A state education evaluator happened to be in the room one Monday and expressed concern that the *New York Times* might not be appropriate material for a "corrective situation." I invited Roosevelt to perform for him. Roosevelt wasn't a good reader, but he could make a box score sound like Moses announcing the contents of the tablets. Still, I think the evaluator would have been happier to see a neatly packaged newspaper kit, programmed and sanitized and normed for appropriate grade levels.

Another state ed bureaucrat visited our classroom and was concerned that every "skill" taught was not carefully linked to an observable, testable, provable objective. He didn't like our learning stations, either, stating that "stations are passé." I didn't tell him we don't operate on the Calvin Klein/Gloria Vanderbilt theory of education. We like what works—for the kids as well as the teacher—and we don't particularly care if our version of learning stations is *au courant* this season. It happens to be a system that works very well as an organizing device in our classroom.

I wonder how I would objectify the ten-foot-high, multicolored ice-cream cone that decorates the corridor. My students made it to illustrate Silverstein's "Eighteen Flavors." Although we are a junior high class, we follow the primary grade practice of decorating the hallway with our work: interviews, polls, poems. (No one is too sophisticated to have his work on display. When I get an article published, I don't just put it in my secret scrapbook and send a copy to Mom; I put it up in the faculty room.)

Underneath our cone we stretched a roll of adding-machine tape the entire length of the corridor. On it the kids wrote every name of ice cream they'd ever heard of. When they ran out of traditional names, we looked at menus from ice-cream shops. Finally, we made up names for ice creams that should be but aren't—yet. We read a *New Yorker* article about the founding and operation of Baskin-Robbins, not worrying about whether the *New Yorker* is certified appropriate reading material for lousy readers. We had contests to see who could read all the ice-cream flavors without a mistake. I can just see my behavioral objective: *Student will read a minimum of 116 flavors of ice cream.*

I am sure the state ed people will be back—to see if we've dismantled our learning stations, found an appropriate reading system, and written up all our objectives. I wouldn't dare be caught with my cloze down. I have a list of standard objectives for all those things that seem to matter to evaluators: the rules about the silent *e*, dropping the *y*, the apostrophe before the *s*, and so on. I'm hoping that after I produce the list, the wit and whimsy with which I try to fill our classroom will be forgiven. If it isn't, I'll console myself with this silent prayer: Yea, though I walk in the shadow of conglomerate criterion-referenced curricula, I will fear no evil; the children, they comfort me.

When the Reading Experts Gather,
What's Their Real Agenda?

Although the convention travels under the name of International Reading Association—and certainly a few of the speakers did have Spanish surnames or British accents—the whole idea of eager teachers flocking to receive the good word of revelation from the university experts somehow seems as American as frozen apple pie. We do, after all, crave the recommendations of experts and celebrities for everything we do—from choosing a deodorant to selecting a popcorn popper. The problem is, of course, that our sought-after music of the spheres turns out to be more of a cacophony; the professors sing many different tunes—all at once. They are joined by publishing chorus lines chanting the ditty, "Follow Me."

Anyone who has not been to an IRA convention may not realize how literally I mean that last remark. I was stunned to be accosted by grown men prancing around the exhibit hall in funny costumes, looking more like mascots for a third-rate football team than people with whom I wanted to discuss basal readers. It was hard for me to get into the spirit of things. When Mr. Fig insisted I have my picture taken with him, I advised him to keep his distance. I admit my prejudices, my hopes, my naiveté: I went to Chicago in search of, if not truth, at least beauty. What I found was the stylized exuberance of the TV game show personified: women scurrying around stuffing their shopping bags. "Just take everything now and look at it later back at the hotel," I heard one lady advise her exhausted cohort. Conventions bring out the acquisitive worst in people. We grab for things we have no use for, worthless junk we can't even use for reading prizes back home. I thought I was pretty selective about what I stuffed in my own shopping bag, and yet I still threw two-thirds of it away before I left Chicago.

Schoolteachers from Dubuque, Cucamonga, and Troy flocked to the IRA convention in Chicago by the thousands (something like twelve thousand people registered) and then were left pretty much to their own devices to pick and choose among the fifteen hundred presenters. A conventiongoer pays her money and takes her chances. She is handed a 176-page program, from which she must choose between what appeals and what appalls. It is difficult to rely on phenomenology when deciding

127

between "Sex Differences in Reading" and "The M & M's of Comprehension." Early on, I began to get the uneasy feeling that the underlying theme of the IRA meeting might be "Trendier Than Thou."

Let the Truth Be Known

If the conventiongoer knew what she was looking for, if she went looking for experts to enhance, elaborate upon, and provide institutional support for her preconvention predilections and prejudices, then she was sure to meet with success. However, if the teacher went to Chicago hoping to find truth, she might have had more trouble. The IRA does not see its function as that of truthgiver—except on certain general, almost pat, issues such as the need for more reading teachers, the problems brought about by federal cuts in education monies, the evils of censorship in any form, and pronouncing the worth of the language of minority children.

Certainly every relevant political-pedagogical-psychological subject seemed to be represented: from reading for the aged to crisis intervention to parent burnout. The medical model for solving the mysteries of reading was well represented, as was the mastery learning model. The language experience approach has moved out of the primary grades and into the middle grades. And as might be expected, computer software was there in quantity and razzmatazz.

It is understandable why teachers hope for a medical answer to dyslexia—or whatever we're supposed to call a child's inability to read these days. Surely hope beats eternal that a clever and compassionate doctor, a cross between Dr. Kildare and Jonas Salk, will come along with a pill or a vaccine to end the problem of lousy readers forever. I suppose it was the vague hope of being able to carry the message of a medical breakthrough back to our colleagues that led hundreds of us to sit in ballrooms listening to learned scientists drone on about the electrical properties of learning, about E.E.G.s measuring the activity of neurons, about the significance of positively charged sodium ions, and so on. God knows why, but many of us sat there dutifully taking notes and felt frustrated when the data we wouldn't have understood anyway flashed on the screen in blurry, unreadable print half-blocked by the speaker's head.

One thing the medical advocates, the psychotherapeutic theorists, and the stress-relief technicians all had in common: their overhead transparencies were shoddy, their handouts inadequate, and their data incomprehensible. Their monotonic presentations were merely proof that they themselves could read. Few made any effort to speak to their audiences. I wondered if I had been out of college too long, if maybe clarity of presentation has never been demanded of professors of education. Classroom teachers know they could never get away with such poor presentations. Apparently professors feel they can get away with anything.

I raise this point because I think it is closely related to what goes on at other meetings of the IRA: those guys making the presentations, whether they be advocates of Mastery Learning or M & M therapy, are laws unto themselves; nobody in their very sacred community of fellows is going to stand up and blow the whistle on them. No one really cares what they do: you present your research findings and I'll present mine. Publish and let publish. Meanwhile, we teachers who are trying to do good in the classroom, or at least to do no harm, are often left in the dark, if not out in the cold. We sit, desperately taking notes on amino acids or a new readability formula, and worry that we're missing Dame Truth. Maybe we chose the wrong session and she's presiding next door.

I was chatting to some people about the convention and complained that if a professor was going to cite a primary student's composition — and display complicated, computer-analyzed data gleaned from said composition — then he should at least be able to decipher the invented spelling. He had completely misread a key word (and was corrected by a third-grade teacher in the audience). An earnest young man spoke up in defense of the professor, "He doesn't have time to work much in the schools. He works mostly with graduate students." It turned out that this young man was one of the learned man's graduate students. I told this story elsewhere, and, amazingly enough, I ended up talking to another of his graduate students. The importance of a professor is displayed in the size of the entourage accompanying him. Watch closely at the next big convention: the person who adjusts the overhead projector is a graduate student; so is the person with the briefcase. That is all fine and dandy, but I still insist that if someone is going to tell me about the language of eight-year-olds, in addition to graduate students he'd better know a few eight-year-olds.

Inane Statements and Electronic Drill

One quickly learns at a big convention that a thing isn't necessarily true just because someone had the nerve to get up in front of 150 people and say it. The IRA's own *Dictionary of Reading Terms* says there is "no clear present consensus about the precise nature of reading disability," which seems to open up the microphones for anybody to say anything he likes at conventions. Professors and publishers tout their theories and their wares, promising to end classroom drudgery forever. I was torn between impatience and outrage. When I got home from the convention and waited for the verbal dust to settle, I began to wonder how it was possible that such words were uttered without the speakers being hooted out of the hall. Should we continue to be polite to people who claim that "the material is self-teaching" or that a manual contains "all a teacher needs"? One speaker insisted that in her program, "Every child responded to every task." I have a few kids I'd like her to meet.

Other statements I couldn't believe I was hearing included: "When the Creator made the brain, He didn't anticipate we'd have to read"; "We must build skills through carefully controlled readabilities"; "Increased metacognitive awareness will improve reading comprehension"; "There is evidence indicating that children are influenced by the textbooks they are asked to read"; "The emerging medium of literacy is very likely to be the cathode ray tube." As to that last comment — the unctuousness and vapidity of the rest stand self-evident — I think it would be fitting if the speaker were made to read a dot-matrix printout of *War and Peace*. Or, even better, he should be sat in a corner until he's read all the IRA publications from a video display.

Some researchers proclaimed that "reading is easy" while others cited the multitudinous discrete subskills involved in this very complicated "unnatural act." Reading as unnatural act is one of my favorite notions gleaned from the convention. Another is "content" reading. The irony of that term seems to escape many people who should know better. If there really is such a thing as "non-content" reading, then surely those awful booklets with a paragraph about the Aztecs, followed by content comprehension questions, followed by a paragraph about the life cycle of a turkey, followed by content comprehension questions, and so on, come as close to content-lessness as anything I care to see. How many decades will it take us to figure out that when we give a kid questions at the end of each paragraph, he doesn't read the paragraph; he only answers the questions? And he learns a terrible lesson in the process: that he hates reading.

There were sessions on parent burnout, sessions on reading-teacher burnout. I would like to propose a session on remedial-reading-student burnout. How much content reading, practice for cloze tests, metacognition training and mastery of short vowels can these kids take? Year after year they read those paragraphs and fill in those blanks. For how many years can a child maintain tolerance for "find the main idea"?

Reading Does Not Compute

In all earnestness I asked a sales representative if I could see the *readers* the children used in her program. She kept showing me isolated paragraphs and the ubiquitous skill drills. "No, no," I insisted. "Where's the reader? What do the kids read?" She replied, "This program is skill based; it *prepares* the child to read." I was looking at a sixth-grade program. Six years in school and the child's day was still almost 100 percent skill filled. If one does not weep at that, what carnage does it take to fill one's eyes and heart with sorrow?

There were plenty of people in Chicago telling us that today's children will find true happiness—and skill development—in computers. I learned that a computer program is available to "calculate the congruence" between a student's reading interests and abilities and those attributes of a book that will capture his interest. Books are analyzed according to the age, gender, and culture of the main characters; the "interest areas" that characterize the text; and the books' linguistic readability. Teachers need no longer fear that a child will encounter anything in print that he could not call kin. That is a relief. We wouldn't want a boy in New York City picking up a book about a girl who was born in India but raised in a strange old house on the moors of England.

Another way in which teachers can "manage" their reading program with the aid of a computer is to store all the basal words in the machine. The unit and story the student is working on in the basal are computer coded. When this code is matched to the classroom library of trade books, the teacher can rest assured that the child, should he ever venture near the "free reading" zone, won't encounter hostile words, words that have not been properly introduced. This guarantee exemplifies what old fogies like me mean when we refer to the chill of computerized instruction. Apparently the designers of such systems have never heard of what Donald Graves refers to as the "joy of new risks." Computers don't take risks. They do what they're supposed to do. That's probably why administrators like them so much.

A lot of computer curriculum seems to be built around our old friends: long and short vowels, blends, consonant digraphs and syllabification. Presenters insist that research has shown that students need forty "exposures" if they are to learn a new skill. I never understood just what you had when you had a kid who could circle all those short vowels, but if one believes that forty drills on blends make good readers, then computers sure do provide efficient means to that end.

An Absence of Beliefs and Books

In my compulsive plowing through publishers' wares at the IRA convention, I found a booklet entitled *Developing a System of Beliefs: The Foundation of Your Reading Program*. Intrigued, I picked it up—and opened it to sixteen blank pages. To say I was stunned is to put it mildly. Was I in the *National Lampoon* booth? *Mad* magazine? Who else would have the temerity to get at the heart of the problem of most reading programs: their utter lack of commitment to a belief? Then I discovered that the blank booklet went with a program for teacher inservice instruction intended to provide a system of beliefs—in three easy lessons or so. I applaud the notion that teachers should have beliefs at the foundation of their reading programs, but I don't think beliefs come in a package, a product, or from an inservice program, or even from an annual IRA convention.

There was one highlight of the convention: a talk by child advocate Lillian Weber. She stood up there, without a note, and *spoke* to teachers. She said that we reading teachers don't have to categorize and label more and more and more; what we have to do is work our guts out. That was a daring message to state at a convention dominated by people who promised they could make teaching easier and easier. It was also a refreshing message. I didn't go to Chicago looking for a piece of cake, and if I couldn't come away better informed, I would certainly settle for some of Weber's inspiration.

I was also delighted to find a new novel by E. L. Konigsburg, a new joke book by Ann Bishop, a witty poetry book by Jack Prelutsky, another outrageous hippopotamus book by Mike Thaler, and a wonder book called *Breakfast, Books, and Dreams: A Day in Verse,* edited by Michael P. Hearne. One of the best things I can say about the IRA is that I enjoyed reading my autographed copy of its award winner, *Good Night, Mr. Tom* by Michelle Magorian, on the plane home. I looked forward to sharing it with my students. I wish publishers could somehow be persuaded to bring more of their trade books to conventions. By and large, though, there was little mention of books in IRA presentations: skills, systems, and strategies, yes; books, no.

A parent recently asked me how I would define a reader. I didn't ponder the question long, and unlike the IRA in its dictionary, I offered no caveat. I said a reader is probably a third or fourth grader who can read a book of more than one hundred pages within a few days. The parent was upset by my definition. His boy brings home wonderful progress reports. A fifth grader, he scored 6.8 on the California Achievement Test and does not encounter any difficulties in "content" reading, completing all his social studies and science assignments in good order. Because of his CAT scores, his school put him in an "enriched" program, one that will help him become "computer literate." To his parents' best knowledge, the boy has never read a book.

IRA President Kenneth Goodman said we're winning the battle against illiteracy, citing the increase in the sale of paper clips as proof positive that literacy is alive and well. I think IRA leaders need to probe the significance of the paper clip consumption a bit more deeply. Even though, as President Goodman also pointed out, people are actually buying more books, if they are mostly books about how to make a killing in real estate, cheat the IRS or flatten your belly, then do we have much to cheer about? Are people buying more real books for their kids? (I'm not referring to those monstrosities that smell, pop out, or light up.) I am not particularly encouraged about the state of literacy just because there exist eight magazines for the pilots of small planes, three for hot tub owners, and God knows how many for soap opera fans. Not when *Harper's* nearly folded and newspapers can't find enough readers. If we teachers are doing such a great job, how come those same kids need that same remedial fix every year? How come one good dose or two doesn't fix them up?

The next time I go to an IRA convention, I will be wary of sessions with words like *psychogenic, neuropsychological, psychophysiological* and *sociopsychological* in their titles. I shall also avoid, whenever possible, longitudinal, multitask data. Such data, one finds, is usually based on eighteen students working with three professors and sixteen graduate students and has no possible application to the classroom. There were a few other terms heard overmuch that I hope will self-destruct before the next convention rolls around: basic skill thrusts, metacognition, writeability, classroom management system, hygiene of writing.

I sometimes wonder if it's easier for a camel to pass through the eye of a needle than for a reading expert to enter the kingdom of children's literature. Confronted with the clutter and clatter of the theories and the materials, maybe we need to be reminded that on the eighth day God did not create the consonant blend. In the beginning was the Word. It would be reassuring to know that reading experts still have faith in words, belief in books. Reading teachers would welcome the IRA as spiritual leader, I think. But can the organization rise to the challenge?

Beware the Rosy View!

Educational camp followers—publishing gurus, methods entrepreneurs, education professors, and curriculum coordinators—are always on the lookout for the package or product or system or technique that can bypass the vagaries of individual teacher-and-student interaction and thus ensure universal quality education. In my eighteen years as a teacher, I have witnessed at least a half dozen such programs presented in my district as the way (at long last) to end forever the need for remediation. One time the administrators were so confident of their product that they abolished all remedial teaching positions at the same time that they handed out the new manuals. Long before the manuals were dog-eared, the remedial teachers were back.

Messiah or Monster?

But now the deus ex machina truly is with us, greeted with loud hosannas and only a niggling bit of doubt. In our time of peril, with no solution to the literacy crisis in sight, a mechanical miracle is offered up to sweep aside low reading scores with a flutter of the video display screen. This time the product is so wondrous that few people are asking whether it's messiah or monster. The administrators in my district, however, are a bit more cautious. Instead of abolishing the remedial positions immediately, they are installing the computers in all the remedial labs.

"Microcomputer-managed information," "Total microcomputer instructional management," "Total skills program," "Enrichment," "Remediation." The microcomputer can do it all. We hear of schools where the SATs went up by thirty points after the introduction of computers, districts where math skills increased 1½ grades in three months. *Time* magazine tells us there is a "new breed of whiz kids" out there, a generation that is "propelling traditional education down promising avenues." We hear that two-year-olds are programming after just an hour's exposure and wonder what's wrong with our humdrum lives. Writing in the *Chronicle of Higher Education* (September 22, 1982), Paul Connolly of Yeshiva University remarked that "parents who cannot compete with their children in video games marvel at the brave new world they do not understand and join the chorus that warns that those who do not rejoice in the new technology may be buried by it."

The computer chorus line is seductive, but teachers must not be diverted from looking at the questions raised by the use of computers in schools, the same old questions that have always plagued the serious educator: who's in charge, what kinds of decisions are they making, and how do they treat kids? In 1832, Emerson wrote in his journal, "Everything is a monster till we know what it is for." What is so monstrous about computers is that in the hands of the bureaucrats, the pencil pushers, and the greedy, they make wrongheaded notions of pedagogy easier to implement. There is evidence abounding that computers can be used as tools for exploration, discovery, and invention. But this electronic capability is irrelevant in schools purchasing packets of computer-aided instruction to push the same old skill drill, materials that insist knowledge is learned in itsy-bitsy pieces of hierarchical process, methods that insist you gotta learn the easy stuff before you can look at the hard stuff.

How can we greet software with anything but contempt when it's marketed with the huckster's spiel that it provides teachers "all they need to know" for curriculum planning, that the computer will "monitor and manage student progress," "prescribe assignments," and make students "progress more rapidly"?

As might be expected, some folks in the reading skill business have been quick to jump at the possibility of another profitable Band-Aid approach to reading instruction. I recently visited a classroom where a reading management system is being installed. The publisher of this system has provided the teacher with a list of all the workbook activities necessary for the "mastery" of a host of objectives. Here I found our old friends: beginning blends, ending blends, vowel dipthongs, syllabification, finding main ideas and so on. Coincidentally, all these workbook exercises happen to be published by the company selling the management system. Some of them were copyrighted in 1927.

As happens so often in education, teachers with twenty years' experience were not consulted; in essence, they were each handed two thousand dollars worth of workbooks. The idea is that the student plows through all the workbook pages listed by the publisher for a certain skill. When he's finished, he punches his *a*, *b*, *c*, or *d* answers to a test into the computer. The computer then generates reports of his performance for the teacher, the parents, the district evaluator, the board of education. . . .

Judging from the number of kids per machine, each kid will have about three minutes a week to punch in his answers. (Good thing the tests are short.) In reality, then, the computer in this management system is being used only to correct tests and reckon students' grades. It can compile individual, class, and districtwide scores, and I sincerely hope

135

school board members will rest easier knowing that reading scores are figured to the third—or thirty-third—decimal place.

McDonald's Rule for Quality Control

For the price of those workbooks, the teacher could have gotten Logo, *Bank Street Writer, Gertrude's Puzzles, Rocky's Boots* and a host of other software to introduce her class to the wonders of computers. Seymour Papert, one of the creators of the Logo computer language, says that if children are allowed to mess around with computers they will become apprentice epistemologists; they will think about thinking, learn about learning. But educational bureaucrats don't understand this notion. Letting kids fool around with the turtle or the mouse or the word processor requires a tremendous amount of faith. You don't get a post-test with *Rocky's Boots,* so you can't prove to the administration that a kid messing around in his own mind is learning anything. Our education managers get nervous at the idea of a kid being in charge. They want the machine to program the child, not the other way around. This attitude isn't new. H. L. Mencken recognized empty technique when he encountered it in 1918:

> The aim seems to be to reduce the whole teaching process to a sort of automatic reaction, to discover some master formula that will not only take the place of competence and resourcefulness in the teacher but will also create an artificial receptivity in the child.

I am told that the virtue of such a computer-managed reading system is that if Johnny moves from School A to School B within the city, the educational leaders feel confident that his educational process won't be disrupted because everybody's teaching the same skills, using the same workbooks, getting the same computer printouts. This, of course, presumes that when you know what page Johnny is on, you know something about Johnny as a learner. It is the McDonald's Rule for Quality Control in Education. Teachers are provided with the franchised formula and are expected just to serve it up "as is." The learning comes prepackaged, presequenced, preordained as useful. Plug the kid in for his electronic fast fix and the management system will do the rest. Nowhere is the phrase "garbage in, garbage out" more applicable.

An interesting sidelight is that some administrators are wondering how they will evaluate teachers under this new system. "After all, you won't be teaching," they say. I suspect administrators will have their hands full checking that the franchised formulas are being adhered to; meanwhile, teachers and kids will soon be looking for ways to subvert the master plan, to introduce individuality, personality, common sense. They will have to do that to stay alive.

People who sell these computerized skill programs like to emphasize that they are a back-to-basic, no-frills approach to learning. But if you buy into this mind set, then everything that isn't a measurable skill becomes a frill. You end up with a new Gresham's law: The curriculum that is quantitatively measurable will drive out the curriculum that is qualitatively justifiable. It would be naive not to admit the appeal this idea has for many people. Marie Winn points out in *Children Without Childhood* (New York: Pantheon, 1987) that our children live in the Age of Preparation. Fostering early skill acquisition has become a much greater priority than encouraging fantasy, imagination, creativity. She quotes a teacher, "Kids in our kindergarten can't sit around playing with blocks anymore. We've just managed to squeeze in one hour of free play a week, on Fridays."

To dwell on computer-assisted reading instruction programs is not to suggest that the other stuff is any better. One could be as critical—or more so—of math-skills programs. According to the *Wall Street Journal*, when three hundred teachers evaluated a batch of mathematics software, only 25 percent of it earned a score of 60 percent or better. Traditional publishers are spewing forth what they know best—only now their workbooks light up and sing. Nontraditional companies have jumped into the marketplace, but they, too, are using the workbook rather than the kid as a model.

And science is no better. Recently I was intrigued by a disk that purported to teach youngsters something about the human body. I should have been warned by the subtitle, "Step-by-step instruction." The program does nothing more than offer up cryptic, dictionary-style definitions of various body systems and functions—just one damned definition after another. "Animation" consists of words occasionally bouncing around the screen for no apparent reason. The lessons are tripe that no reasonably healthy student would sit still for. Following the so-called instruction is a test of sixty-seven questions, a test of the worst kind: choose *a, b, c,* or *d* and a true/false regurgitation of definitions. There is no invitation to explore, elaborate on, or integrate information. I had thought that the program, at the very least, would show some dynamics of the body processes: the blood circulating, the food digesting. I was wrong. Programmers of such material operate under the phenomenological principle that it's enough to light up, wiggle, and bleep.

All these junky materials are marketed both as skill developers and as tools that bring "computer literacy" to the schools. This, of course, is just the newest educational buzzword, one employed to intimidate teachers, impress taxpayers, and enrich publishing conglomerates. In the name of computer literacy, children are learning a few purely mechanical skills: where to insert the disk and which buttons to push. As implemented in most schools today, computer literacy is a fraud that has nothing to do with the significance computers can play in people's lives.

For Whom the Bleep Tolls

Teachers always need to become knowledgeable about educational theory and apparatus, but it is very likely that most of us do not ourselves need to become truly computer literate. Paul Connolly gives us hope when he questions the notion that data processing is at the core of every enlightened being. It is refreshing to hear, amidst the apocalyptic blather about the uninitiated being left crippled and helpless in the wake of the technological revolution, that maybe there are some worthwhile people in this profession for whom the computer's bleep does not toll.

It is tempting, however, for someone like me, a third-grade teacher who knows firsthand of the physical difficulties eight-year-olds have in getting words on paper, to embrace the word processor as the heaven-sent answer to my woes. Sure, the novelty of the keyboard will appeal to the kids. The erasing capabilities alone make it seem worth the price.

Contrary to the claims of certain proponents, however, the bland screen is not really "friendlier than a blank sheet of paper." Once the child has tired of typing his name, the names of all his friends and relatives, the alphabet, all the jokes he knows, the time will come when he is supposed to produce words of his own: he will need something to say. Actually, most young children, if properly encouraged, have a lot to say. The problem is that once it is said they seldom see any need to change it. Donald Graves, author of *Teacher and Children at Work* (Portsmouth, NH: Heinemann, 1983), although cautiously optimistic about the possibilities word processing offers young children, warns that seeing their words neatly printed might make children even less anxious to revise. Words typed are already more final and official than words handwritten.

More important, says Graves, is the fact that a word processor won't make a good writing teacher out of a bad writing teacher. Graves is one of those educators who speak to the fact that the child needs time to explore, to discover, to create. This time cannot be preprogrammed; there are no shortcuts. The good teacher knows that and gives the child room.

Bertram Bruce, codirector of the Massachusetts-based company that developed *Quill* (a set of microcomputer-based writing activities for children in grades three to six), notes that sometimes the students with the best teachers don't use the computer writing program as much as expected because there are "so many interesting competing activities in their classroom." This point cannot be overstated. When a teacher decides to use the computer, she has to make time for it. She has to decide *not* to do something else. When a teacher introduces a computer program, she and the children have a right to demand that it be better than the alternatives.

Bruce proudly adds that his company's computer-writing activities are so powerful that some children come in before and after school to work on them. I believe that and am happy kids are being encouraged to write. We don't need a computer, however, to get the kids back into the building. They will come for optical illusions, bones, the solar system. I've had kids show up to practice borrowing in subtraction. Kids will even come to write stories with pencil and paper. If a good teacher offers to stay after school, she will always find plenty of company.

Another Shot of Novelty

Recently I attended a reading conference where a teacher-presenter said she liked working with computers because they made her feel important. "Reading teachers are so ordinary," she said. "This makes me special." At first her naiveté made me sad, but the more I thought about it, the angrier I became. This is a parody of the professional, someone who needs a triannual shot of novelty to keep her going. The true professional needs stamina for the long haul; she needs to be able to face the fact that things are probably going to be more the same tomorrow than they are today.

In *The Micro Millenium* (New York: Viking, 1980), Christopher Evans predicts that teachers will be replaced as "exclusive repositories and disseminators of specialist knowledge." While acknowledging the failure of the old-style teaching machines and programmed learning, Evans asserts that the teaching computers will be genuinely "smart"; they will "adjust their responses . . . to meet the needs of the moment," giving the impression that they are "interested" in teaching. A person who is capable of believing such hogwash has no notion of what goes on in a real classroom.

It is likely that I make myself an endangered species by admitting this, but I don't leave my classroom at the end of the day proud that I taught three — or thirteen — skills. When I recall my crystal moments in teaching, I'm not thinking of the day 96.4 percent of the class scored 98.672 percent on a long-division quiz. I am likely to be thinking of something that had nothing to do with the *cr* blend, the eights times table, or any of the other minutiae of the ostensible curriculum. I am probably recalling something serendipitous, something unforeseen that happened only once and will never happen again — like the day one of my deaf students learned a knock-knock joke.

I don't offer my students a glut of information; instead of factoids, I present an attitude and approach to learning. I like to think that children with me for ten months develop some self-reliance, a love for the sound of our language, and at least a beginning awareness that they can experience joy in words, both in their own words and the words of others. I also throw in a bit about the power of numbers and the wonders of messing around in science. I try to help children get a feeling of the *connectedness* of things. I believe that for this job I am uniquely qualified. On my good days I have faith in my own judgment, sensitivity, and skill. Even on my bad days I know that I will get another chance. To do my job as I have defined it, I am in charge. I yield to no higher authority. None.

That doesn't mean I don't look for help. I make sure I am knowledgeable about as many theories and as much material as possible, even the tiddly-pom that lights up and whistles Dixie. I need the experts to help me separate the pap from the prophecy, but I don't need them to make me feel special. For that, the kids are enough.

How Today's Software Can Zap
Kids' Desire to Read

MOST READING SOFTWARE is foolish and impudent, an odious endeavor. And the mistake is right up front—in the endeavor itself, not in the execution. I like clever graphics as well as the next person, and today's software certainly drills with pizzazz. But what I find foolish is the basic premise—that reading can be achieved by drilling students on discrete skills.

Plenty of folks are fond of consonant blends and their assorted kin. A skill is comfortable. It is easy to spot; it can be measured, charted, graphed, put in a data bank, brought out on parent conference night. Certainly these skills are nothing new and I do not blame the computer parvenus for their existence. But neither do I thank them for making things easy for the educational bookies who insist we can know a kid by the numbers in his folder.

Folks who play the educational numbers game never ask what a collection of 1,392 of these skills is good *for*, what the kid should do with them. Acquisition is the only goal. Computers, which allow isolated skills to multiply faster than the biblical tribes, merely encourage the foul bureaucratic impulse for collection, storage, and retrieval. I can only express my gratitude that, when I taught reading in New York from 1969 through 1983, I was unaware that the New York State Education Department had eighteen hundred-plus reading objectives stored in its computer bank.

Consonant Blends That Dance a Jig

People ask me what I have against the consonant blend and other wonders of phonics. Absolutely nothing. I show my students that these devices are helpful—but only to help them read books, not to fill out skill sheets. In my years as a reading teacher, I watched any number of fancy skill-drill programs pass through the coordinator's office. But those who offer only a choice of how skills are to be presented—filmstripped, tape-recorded, televised, or computerized—offer no choice at all.

Bureaucrats seem ever able to find thousands of dollars for up-to-date ways of delivering the same old skills at the very time they cite budget deficits as the reason for laying off librarians. A computerized skills checklist may be convenient for justifying one's application for federal monies (to purchase more electronic checklists), but we must demand more of our reading paraphernalia. We must insist that it be good for kids. We teachers must not relinquish our savvy about kids and how they learn to read.

Disk-drive partisans justify their use of computers by bragging about the bonanza of "immediate feedback." If one can't think of anything else to say about a program, there is always "speedy correction." And yet thoughtful scholars such as Frank Smith caution us against being too quick to offer feedback. If a child is to become a reader he must be willing to take risks. Do we want to be too quick to label such risks as error? I, for one, am not grateful to the guys who bring me the nasty combination of silly questions and speedy corrections. I find no charm in immediate numerical gratification.

And then there is "impersonal feedback." Now there's a notion to make a granite wall weep. I want my students to become personally involved with books—to puzzle over them, laugh over them, and, when necessary, get angry with them. For this to happen, I need to be passionately involved. I need to offer myself—my intuitions, experience, knowledge, and, yes, also my pleasure, my ire. Better I should wrongly holler at a kid than abrogate my teaching role in the name of impersonal feedback. I did not become a teacher in order to replace enthusiasm with anomie.

But then I don't see reading as a steady progression along carefully sequenced rungs of skill development. Reading has always seemed a more pesky enterprise to me. We must recognize that the hucksters of skills systems have a disarmingly optimistic view of skills but are propelled by a dismal view of children. Reading cannot be handed out like scratch-and-sniff stickers. The skill-and-drill fix is about as helpful to children's intellectual development as sucking on jujubes.

Skill-Drill Thrills ... and Chills

So how do we keep our feet firmly on the rock of pedagogical principle when faced with so many reading programs on disk? How do we find the few that are worthwhile? We can't rely on software reviews. They seldom measure the electronic hugger-mugger against, say, *Charlotte's Web* or *King Arthur* or *Never Cry Wolf.* Instead, reviewers say, "This is better than a workbook." Paltry praise indeed. The students shouldn't be wasting time with a workbook either.

No, we have to look at the stuff ourselves. I recently did that and I doubt that anyone could possibly believe what I saw. You had to be there.

The dim-wittedness offered up by much current software in the name of reading comprehension and thinking skills is quite amazing. Let it suffice to say that there exists a junk category of software totally fascinating in its foulness. I spent hours punching in wrong answers just to revel in the stupidity of the "explanations," except that I often erred in my anticipation of errors and got answers right that I intended to miss. (That meant starting the program all over, since I was determined to see every one of the wacky explanations.)

Anyone who is in awe of the technological breakthroughs in education should work through the 815,000 ugly little sentences generated by one program — a program that purports to teach the thirty-eight rules for capitalization. This software operates on the principle that if the kid doesn't get it the first time, then make him try the same thing 814,999 more times. Or consider *Vocabulary Development, Phonics in Context, Spelling Mastery, Choosing Titles, Prefix Tutor*. The titles alone tell us we don't need this nonsense. There's no wit here. No whimsy. Just whistling in the pedagogical dark.

I am stunned by the wrongness. These products are billed as research based and dazzlingly up-to-date, but they give me a prickly feeling of déjà voodoo, proving over and over that anything that can be put in a dimestore workbook can also go on a floppy disk. I recall Dorothy Parker's advice about a book she was reviewing: "This is not a novel to be tossed aside lightly. It should be thrown with great force." Likewise, I recommend rubbing these skill disks with a nice big magnet.

Or how about the program that asks students to reconstruct on a blank screen a passage from *Magic Mountain* by Thomas Mann? If that task seems rather strenuous, the student can choose instead to supply every other letter or all the vowels. I'll admit there is an interesting principle at work here, one involving *structural clues*, but I cannot fathom the choice of literary selections. Nor can I believe that a student, assuming she does re-create the passage, would ever be inspired to read the real thing. (But I confess to never having finished *Magic Mountain* even when all the letters were there right from the start.) When I see such an excerpt in a program purportedly designed for students age nine and up, I wonder who is kidding whom.

Tremendous effort seems to have gone into producing software that spews out readability formulas for any literary passage you care to input. In my survey, I discovered programs based on most of the major word- and syllable-counting schemes, including Flesch, Lore and Fry, Dale-Chall, the Navy, General Motors, Bell Laboratories, the Department of Defense. But such software only encourages teachers to dump the delicate art of guiding students to books best able to capture their interests and imaginations in favor of academic numerology. And I say to hell with it.

I also uncovered numerous computer versions of word scramble, hangman, Go Fish, and Old Maid. Certainly kids like such stuff, but I can't see that the computer enhances these old chestnuts. I'd rather see a child playing Go Fish with a friend than a machine. I'm not even convinced that kids would choose to play hangman on the computer rather than on the chalkboard—not without some moments of deliberation. (Kids love the word-processing capabilities of chalk and eraser.) But if a teacher is determined to find some use for the electronic beastie in her reading classroom, better she let the kid play hangman than insist he search-and-destroy all the *cr* blends he spots or shoot down vocabulary words. And for teachers who laboriously construct crossword puzzles and word searches, the good news is that programs exist to simplify their lives.

A Glimmer of Hope Amid All the Bright Lights

If we do not set our expectations too high, then there *are* some software programs that can be useful in the classroom, programs worthy of some celebration. I've looked at various programs traveling under the name of poetry that are fun and even intriguing the first few times one plugs in words. But I hope that teachers will help children to see that poetry is the careful, meaningful choice of words, that writers work hard at their craft, that even though plugging in words at random can be fun, it isn't poetry. A program such as *Suspect Sentences* (Ginn), in which a student tries to hide an original sentence in a literary passage so that his peers can't find it, seems to have more potential than most language arts programs. To play this game successfully, students must read critically and then model their own writing after an author's style. They certainly won't come away thinking that any old word will do.

The *Sentence Maker* portion of *Word Worx* (Reston) encourages children to use their understanding of grammatical structure to create sentences. The computer presents five letters, and players try to make sentences using those letters. Once a word is used, the computer will not allow it to be used again. Kids keep making sentences until they run out of ideas—or guess the computer's sentence (an adage or famous quote). Although critics might point out that such an exercise addresses only surface and not deep grammar, it is nonetheless one of the better programs available, and teachers need not feel apologetic for allowing it into a classroom.

Never Forget the Pageantry of Peas

When all is said and done, the computer is not going to stimulate much reading. Reading a screen filled with type is neither amusing nor inspiring.

It is actually painful, and people who are forced to do it should receive adequate monetary compensation. Certainly it is not something we should inflict on children we are trying to encourage as readers.

Long ago, E. B. White commented on the great technological breakthrough that promised to revamp the kitchen so that we could push a button and peas would appear on a paper plate. White pointed out that the technocrats had misunderstood the "pageantry of peas." Similarly, though I am bombarded by an electronic hailstorm, I'm not willing to let the skills people get away with obscuring the pageantry of reading with their flood of state-of-the-art sound-and-light shows. I don't care if the kids down the hall stay a skill lesson or two (or even fifty-six) ahead forever.

No. Instead, I hope to nurture my students in an environment that convinces them they might want to read a book someday. I see too many proficient decoders, kids who perform extremely well on standardized tests but never willingly pick up a book. They have mastered an incomplete system, one they find lacking in marvel or mystery. As Mark Twain reminds us, the man who doesn't read good books has no advantage over the man who can't read them.

So I say to those fellows with their whistling curriculum: I am wary of mistaking convenience for progress. The worth of a machine depends upon the use to which it is put. Marching children through reading systems in the name of efficient record keeping has the pedagogical justification of a No-Pest Strip. One good book is worth a thousand floppy disks. Or more. I'd trade my *WordStar* disk for almost any one of E. B. White's sentences. Or Gore Vidal's. Or Calvin Trillin's. Or Max Apple's. My list is wonderfully long. And I would not trade my memory of Jennifer's face when she first read *Amelia Bedelia* for a whole skills-management system.

Even such a rationalist as George Bernard Shaw confessed to a fascination with machines, saying he once nearly bought a cash register "without having the slightest use for it." We teachers are probably more vulnerable to things mechanical than most. We live harried, hassled lives, beset by hucksters and inspectors alike. But we must keep track of what matters, what the children need. We must not allow bored, restless managers or sharpshooting wheeler-dealers who are ever reaching for some pie-in-the-sky to turn our reading programs into techno-skill dumps, wastelands hazardous to the well-being of the children. Do not go gentle into that computer lab. Question. Judge. And, if necessary, rage. And always, always: Resist much.

Who's Afraid of Old Mother Hubbard?

I<small>F</small> E. D. H<small>IRSCH</small> is to be believed, my husband needs literacy remediation, and he needs it fast. After reading Hirsch's assertion that nursery rhymes provide essential building blocks for future literacy, I grilled my husband on his Mother Goose literacy. I discovered that out of the whole canon he has a vague notion that Humpty Dumpty had some sort of fall. He claimed he'd heard of Old Mother Hubbard but when pinned to the wall admitted he didn't know anything about a dog or a bone. "No points!" I insisted. "No points without a dog!"

According to Professor Hirsch, alarm bells should ring. Contending that knowledge is sequential, that small bits of information lead to larger pieces of essential understanding, Hirsch insists that nursery rhymes are the essential foundation on which cultural literacy is built. In his words, "If there's one nursery rhyme you don't know, it might not matter. But multiply "Humpty Dumpty" by one thousand and, eventually, you'll be missing what you need to know to understand more demanding material and to make progress" (1988a, 43).

Don't you believe it.

My husband, for one, would have an easier time whistling "Dixie" (if only he knew the tune) than coming up with any information about the dish that ran away with the spoon or Little Boy Blue or any of the additional 998 nursery rhymes Hirsch deems essential for something called culture and something equally elusive called progress.

Hirsch's agenda for the schools is often linked to that of former Secretary of Education William Bennett and *The Closing of the American Mind* author Allan Bloom (1987). Although there are profound differences, with Hirsch setting out an agenda that might be called Culture for the Millions—without the Pain of Reading—and Bloom setting up criteria for membership in an exclusive, elitist club, and William Bennett trying to keep a foot in both camps, all three have a profound distrust of teachers and students. And like the Plato they revere, they don't trust books much either. All promote a core canon regulated by experts on high, insisting on what Hirsch calls "a systematic approach to knowledge." While Hirsch promotes his idea of a national vocabulary for third graders, Bennett publishes his list of recommended books, and Bloom laments the bewildering variety of courses available to the university students and complains about the lack of university-wide agreement about what every student should study.

As a teacher, I am well aware of bewildering variety. My desk is messy, my plans subject to change as soon as a child walks through the doorway. Instead of seeking a national vocabulary or a core list of books to be read by every third or seventh or eleventh grader in the land, it has been my credo as a teacher to celebrate the bewildering variety of the children placed in my care by encouraging them to find their own books, books both personal and individual. My goal is not that every child will read the same few books appearing on someone's recommended list; my goal is that every child will grow up to be an adult who reads when I'm no longer there watching and guiding.

I hope every child leaves my care wanting to read another book tomorrow and tomorrow and tomorrow. And in building these readers for tomorrow I cleave to what Edward Abbey calls

> that great, bubbling, disorderly, anarchic, unmanageable diversity of opinion, expression, and ways of living which free men and women love, which is their breath of life, and which the authoritarians of church and state and war and sometimes even art despise and always have despised. And feared. (1977, 230)

I think back to my first year of teaching. Granted an emergency credential by the New York City Board of Education, I entered Grover Cleveland High School in the middle of someone else's lesson plan for ninth- and tenth-grade English. I had not trained to be a teacher and had not the slightest notion of how to begin being one. But it didn't take forty-eight units in education courses for me to see that our class reading of "Paul Revere's Ride" was not successful. And two days into *Silas Marner*, I complained to the department chairman that this piece of literature did not seem appropriate either to inner-city youths or to their teacher. He advised me, "Just skip the descriptive passages." And that is Hirsch's advice, too, except he would have us skip even more. While Bennett and Bloom would have students slog through impossible classics, Hirsch claims it is enough for the literate person just to recognize the titles and authors.

In *Cultural Literacy: What Every American Needs to Know*, Hirsch takes great pains to make a distinction between cultural literacy and the more traditional book literacy championed by what he calls the "literary specialists." For the purposes of cultural literacy, Hirsch explains, a literary work is not a text to be read but a word or phrase to be recognized. Hirsch calls this recognition information about literature and asserts that it can come from "conversation, criticism, cinema, television, or student crib sheets like *Cliffs Notes*" (1987, 147). In both *Cultural Literacy* and *The Dictionary of Cultural Literacy* (1988b) Hirsch spells out how to be "culturally literate" in, say, *Romeo and Juliet.* We need to recognize that this is a play by a man named Shakespeare and that the notable lines are "Romeo, Romeo, wherefore art thou Romeo?" and "What's in a name?" and that the phrase "star-crossed lovers" is associated with this play. And that's it.

Which is worse: to bar twelve-year-olds from the wonder of words by taking Bennett's advice and force-feeding impossible tomes like *Ivanhoe, The Virginian,* and *A Connecticut Yankee in King Arthur's Court* or to insist along with Hirsch (1988b) that knowledge of six hundred discrete items is all that stands between the eight-year-old and third-grade cultural literacy?

If the choice is between classical literacy and cultural literacy, I suggest we read a bit further in *Romeo and Juliet* and borrow a phrase that did not make Hirsch's list. I say, "A plague o' both your houses!" I want more for my students, much, much more. I want for them whole literature; I want for them a personal literacy. And toward that end it is my responsibility as teacher to welcome my students into the magical kingdom of good books and to help them find the one wonderful book that will make them want to find another.

What would these expert information advisors make of a child like Mildred? Sixteen years old and in the eighth grade, Mildred had never been in a remedial reading class because her recorded IQ score made her ineligible for federal programs designed for underachievers. Should I pretend that Mildred would read *Evangeline* along with all the other eighth graders (assuming, of course, that I would make any eighth grader read that poem or much of anything else in the text handed out by the board of education)? Should I follow Bennett's advice and find a simplified version? Or follow Hirsch's prescription and simply make sure Mildred could recognize the name Henry Wadsworth Longfellow?

Mildred was something of a basketball fanatic and so I gave her a book containing biographical sketches of current pros. The book was written on a fourth- to fifth-grade level, and it took Mildred at least a month to read it. She covered it in plastic to keep it safe and carried it home every night. When she finally finished it and returned it to me, she had tears in her eyes. "You know," she said, "I read it. I really did. I read the whole thing." And as she left the room, she added, "Best book I ever read." Up to that moment, of course, it was the only book she'd ever read.

The shame of our schools is not that students graduate without recognizing the name of Henry Wadsworth Longfellow. The shame of our schools is that they leave us never having loved a book. Not one.

I read aloud to my students every single day, and they read to me. We have laughed and cried together over thousands of wonderful words. But most of my crystal moments as a teacher center on individual children connecting with individual books. In third grade: Leslie, the indefatigible deaf child, reading a knock-knock joke correctly after months of practicing and screaming, "I get it! I get it! Let me read another one!"; her friend Jacqueline defying all notions of readability and immersing herself in *Wind in the Willows* for two months; Charles, developmentally delayed and mainstreamed into our classroom, starting each day with *Rumpelstiltskin* (even though I still puzzle over why this book was so important to him, his "I like it" had to be reason enough for me to stop counting after the sixteenth time he read it); Chris finding out from a handwritten reply to his fan letter that his beloved Jack Prelutsky's penmanship is as bad as his own. In junior high: Nick's mom phoning to report that this boy, who had so steadfastedly resisted books for his entire school career, had insisted his parents stop the car as they were pulling out of the driveway on spring vacation so he could go back in the house and get the copy of *Can You Sue Your Parents for Malpractice?* (Danziger 1979) he had borrowed from my desk; Sylvia, a tough, belligerent seventh grader, leading her group of friends through *Soul Brothers and Sister Lou* (Hunter 1968); Keith, a very troubled fifteen-year-old, finally dropping his elaborate defenses and proudly figuring out how to read Dr. Seuss' *Hop on Pop* (1963); Jack reading a *Funk and Wagnall's Dictionary* for six months straight so that he could become a champion Scrabble player; a whole group of boys who grumbled every day that they hated reading insisting I buy more copies of a nonfiction book depicting the terrible repercussions of a teenager's drug involvement; Michael, coming back three years later to tell me that even though he made his whole family watch *Acorn People* (Jones 1977) on television, the book was a whole lot better. Michael, beloved Michael, who had whined at my elbow for two years that there wasn't a book written that he'd like. I couldn't resist asking, "Did you ever think you'd say that about a book?" He grinned and admitted, "No, I never did." And as he left the room, the magic words came. Michael turned in the doorway and asked, "Say, did that Jones fellow write anything else?"

Sometimes I feel the need to defend myself against bureaucratic assault by adding that those kids who read Dr. Seuss and popular teen-age novels also read Newbery winners and Poe and Faulkner and Thurber and T. H. White and hundreds of others. But the crystal moments—for them and for me—were magic, electric moments of personal connection.

My desk is messy and my plans ill-formed, but as I look back over a twenty-year career in the classroom, I can see a very clear pattern. From that first disastrous round robin-reading of "Paul Revere's Ride," I have rejected all attempts to systematize what I do with my students. For me, basal readers, assertive discipline, Madeline Hunter, William Bennett, and E. D. Hirsch are all variants on a misbegotten theme of trying to regulate learning: to sanitize, standardize, and pigeonhole what for me has been a creative, quirky, soulful, oddball activity. In their attempts to regularize education, this crew of conformity would stamp out what philosopher-teacher David Hawkins (1974) so movingly describes as "the bird in the window": that elusive bit of magic that enriches our classroom lives if we are lucky enough to catch sight of it and if we are worthy enough to take advantage of its unexpected appearance. I affirm the bird. And to the regulators, the makers of hierarchies, lists, steps, graphs, wall charts, and agendas, I just say no.

I understand and even sympathize with Hirsch's intent but nonetheless find it as loathsome as all other attempts to standardize the classroom. In the end, Hirsch's system may be worse than the rest because of its false promise. He defines the culturally literate as one who, by the end of high school, can identify some five thousand factoids, separate, disjointed little slugs rooted neither in context nor purpose. People who haven't read Hirsch's explanation of just what he means by cultural literacy are always surprised to learn that you don't have to read to qualify. But I reject this game-show notion of literacy. Name recognition is not literacy. If you want to be literate, you have to read the books.

Literacy ultimately depends on the individuals acquiring it and the uses they make of it, not a narrow content, particularly a content that excludes rather than welcomes. A parent once asked me how I'd define a reader. After about a fifteen-second hesitation, I declared that a reader is an eight-year-old (or a thirty-year-old) who can read a book of more than 150 pages within a few days. If we teachers are to foster these readers, then we must know the individual students in our care and motivate them with the best literature possible. We must trust the power of the words to motivate and the desire of our students to learn and grow. Offering up a few stale chestnuts or a few thousand discrete items as a definition of literacy sells short both the word and the student. Such pre-packaged, regimented offerings ignore the important educational issues of our day: the plurality of our culture, the condition, both spiritual and physical, of the children in our care, and the needs of these children today as well as the needs of the society into which they will emerge.

I find it wonderfully loony to position "Hickory Dickory Dock" as a critical first step in the systematic acquisition of a Ph.D., a two-family garage, and a favorable balance of trade. But it is worse than loony to choose a four-year-old's bedtime story or a first grader's read-aloud with an eye on his or her SAT scores and his or her acceptance to law school. Treat children's exposure to literature as a duty or a means to an end, treat it as an information delivery system, and you kill their joy in books. We must read to children for the joy of it, ours and theirs. We must never lose sight of the fact that a joyful encounter with words is the greatest gift we can give the children entrusted to us.

In the words of language, literature, and culture critic George Steiner, "That which you have not heard will not sing for you later." And that is why we read aloud to children: to entertain them and also to provide the essential function of helping them to "make music" with words. For very young children, the sense of the particular words matter not. What matters is the pattern and the pleasure: the rhyme, the rhythm, the repetition—the joy of it all.

It seems especially ironic that Hirsch would single out nursery rhymes as a necessary foundation for the classics. As much as they love to parrot nursery rhymes, children don't *understand* them. And neither do adults unless they search out an annotated version that explains obscure historical and political references. We don't share nursery rhymes with children for any information they contain; we share nursery rhymes for the pleasure children find in the rollicking rhymes, their irresistible rhythm, and the pure nonsense of it all. It's the sound that matters, not the sense.

I, for one, am not particularly fond of Mother Goose and do not particularly care whether my students are familiar with that canon or not. And so, I choose different materials to deliver the rhymes and rhythms so important to beginning readers. I read poems, not just once or twice or half a dozen times a day, but all day long. My students who were lumped together as the rotten readers of third grade soon learned they could make me happy by requesting Shel Silverstein's "Sarah Sylvia Cynthia Stout Would Not Take the Garbage Out" (1974) right before lunch. And we had a medley ranging from Robert Louis Stevenson to Myra Cohn Livingston through the rest of the day. When I wasn't reading poems I was reading word-rich stories, outlandish stories, heartbreaking stories, stories of every size and shape.

Probably those third graders left my class knowing no more nursery rhymes than when they entered, but they were intimate with the rhythm and reason of wonderful words. And in that third grade classroom I witnessed the magical leap into independent reading that occurs when children who seem resistant to reading suddenly read—and hear—with an internal ear for the first time. It is a thrilling moment for teacher and child. It happened twenty-one separate times in that classroom: twenty-one individual children making that first, magic connection with a real book.

From the first half-hour of school, they liked listening to me read aloud, but they did their best to avoid being stuck with books on their own. I persisted and the books won out. One at a time, those children encountered that flash of illumination, what Emerson calls a "chief event of life . . . the day in which we have encountered a mind that startled us." For my third graders, Peggy Parish, Arnold Lobel, Steven Kellogg, Daniel Pinkwater, James Marshall, Arthur Yorinks, and William Steig were startling minds, authors who showed them what words can do. Although there are universals in children's literature, books every child loves, and although I eagerly pay loving tribute to the power Beatrix Potter's little books and big books like Gelman's *More Spaghetti, I Say!* (1984) have to move an entire class, we must not forget the uniqueness. Each child must find his or her own special book that gives special joy in words and sparks that illuminating intellectual leap into reading independence.

And what about my husband? Since English is not his native language, it is no surprise that Mother Goose is not part of his repertoire. If Hirsch were correct and this nursery rhyme deficiency did indeed mean he is missing what he needs to know to understand more demanding materials and to make progress, then I could offer him nursery rhyme remediation. But why would I pull my husband away from Wilde and Conrad, Theroux and Selzer, Kinglake and Wedgewood to teach him "Hickory Dickory Dock"? My husband would not do well on *Jeopardy*, but he doesn't need Hirsch's new book *The Dictionary of Cultural Literacy* to make sense of the *New York Review of Books, Scientific American,* and the *Atlantic.* So why worry?

Likewise, why worry when I discover my third graders have information gaps? Let's stop looking at the hole and pay more attention to the bagel. Yes, like my husband, our students come to us with all sorts of idiosyncratic gaps in their store of information. But mere information is a dead end. It is our job to help students find those startling wordsmiths who will knock their socks off and to inspire them both to search for understanding and to reach for another book. We must have faith that, given time, space, and freedom to find joy in words, our students will indeed reach for another book. We must fight against the easy solution of filling their school day with some intellectual silly putty designed to cover up the gaps.

Hirsch contends that the leading cause of illiteracy in the U. S. is the lack of basic information. His remedy is to advocate that the schools put more stress on memorization, starting in kindergarten. Indeed, Mr. Hirsch has got a little list—some six hundred items every third grader should know. So when kids aren't taking courses in compensatory nursery rhymes, they can drill and practice items on Hirsch's list. Then their school will rate above average on a national test of this thing called cultural literacy.

Figuring out exactly what human beings need to know is a tricky business. My school district once set up committees at each grade level to discuss what our students needed to know and when they needed to know it. The stated goal of each committee was to establish the entry-level skills necessary to succeed at each grade level. Surprise, surprise: fifth-grade teachers said incoming students needed to read at a fifth-grade level; fourth-grade teachers said incoming students needed to read at a fourth-grade level, and so on. Everybody wanted kids to know math facts, periods, and commas. Sanity did prevail, however, and we stopped short of making apostrophe literacy mandatory for entry at any grade level. We made these lists, turned them in to the administrators who had mandated our committees into being, and then . . . we laughed. In our laughter we acknowledged that there is no such thing as "McKid," prepackaged and guaranteed to meet anybody's wishful thinking or any gatekeeper's bureau of measurements. To my knowledge, these standards committees never met again. And kids still get into fifth grade even though their commas are unreliable and their math facts bumpy.

Let the buyer beware. Before we rush out to get Hirsch's third grade list and Bennett's recommended books for the James Madison Elementary School, before we worry and fret about how many items our children know, let's remind ourselves that a list—any list—is a paltry thing. It is also dangerous. A list that prescribes content is easy to make but hard to live with. Any list manufactured in a time and place separate from me and my current students cannot take into account our diverse needs. Twenty years of working with kids has shown me that different folks need different challenges. And that applies to teachers as well as to children. I can't take my own well-considered book list from one year and use it again the next year, so how can a distant Washington, D.C., bureaucrat or university professor decree what books I need in my classroom?

Hirsch's list starts, and ends, with a grimness of facts, disjointed bits of information that make no connections and add up to nothing. It is hard for me to characterize Bennett's list: I read it and weep. Then when the school district administrator puts it in every teacher's mailbox, I rage, knowing that such a list will easily become a mandate that shuts teachers off from a discussion of books that is their need and shuts children off from the joy in words that is their right.

We must realize that illiteracy results not from our failure to expose our students to information; illiteracy results when we fail to help students make the necessary connections between one piece of information and another, connections between books and their own lives. People who don't read are people who have never known the illumination written words can bring. What we need to bring to our classrooms is not 600 or 6,000 facts, not 16 classics; we need to bring the power and possibility of words that connect.

The road to literacy is illusory and filled with false promise. Hirsch's road map is indeed too simple. The sequential, building-block theory of cultural literacy is neat and tidy. It is logical; it is also wrong. I offer no guidebook for the successful classroom, no list of essential books. I can offer only a testament of faith, a spiritual commitment that defies codification.

What matters is not what kids know and when they know it. What matters is the teacher's belief in children and belief in good words, the teacher's conviction that despite all socio-economic-bureaucratic impediments, both the child and the words *will* triumph. I know first hand that given a teacher who provides a joyful, sensitive literacy model, given free choice and the chance to explore, children *will* choose good words. They *will* choose words that inform, inspire, and enlighten as well as entertain. After all, children have made the *Amelia Bedelia* books best-sellers for twenty-five years; they have kept Shel Silverstein's *A Light in the Attic* (1981) on the *New York Times* (adult) best-seller list for more than three years (192 weeks as of Dec. 4, 1988). These writers don't offer information to be codified in neat and tidy lists. Instead, they offer their own startling minds, demonstrating for children great possibilities.

If seventeen-year-olds (and their parents, grandparents, and great-grandparents) don't know as much as we wish they knew, or don't read as much as we wish they read, the answer is not to be found in more of the same — more information-cramming, more testing, more codification. Hirsch and his colleagues do not explain just what a middle-aged man who has never heard of Jack Sprat is missing; neither do they explain just what you've got when you've got a nine-year-old who recognizes "Fresno." The answer in both cases is, of course, "Not much."

References

Abbey, Edmund. 1977. *The Long Journey Home.* New York: Dutton.

Bennett, William. 1988, August. *James Madison in the Elementary School: A Curriculum for American Students.* Washington, D.C.: U. S. Department of Education.

Bloom, Allan. 1987. *The Closing of the American Mind.* New York: Simon & Schuster.

Danziger, Paula. 1979. *Can You Sue Your Parents for Malpractice?* New York: Delacorte.

Gelman, Rita Golden. 1984. *More Spaghetti, I Say!* Ontario: Scholastic-ATB.

Hawkins, David. 1974. *The Informed Vision.* New York: Agathon, pp. 78–98.

Hirsch, E. D., Jr. 1987. *Cultural Literacy: What Every Person Needs to Know.* Boston: Houghton Mifflin, pp. 147, 201, 213.

——— . 1988a. "Faculty Lounge." *Learning 88* 17(8): 46.

——— . 1988b. *The Dictionary of Cultural Literacy.* Boston: Houghton Mifflin.

Hunter, K. 1968. *Soul Brothers and Sister Lou.* New York: Scribner.

Jones, R. 1977. *Acorn People.* New York: Bantam.

Seuss, Dr. 1963. *Hop on Pop.* New York: Beginner Books.

Silverstein, Shel. 1974. *Where the Sidewalk Ends.* New York: Harper & Row.

——— . 1981. *A Light in the Attic.* New York: Harper & Row.

Ruffles and Flourishes

"CHILDREN LIKE A fine word occasionally," Beatrix Potter once told her publisher, when he complained about the use of the word *soporific* in her book *The Tale of Flopsy Bunnies*. I taught grammar-school students for the better part of two decades, and I count myself firmly in Ms. Potter's camp. It follows, of course, that I can muster little enthusiasm for basal readers, those homogenized and bowdlerized grade-school texts—edited according to elaborate readability formulas and syllable schemes—that constitute the bulk of the average child's officially sanctioned reading material in American schools. Basal readers can be criticized on a lot of grounds. Their worst fault, I think, is that for no good reason they squeeze the juice out of some very fine tales. Here is a passage from the Paul Leyssac translation of Hans Christian Andersen's "The Emperor's New Clothes":

> "Magnificent!" "Excellent!" "Prodigious!" went from mouth to mouth, and everyone was exceedingly pleased.

Here is the same passage as rendered in a modern reader:

> "How marvelous," they echoed the emperor. "How beautiful!"

Sure, *prodigious* is a tough word, but it's a word that young readers would be pleased, perhaps exceedingly pleased, to try out, to repeat, to save.

Admittedly, the publishers of basal readers encounter prodigious difficulties in the preparation of their texts. They are under acute and conflicting pressures from educators, from parents, and from organized interest groups of every kind. Too, the sensibility of many old stories may often be at odds with the tenor of our times. In many instances, however, the sense behind the censorship seems impossible to fathom. The difference between many familiar children's stories in their original form and the way they appear in basal readers is, indeed, so striking and the changes, it seems to me, so unnecessary that several years ago I began comparing old and new versions line by line.

A good many of the editorial changes are of a kind that one would never write an angry letter about but that nevertheless give one pause. I have in mind changes like the following:

Original	Basal
Do a tapdance!	Chirp like a bird!
Cook spaghetti!	Cook pancakes!
"Trust me," I said.	"You'll see," I said.
Come to my house at eleven.	Come to my house around twelve.
The sea is our enemy.	The sea is not our friend.
wily swindlers, crafty rogues	weavers
cornflakes	potatoes
Rubbish!	Why?

This sort of thing does not, I suppose, amount to extreme literary depri-
vation, but the average classic children's tale — a work by, say, Andersen,
Kipling, or Pearl Buck — in basal form contains hundreds of such alterations. Taken together they suggest a preternatural disposition to tinker,
which in turn perhaps reinforces a parallel disposition to cut and trim and
simplify, to tame and domesticate what is powerful, florid, and wild in
the way that good writers use our language.

The latter disposition is pronounced. Consider how, in Kipling's "How
the Camel Got His Hump," "sticks and thorns and tamarisks and milk-
weed and prickles" becomes, in basal form, "sticks and shrubs"; or how a
"great big lolloping humph" turns into a "great big humph." You lose a
great big lolloping lot when you lose the humph's gerundive. Consider
how, in Walter Blair's "Pecos Bill," "giving a coyote yell of a size to make
any state that was less tough than Oklahoma split right down the middle"
becomes, in basal versions, "howling like a coyote." One of the stories my
students have most enjoyed over the years is *Flat Stanley*, by Jeff Brown.
As the title implies, Stanley has gotten himself flattened, and the story goes
on to describe the very special things that a flat boy can do, including travel
across the country by mail. Here is a passage from Brown:

> The envelope fit Stanley very well. There was even room left over, Mrs. Lamb-
> chop discovered, for an egg-salad sandwich made with thin bread, and a flat
> cigarette case filled with milk.
>
> They had to put a great many stamps on the envelope to pay for both air-
> mail and insurance, but it was still much less expensive than a train or airplane
> ticket to California would have been.

Here is how the passage appears in a basal reader:

> The envelope fit Stanley very well.
> There was even room left over for a sandwich.

My students always loved the author's mention of thin bread—they knew he was being very deliberate in his choice of words, and they appreciated his nod to their intelligence, his acknowledgment that they would know he was sustaining a joke. They appreciated, too, the humor of egg salad—a much yuckier substance than, for instance, bologna, and one with which you would certainly not choose to be sealed in an envelope. I appreciate the taboo governing allusions to cigarettes, and yet what my students tended to note is not the reference to tobacco but rather Mrs. Lambchop's ingenuity in finding a way to make sure that her son, while in the mail, is able to drink his milk. Eventually, Stanley's friends mail him back from California in

> a beautiful white envelope they had made themselves. It had red-and-blue markings to show that it was airmail, and Thomas Jeffrey had lettered it "Valuable" and "Fragile" and "This End Up" on both sides.

Basal readers simply stuff the kid in "a beautiful, large white envelope" and get on with the story.

I have compiled notebook after notebook of alterations of just this kind, which probably makes me some kind of a nut. I find it hard to believe, though, that the unscrupulous editing of basal readers doesn't matter. Like Bartleby the Scrivener, modern reading textbooks are "pallidly neat, pitiably respectable, incurably forlorn." There is room in our children's literature for silliness, for unpleasantness, and for difficult words that children do not know. Above all, there is a place for detail and nuance and subtlety, which children admire perhaps more than adults do. Young readers are not like the Emperor of Austria, who told Mozart that his music was great but complained that there were too many notes. Perhaps a few of them could be cut?

Mozart was lucky. He succeeded in silencing his critic with the question, "Which few did you have in mind?" The editors of modern basal readers, unfortunately, would have had a reply. There is a book kids love called *Nate the Great*, by Marjorie Weinman Sharmat, and here is a passage that does not appear in any of the basal versions:

> "Fang has sharp teeth and I, Nate the Great, say that we should keep anybody happy with sharp teeth. Very happy."

I never used the basal texts, and so my students could sigh and grin over that phrase "Very happy." They copied the device, as they did other devices, in their own writing. Children notice and savor the ruffles and flourishes in special writing. It is these, in the end, that keep us reading books.

References

Brown, Jeff. 1964. *Flat Stanley.* Illustrated by Tomi Ungerer. New York: Harper & Row.

A Plea for More Disorderliness

I saw a lot of happy whole language teachers browsing in the exhibit hall at the IRA Convention in Toronto. It was indeed an impressive sight to see so many publishers using children's literature in their basals, to see so many professors using children's literature in their presentations. I confess I taught for twenty years thinking it would be easier for a camel to pass through a needle's eye than for a big biz professorial consultant to enter the kingdom of children's literature.

So with all this children's literature filling the convention, how come I'm so glum? The key to my discontent is to be found in the word *using*. Publishers and professors—and classroom teachers—aren't saying, "Kids should read this story because it will knock their socks off." They aren't saying, "Kids should read this book because it will make them want to read another book." No, the publishing conglomerates with their attending professors are spewing forth the same old promises about the multitudinous skill acquisition that can be dredged from wonderful literature. And too many teachers are too anxious to become fellow travelers to this skill acquisition. In session after session, in brochure after brochure, I found the claims that, as a result of reading this or that award-winning story, the student will:

Learn vocabulary in context;
Understand adjectives;
Recognize cause-and-effect relationships;
Draw conclusions;
Learn techniques for applying cooperative learning.

And so on. I'm not against cooperative learning, cause and effect, or even adjectives, I suppose. But teachers who try to milk the "new" children's literature for as many skills as were in the "old" basal programs are missing the point. Even worse, they may be ruining wonderful books for kids forever.

Take *Amelia Bedelia*, for example. Jennifer introduced me to the wonders this book holds for children when I transferred from seventh grade to third grade. Those children, the worst readers in third grade, also suffered from a lot of physical, emotional, and intellectual disabilities, and they assured me every day that they "hated reading."

Jennifer discovered *Amelia* in December. By that time the children's period of independent silent reading had extended from the initial torturous time of five minutes to a fairly willing forty minutes. The first thing every morning we all read our separate books for forty minutes.

I knew the instant Jennifer discovered something startling in *Amelia Bedelia*. Her eyes opened wide; she turned back a page and read it again, mouthing each word. Then she giggled and looked up at me. I nodded and winked. She grinned and nudged Sophie, showing her the page. Then David demanded to see what was so fun, and before he realized what was happening, David, the boy who whined the loudest every single morning, "I hate reading!" was enjoying a book. Before long, twenty rotten readers were scrambling to get their names on a waiting list for, of all things, a book. And then Jesse discovered that there were more *Amelias* and we had an Amelia celebration.

But it was a celebration of reading. We didn't use the book as an excuse to do something else. I didn't interrogate them about main idea; they didn't make puppets. We used each book as inspiration to read another book. I don't recall ever asking a single question about an Amelia book. What is the need for questions when the children's pleasure is so evident? I was appalled a few years later, in the course of doing some research on the basal, to discover *Amelia* in a basal. The good news is that it is printed pretty much as the author wrote it. The bad news is that the teacher's manual carefully lists the objectives to be taught with the story, including:

> decode words based on the spelling pattern generalization that a vowel letter followed by a consonant and final e *represents a glided (or long) vowel sound.*

Never mind that research has shown that the *final* e *rule* is true no more than 53 percent of the time. Even if the rule were 99 and $^{44}/_{100}$ percent pure, a child who can decode—and enjoy—*Amelia Bedelia* has no need to practice the *final* e *rule*.

Teachers traveling under the banner *whole language* need not feel too smug when they see the travesty wrought by a publishing conglomerate. I have seen reputable whole language advocates milk *Amelia* for:

• Comprehension Questions

"Amelia Bedelia _____ colored balls on the tree."
a) bounced   b) threw   c) tied

• Spelling Demons from the Story

"*laughed:* the *gh* has an *f* sound here"

• Problem Solving Skills

"Pretend you were Mrs. Rogers. What would you have done when you came home and found the towels ruined?"

• Higher Order Thinking Skills

"Write a new ending for the story."

• Projects

"Make puppets and put on a play."

• Eating

"Make a cake with a surprise (such as gumdrops) in it."

On and on it goes. Whole language people, and everybody else, are in for a wondrous revelation if they ever let kids read. And read. And read. Amazing as it seems, even rotten readers, kids repeating the grade, kids mainstreamed from special class, kids from one-parent families, kids on probation, bilingual, minimally brain-damaged, deaf, one-eyed kids *will* read willingly and with enthusiasm—if given the chance. School rarely gives them the chance. I tell teachers that by February my third graders were moaning and groaning when I called a halt to sustained silent reading at the end of one hour, and those teachers are amazed, shocked, and mystified. "When did you find time for skills?" they ask. Honest. It's the first question I'm always asked.

The skills *are* in the books. After all, the writers do use adjectives, words that obey the silent *e* rule. They even use apostrophes on occasion. But to rigorously plumb the books for these discrete skills is to miss the point of reading. If we are going to dredge wonderful literature for the same discrete skills found in the dreaded workbook, then what have the children gained? At least commercially prepared workbooks offer four-color art and are a lot more attractive than the stacks of purple plague that roll off faculty room ditto machines.

If we are going to invite our students to read *Charlotte's Web* so we can milk it for every "sequencing activity," "summarizing main ideas," "understanding vocabulary in context," and so forth—across the curriculum, mind you—then for all the wonder the kids will get from the book, E. B. White might have done better to spend his time feeding the chickens. A well-meaning teacher sent me a list of sixty-four projects kids can do on *Sarah, Plain and Tall*. If this doesn't make one weep, what will?

Leaving a child alone to savor a book, to get from it what he will, and then holding one's tongue when that child closes the book requires a tremendous act of faith—faith in children and faith in books. Sad to say,

161

school systems are not designed to easily accommodate acts of faith. They demand records: competency checklists and adherence to scope and sequence.

Trusting children and books is a revolutionary act. Books are, after all, dangerous stuff. Leave a child alone with a book and you don't know what might happen. But to the teacher who feels she must be in control — of the skills, the books, and the children, I commend Arnold Lobel's lovely little fable, "The Crocodile in the Bedroom" (*Fables*, [New York: Harper & Row, 1980]). A crocodile who loved the neat and tidy rows of the flowers on the wallpaper in his bedroom was coaxed outside into the garden by his wife, who invited him to smell the roses and the lilies of the valley. "Great heavens!" cried the crocodile. "The flowers and leaves in this garden are growing in a terrible tangle! They are all scattered! They are messy and entwined!" Whereupon he went back to his room, seldom leaving his bed. He stared at the neat and tidy rows of flowers on the wallpaper and "he turned a very pale and sickly shade of green."

I would ask whole language enthusiasts to remember that Lobel's moral, *Without a doubt, there is such a thing as too much order,* applies as much to school reading programs as it does to wallpaper.

Literature Has No Uses

IN A COLUMN titled "Internal Combustion Prose," Russell Baker noted the defeat of a proposal to emblazon Wisconsin license plates with the slogan "Eat Cheese or Die." Maybe the born-again Whole Languagelicals who have recently discovered books should take up from where the folks in Wisconsin left off. Certainly schoolmarm slogans, which run along the lines of "I love reading," could use a bit more oomph. The battle-cry rhetoric of "Read or Die" has the kind of zip to wake people up. Some professional organization might even want to stick it on their next batch of T-shirts, coffee mugs, and bumper stickers.

Reading, as everyone knows, deserves all the help it can get. Some folks think schools are filled with reading. They are wrong. Reading disappears about midway through the third grade. After that, students spend their time writing term papers and getting ready for the SATs. They copy passages out of encyclopedias and answer questions on ditto sheets titled *How Well Did You Read?* The gifted get enrichment courses in footnoting. And it doesn't take any of these kids a day and a half to figure out that when you gotta write a term paper and answer the questions at the end of the chapter, reading only slows you down.

I once taught in an alternative high school where I was responsible for forty disaffected students who can best be labeled as "None of the above." Our classroom was filled with daily copies of the local paper, the *New York Times*, and the *Daily News*, and paperbacks of every type—best-sellers, thrillers, mysteries, romances, joke books, science fiction, sports, biographies, essays, "how-to" books. Every few weeks I took a few students to the local bookstore to help choose more books.

We had a lot of single copies of traditional English classroom books on the shelves. Students seemed to get reassurance from seeing *A Tale of Two Cities, Julius Caesar,* and so forth. They had no intention of reading such books, but they liked knowing the books were there. A student would pick up *A Tale of Two Cities,* exclaim, "Oh, yeah," and put it down. These books made the place look like a real school. In this, my students' attitude toward the classics was akin to the position espoused by E. D. Hirsch— actually reading the classics is not necessary, but name recognition provides some comfort.

All of my students *could* read; they just didn't. I insisted that the first rule of our classroom was that every student read for half an hour a day. They were all expert at faking reading. How I got them reading is a rather involved story, but it wasn't by ordering forty copies of *The Old Man and the Sea*. Once a student got hooked on a book—be it *Flowers for Algernon*, *The Outsiders*, *Temple of Gold*, *Richie*, or something else—other students noticed and demanded, "Let me see."

I kept tabs on things but didn't interrogate those students about their understanding of plot, theme, rising action, and so forth. I judged a book a success when a student closed the last page and asked, "Do you have any more?" On their own, about three-fourths of the students began stretching the obligatory half-hour period into an hour a day. And more. Even those who stuck to the half-hour reading were amazed. They told me they'd read more books in the three months in my classroom than they had read in eleven years in regular school. In traditional classrooms, kids are too busy answering questions to do much reading.

[margin annotation: True — Provided so much]

I know some colleagues will agree with the inspector from the State Education Department: All this reading may be fine in its place, but it isn't *literature*. He saw students reading Dick Francis, Paul Zindel, Adam Hall, William Goldman, Paula Danzinger, and Cynthia Voigt and complained about the quality of our *literature*. I pointed out that many of the students had also read John Updike, Frank Conroy, *Unicorn in the Garden*, *Incident at Owl Creek*, Poe stories, excerpts from Anne Frank's *Diary*, *Hiroshima*. After watching the movie *Night and Fog*, we examined the rhetoric of Hoess' testimony at Nuremberg and accounts of responsibility at Mai Lai. One student and I had a very impassioned discussion following his reading of Bettelheim's *Truants from Life*. And so on. But the inspector complained of our lack of class sets of "the standard books." He asked, "What major work do your sophomores read?" I replied that I didn't think we had any sophomores at the moment. And I wrote a letter of protest to the State Education Department, insisting that if they wished to send out any more inspectors they should do it after school hours, as I would not again subject my students to anybody sneering at the books that overflowed our shelves and stimulated their minds.

State Education bureaucrats, of course, are not the only folks who worry about real *literature*. Very early in my career I taught at a technological university. My freshman engineering students, able readers all, hated English class as much as any reluctant reader I have ever encountered. It became my mission to find wonderful words—to demonstrate the power of language to them. Every day I wrote snippets on the board for their wonder, amazement, laughter. And every day I worried and fretted over what novel we would read in the spring. And then *Harper's* ran an excerpt of Norman Mailer's *On the Steps of the Pentagon,* announcing the book would be published simultaneously in hardback and paperback.

I read that magazine excerpt and knew that I had found our book. My professorial colleagues stewed and fretted and muttered, "Well, yes, it is powerful, but is it *literature?*" My students and I read that book. We laughed, argued, fumed, worried, and reached no consensus. We were moved, angered, challenged, and, I think, changed by it,

I told my students about the faculty concern that the book might not be *literature* but that if it wasn't then I had no idea what *literature* was. And then, weeks after we'd finished the book and moved on to others, *On the Steps of the Pentagon* won the Pulitzer Prize for Literature and the National Book Award. My students, the fellows who hated English, came dashing into the room to congratulate me. I think they must have been nearly as pleased as Norman Mailer. I never taught the book again. It was a book that was perfect for those particular students at that particular moment. And the next term, the book, certified *literature,* was on the reading list in half a dozen *literature* courses at the university.

Am I contradicting myself? First I say "Don't make twenty-five third or eighth or tenth graders all read the same book," and then I tell of making one hundred college freshmen all read the same book. College freshmen have tougher constitutions and they are a whole lot easier to teach, mold, coerce, and dominate than eighth graders. College freshmen have similar purposes and goals. But whom are we talking about when we talk about an eighth grader? The girl who spells her name "Sherri" and hides a copy of *True Confessions* in her binder? Or the "Sherry" who sucks her thumb and wants to listen to a tape of "Rumpelstiltskin"? Sherri/Sherry can't be pinned down to read the same book on different days of the week, let alone the same book as all of her classmates.

This sort of problem did not seem to trouble William Bennett when he compiled the list of recommended books for seventh and eighth graders in his James Madison Elementary School. And I don't hear an outcry against Bennett's list from teachers or professional organizations. As a profession we find it easier to run for cover than to stand and fight. When governors and industrialists announced their concern for excellence in the schools, my professional organization, instead of pointing out that these emperors of excellence were naked, issued an excellence sweatshirt. I worry that at this very moment they might be appointing a joint subcommittee to figure out ways to turn such Bennett favorites as *The Scarlet Pimpernel, The Yearling, Ivanhoe,* and *The Virginian* into memo pads. Or a bumper sticker.

As for me, I want my T-shirt to read "Literature Has No Uses." Certainly it is foolish to call on *literature* to redress the trade deficit, increase the gross national product, and help kids say no. Worse than foolish, it is wrong.

William Bennett thinks that seventh and eighth graders should read the recommended books closely "for theme, style, point of view, plot, setting, character, mood, irony, and imagery." And that's not all! Like those ads on TV for the $14.95 kitchen knife that also waxes, polishes, and whistles "Dixie," Bennett promises that these books will also "serve as models of fine composition and as subjects for writing assignments that stress a mastery of elementary vocabulary, grammar, usage, mechanics, description, persuasion, narration, and exposition."

Before we try to decide what the kids should read and how they should read it, maybe we'd do well to think about why we want them to read. What is this thing called *literature*, and why do we want kids to do it? That is a serious question, one every teacher should face. And I'm not talking about such tripe as pre-reading, setting purposes, and getting the lesson objective on the board. One of our professional journals printed an unwittingly hilarious article that should be the final word on pre-reading piffle. The punchline to the good professor's advice was that if the children were going to read about ducks, then the teacher could set the purpose by waddling into the room like a duck. Twenty years in classrooms from grades one through fourteen have proven to me that when we bring the best words possible to particular students at a particular ready moment in their lives, that is a great big lolloping enough. There's no need to quack, waddle, or pop.

But looking neither to the right nor to the left, many teachers will feel compelled to jump to add a classic or two to their curriculum. Too many of us would rather jump than be shoved. And these days we worry as much about the media as the principal and the board of education. Any day now I expect to find a Gallup pollster on my doorstep, taking a body count to find out how many of my students have read *The Virginian*. And then *USA Today* can print a front-page, colored graph on the state of classics in the classroom as related to gross national product. The *New York Times* will run the same graph in black and white on page 46.

And nobody will ask, "Did anybody enjoy the book?" Does any thirteen-year-old ask, on finishing *Ivanhoe*, *The Red Pony*, or *Rip Van Winkle*, "Are there more?"

People get nervous when I poke fun at Sir Walter Scott. But I would advise any defenders to pick up *Ivanhoe* and read it before sending me their angry letters. Nobody reads *Ivanhoe* these days, but nobody wants to be quoted as denouncing it either. I asked teachers, librarians, and professors from all over the country about Mr. Bennett's list and the even-more-ridiculous *Summertime Favorites* list put forth by the National Endowment for the Humanities. (Would you believe *The Pilgrim's Progress* as a summertime favorite for seventh and eighth graders?) The general reaction was one of relief: "Yes we do this one and this one...." *Doing a*

166

book, of course, means watching a movie, making puppets, listening to the teacher read aloud, answering questions, looking up vocabulary. *Doing* is far different from reading.

I suppose that one time or another in my career my students and I have talked about the theme in one book, the style of another, and maybe even the setting in another. Never all at once. Most often, I keep my mouth shut when a student finishes a book. I certainly don't ask how many ducks were on the pond. Such interfering school talk makes one reluctant to pick up another book. When I phoned a friend long distance recently and told her, "You must read Tobias Wolff's *This Boy's Life* — and while you're at it read Geoffrey Wolff's *The Duke of Deception* written ten years ago," I talked about the Wolffs' incredible memoirs of childhood for half an hour without ever mentioning setting, plot, theme, or whatever. That's just not the way real people read real books. Not when they are really excited by them, anyway.

For me, reading, like writing, is a private act. I regard committees as the last refuge of the scoundrel, and collaboration is just a fancy word for committee. Certainly there are times when beginning readers help each other learn to read; there are times when passages scream to be read aloud to a friend. But ask yourself: "When was the last time you and twenty-four other people sat down and read the same book together?" I can't even get my husband to read the same books I do. And I sure don't know twenty-four other people who want to read the books I want to read. When I want to read them. Once I actually tried to get about twenty people all involved in the same story. When Max Apple's "Stranger at the Table" appeared in *Esquire*, I was so moved by the story I photocopied it and sent it to everybody I knew. I mean that quite literally. I was working in California at the time and all my ex-colleagues in New York began getting thick envelopes with the imperative "READ THIS!" scrawled on the ten-page story inside. I was surprised when I didn't get ecstatic phone calls or letters back. I thought at least half a dozen people would report that the story inspired a moment of epiphany. But then I made a few calls and I could sense people were as puzzled as hell. I'm not Jewish, they weren't Jewish, so how come I was sending them this story about keeping kosher? A few people said, "Uh, it was interesting." I got so wound up in the whole thing that I ended up writing Max Apple to clarify an argument I had with my boss over that story and another one he wrote. I'm not sure Apple's reply was at all clarifying, but it sure was fun.

The only other time I wrote to an author was when I was a college freshman and I asked E. M. Forster a straightforward question about "The Celestial Omnibus." He sent me a straightforward answer, and I was startled by my professor's astonishment when I showed him Forster's reply. "Why would you do that?" he demanded. Ever since, I have

By discussing it in one way it took the joy out of others

Very personal

wondered if maybe that's why teachers like teaching dead authors: smart-aleck kids can't write letters behind their backs. And all this makes me think I'd like to write Tobias Wolff. I really want to know if that sneaking, lying, irrepressible boy is okay. I care a lot about that boy. I feel certain any teacher would.

In *The Call of Stories*, Robert Coles quotes William Carlos Williams' worry that teachers elicit dependence rather than independence in their students: "When you graduate from college and read a book, whose office hours do you visit when you have a question?" Do we convince our students that they need either a teacher or *Cliffs Notes* to read a book? Will they ever be tempted to pick up a book without one of us peering over their shoulders? Do we ever convince them that reading can be a whole lot of fun?

We must beware of what Walker Percy calls the "busy disregard" of the tourist. He is so preoccupied with his camera or how much to tip or whether to drink the water—the mechanics of the matter—that he misses the foreign locale entirely. Literature teachers are in danger of that same "busy disregard"—getting caught up in the mechanics of *literature* and missing the point of why anybody would want to read.

Back in the seventies I polled six hundred seventh, eighth, and ninth graders, asking them a number of questions about what language arts is and why they are required to study it. The student response to "How can language arts help you when you get out of school?" was depressingly utilitarian. The majority of students felt that language arts was the ticket to getting a job—in the narrowest sense: "L.A. trains you to fill out job applications and to write business letters." One hundred and thirty-eight students mentioned everyday survival skills such as understanding prescriptions and recipes. A sizable number thought L.A. would be useful only if a person wanted to be a teacher of L.A., a secretary, or a newscaster. Thirty-four students answered this question with a flat, "It can't." Forty-five students didn't reply.

I challenge you to ask students you know a similar question: "Why do we read?" But don't do it if you haven't first asked yourself—and been able to answer, "Because occasionally I come across a book that knocks my socks off."

Kurt Vonnegut once proposed that anybody running for the school board should be hooked up to a lie detector and made to prove that he'd read a book—all the way through—since graduating from high school. I'd like to propose a similar sort of test for literature teachers. Ask yourselves, "What piece of literature have you read for the first time in the last year that knocked your socks off?" It is important for your students that you encounter such literature. It is even more important for yourself.

HIERARCHIES, OR WHO'S
IN CHARGE?
· ·

THE TITLE OF this section has a double meaning for me. Almost every one of these pieces came about because of a phone call from an editor asking for an article. The editor named the topic. (Surely this is a fitting subject for doctoral students of the writing process.) I admit my own bias. Experience tells me that it matters little who conceives of a topic. What does matter is if the writer embraces that topic, nurtures it, worries over it, nags it along. I was never assigned a topic I didn't end up liking.

The first time an editor called asking for an article, he asked me to write about discipline. My immediate feeling was that I'd just swallowed cement, but I managed a quick and cheerful, "Sure!" That's always my immediate response when an editor phones. As soon as I hung up the phone, I began to worry. Discipline? I was sure that I didn't know anything—or care at all about—discipline. I resorted to what I always resort to: I read every book and article I could find on the topic. My strong reactions to what I read showed me that of course I had strong beliefs about discipline; I even had a discipline philosophy. Probably I would never have known this had that editor not given me the topic to write about.

This is not to say that an education writer has the luxury of waiting for editors to call. Although *Washington Monthly* ended up asking me to write "'Yes, But Where Are Your Credits in Recess Management 101?'" I had carefully primed the pump a year before. I read lots of journals, waiting for the chance to pounce, writing a letter-to-the-editor to set them straight about educational matters. In response to an article about bureaucracy, I spent a week working on a letter—getting it short enough to be printed but with enough punch to attract the editor's attention. I was very much aware of that journal's particular editorial philosophy as I wrote the letter. I hoped the editor would see my letter as a funny and passionate preview of the kind of article I could write. *Washington Monthly* printed the letter and one year later the editor did ask me to write the article.

Nobody asked me to write "On Stir-and-Serve Recipes for Teaching." This is the only piece I've written that started out as a game. I wondered if I could translate principles from Chinese art to teaching. (Like the titles of all my articles, it is the editor's, not mine. When I confess I wanted to call it "The Sound of One Piece of Chalk," the reader may understand why editors get to pick the titles.) I had written a final exam for a graduate course in Chinese art that both the professor and I thought was pretty good stuff. The professor cited my exam as proof that I should "stop wasting time" with marginal kids and come down to his university to work on a Ph.D. In four years of working in our district to retrain teachers, this professor steadfastly pursued a policy of minimal contact with the locals, never stepping foot in my classroom. Finally, his put-down of my life's work provoked me to translate my exam on Chinese art into a pedagogy of classroom practice. I tried to explain to the good professor—and to myself—why I would stick with teaching. Once *Kappan* printed the article—with the title they chose—I sent a copy to the professor, along with my explanation of its genesis. He did not acknowledge receipt. It is in a bittersweet mood that I offer this footnote: the article won an education prize and has been reprinted in more college texts than anything else I have written.

"'Just the Facts, Ma'am'" provides a cautionary note on self-censorship. Although I was staff writer for *Learning* at the time I wrote "'Just the Facts, Ma'am'," I did not submit the piece to them. I was very conscious of the fact that the circulation of *Learning* was ten times that of *Education Week* (and surely every writer has to have one eye on her audience), but I was sure *Learning* would not let me get away with leading off with a story about my cat not peeing in the litter box. *Education Week* published the article and, without asking me, changed the expression to "stopped using the litter box." I showed the article to the then-editor of *Learning* who expressed great regret they didn't get it, insisting of course I could have said "peeing in the litter box." Easy for her to say after the fact.

I would add that I have stopped telling the story of the mystery of my cat and the litter box on the lecture circuit because I am tired of fielding the anxious question, "What color was that new litter box?"

"Not-So-Super Superintendents" cost me a lot of money to write, but I couldn't resist the deliciously awful prospect of seeing George Steinbrenner as keynote speaker to an education convention. He did not disappoint me. Shortly after the article appeared in *Washington Monthly*, ASCD sent me an invitation to cover their convention, offering to waive the registration fee. I looked at the program: their keynote speaker was Lee Iacocca. Apparently some of these organizations operate under a modified Barnum principle: "We don't care what you say about us; just get our name in print."

"What Makes Whittle Qualified . . ." seems like a pedestrian title to me, but my recent career in writing for newspapers shows me that newspaper editors took a different title-writing course than did magazine editors. I care a whole lot about what Whittle is doing to education. I hope my piece might make a few more people care.

"Huffing and Puffing and Blowing Schools Excellent" stays amazingly current even though it talks about ten-year-old reports to the nation fixing blame for the uneasy zeitgeist on the schools. We are currently undergoing another round of such finger pointing. This time they're saying that if teachers just get certified, and the curriculum gets standardized, schools will be better, the GNP will improve, and somehow our crumbling infrastructure will be shored up. This time our professional organizations are jumping in to say, yes, the teachers have been at the heart of the problem; teachers need to pull up their socks and do better. All I can say is that I've never read a curriculum guideline that made sense to me or a booklist that I didn't find fault with. I once thought that if I had to choose, I'd choose competence over good heart. I have changed my mind. And I don't know how you test for a good heart. The battle is never over. The deep issues don't change.

I include "The Paper Chase" as a reminder that teaching is a lonely calling; in the end we can rely only on ourselves. Of course some folks think "The Paper Chase" is about toilet paper. When *Phi Delta Kappan* published the piece, school administrators wrote letters denouncing me. They said anybody who spent so much time worrying about toilet paper obviously couldn't care much about children. The piece won the EDPress Award as best education article of the year, beating out a *Newsweek* submission. Somehow I don't think the judges were awarding a prize to a teacher who cared only about toilet paper. When the editor of *Vital Signs* asked me if I would like to write a piece about restructuring the English classroom, I seized the opportunity to write a sequel to the toilet paper saga. "Inside Classroom Structures" is the result.

The principles underlying the particulars are what teaching is all about. At a time when committees on something called teacher empowerment are accumulating faster than dustballs, we know we are already empowered. Our own importance sits, sometimes heavily, on our shoulders. Does anyone believe that power will come with some consortium's proclamation that we are, at long last, "professional"? When a teacher walks into a classroom she has infinite power: power to wound, power to heal, to defeat, to inspire.

We can survive and even triumph in the classroom only by informing our own best instincts and finding our voices. In the end, we must look not to the politicians or the managers of our profession for the words and deeds of our craft. Emerson reminds us that "nothing can bring you peace but yourself. Nothing can bring you peace but the triumph of principles."

The Paper Chase

MANY OF MY colleagues thought that my zeal for the paper chase was, if not misinformed, then certainly misdirected. I can understand their concern. Especially in these days of media hype, with committees on excellence proliferating like ragweed, a teacher doesn't want to be caught with her dignity down. If teachers around the country were polled on their professional priorities, no doubt securing toilet paper that fits the dispensers in the faculty rest rooms would not rate very high.

Even in the heat of the moment, I knew that marching in the school hallways brandishing my roll of toilet paper looked slightly nutty. But, as I kept insisting to my more reserved colleagues, it wasn't merely a tissue issue: I was fighting bureaucracy; I was fighting for the rights of employees—yes, even teachers—to decent working conditions. And before I finished my paper chase, I learned a lot about how bureaucracies function and about where teachers fit into the scheme of things.

People unfamiliar with the way schools are run might think a toilet paper dispenser is something you can take for granted, but we hadn't been in our new multimillion-dollar school for half an hour before we found out that we'd better not take anything for granted. An outside door couldn't be opened; the gizmo that's supposed to bring in fresh air to windowless interior rooms didn't work; the fire alarm bell sounded for no apparent reason; and that same fire alarm bell was audible in only half the building. Later, we found out that the roof leaked badly every time it rained and that the heating/cooling system required one to wear parkas in some parts of the building and sleeveless T-shirts in others.

And the toilet paper didn't fit the dispensers. After a single piece was pulled out, the rest remained jammed up inside the dispenser, unreachable by even the longest fingers.

The janitor told me that the district had gotten "a deal" on the paper. Some deal. The bargain paper was a different size from the dispensers. This size discrepancy was also a problem with the paper towels. Custodians bypassed the towel dispensers and stacked towels on the counter. Picking up one towel with wet fingers would inevitably soak six more. I hoped that the bargain, cut-rate price was no more than one-sixth the price of regular towels.

At first, people muttered about the toilet paper. We brought it up at a faculty meeting, and the principal promised to "look into the matter." Finally, he got the idea of bypassing toilet paper dispensers, too. We came to school one day to find the toilet paper stacked behind the toilet seats — next to the handle that people kick to flush. That system didn't last long. Even teachers who never complained about anything weren't going to put up with kicking the toilet paper all over the floor and then having to retrieve it.

So another plan was devised. The toilet paper was stacked in shoe boxes on the floor; each cubicle had its own shoe box. But people didn't want to use paper that someone else had touched, so pretty soon the shoe box was a nest of paper that had been ruffled through. The boxes were kicked around and knocked over. Paper was scattered all over the floor, and even the paper that remained in the boxes was in a sorry state. Once again, even the noncomplainers began grousing about this new system because it wasn't sanitary.

One should not suppose that all of this happened overnight or even in the course of a single year. While the wheels of all bureaucracies turn slowly, in school bureaucracies many of those wheels have flat tires.

When there was no response other than annoyed shrugs from administrators who didn't want to be bothered with such trivial details as toilet paper dispensers, a few teachers tried to lodge an official complaint with the union representative. But the union rep wasn't at all certain that toilet paper was a grievable item — or that he wanted to find out. Finally he agreed to put the tissue issue on the agenda of a meeting of the Teachers and Administrators Liaison Committee (TALC), a group formed to iron out annoyances, disputes, and common concerns, so that teachers would not resort to formal grievance procedures.

And the TALC solved the tissue problem. Or so it said. That's when the tissue appeared on the backs of the toilets. After we complained about that solution for six months or so, the TALC solved the problem again: this time with the shoe boxes.

After fielding complaints about the shoe boxes for a year or so, the principal solved the problem himself. He went into each cubicle and "personally adjusted" each dispenser. Since I was one of the most persistent complainers, he interrupted my class with the good news that the toilet paper was back in the dispenser and that it worked. You can imagine the stir this caused in a class of seventh graders.

And in a way, the principal had fixed the problem. Certainly the paper no longer got stuck. But when you pulled out one sheet, thirty-two more came with it. By 10:08 A.M. there was lots of paper on the floor but none left in the dispenser. I can be precise about that time because by then I was really getting into the spirit of documenting bureaucratic ineptitude. My malcontent colleagues and I began keeping notes on the precise time by which paper was no longer available in the dispensers. When I complained to the principal about this new wrinkle in the tissue problem, he announced that the problem was not in the dispenser but in the way "you ladies pull the paper."

The TALC refused to put toilet paper on its agenda again. The TALC members wanted to concern themselves with real issues. Our contract specified a twenty-seven-minute lunch break for teachers, and the union was fighting against taking "walking time" to report to hall duty out of that brief lunch period. The union representative showed me the minutes of the TALC meeting announcing that the dispensers had been adjusted and the problem solved. "The paper is out of the dispenser and all over the floor before noon," I protested. He suggested that I find a different lavatory.

The custodian followed orders and filled the dispensers every night, but the shoe boxes reappeared so that paper would be available after 10 A.M. That's when "the ladies" decided to march, each carrying her own personal roll. All we did was gather at one end of the hall and walk down to the other end, each of us brandishing a roll of toilet paper on the end of a broom handle. When kids asked us what we were doing, we told them that since the school wouldn't provide us with paper we had to bring our own.

The principal confiscated my roll of toilet paper, saying that the sight of "you women carrying rolls of toilet paper in the hallway — in full view of the students — is one of the most disgusting sights imaginable." I could easily have pointed out two dozen more disgusting sights in our school, but I kept silent. He said that if I didn't like the toilet paper supplied by the district I certainly should bring my own, but he insisted that I keep it out of the sight of innocent children.

It soon became clear that the Toilet Paper March was an unsuccessful tactic. We teachers who had hoped to draw attention to the unsanitary conditions in the lavatories succeeded only in earning administrative letters of reprimand. What's more, such hooliganism scared many of our colleagues into insisting that the tissue was fine, that there never had been and never would be a tissue problem.

But I couldn't let it rest. I decided to carry the tissue issue beyond our school. The first phone call was the hardest. I was shifted through four different offices at the County Health Department in search of someone willing to discuss public school lavatory requirements. Each time my call was transferred, I heard the incredulous question, "You say your tissue is in a shoe box? On the floor?"

Finally, I was transferred to someone in the Environmental Protection Unit. He told me that there is no question that "rolls are more sanitary than single sheets and are recommended for toilets in public buildings."

"Would you write a letter to that effect to my principal?" I asked. There was a long silence. "Actually," I offered, "it would be fine if you wrote the letter to me. I could pass it along."

Suddenly, the fellow who had been so forthright about the preferred installation of tissue in public buildings became cautious in the extreme. It is one thing to make statements over the phone; recommendations in writing are apparently an entirely different kettle of fish. He told me that he did not have the authority to write letters. I asked to be transferred to someone who did have letter-writing authority, and then the bureaucratic waffling began in earnest. I talked to three more people. But, after agreeing that roll dispensers are preferable to single-tissue dispensers, each one clammed up when I asked for a letter to that effect.

A public-health nurse was sympathetic. Drawing on her experience in field work in Appalachia, she gave me directions for making a toilet paper roll out of a coathanger. But she wouldn't write a letter either, pointing out that that was not her area of responsibility.

The Senior Public Health Sanitation Officer informed me that "all standards for the maintenance of health in public schools are the responsibility of the New York State Education Department." He further informed me that the County Department of Health cannot enter a school unless invited by school officials. He agreed that, if we had an outbreak of bubonic plague, the health department would not wait for an official invitation to investigate. But he suggested that the dispensing of toilet paper fell short of such an emergency. He would not write a letter either, because he did not want to infringe on someone else's responsibilities. Everybody at the Department of Health asserted that someone there did have the authority to write letters, but I finally gave up trying to find that someone.

My next call was to the setter of school health standards and codes: the New York State Education Department. It took just three transfers for the functionaries at the state department to decide that they did not have any lavatory regulations. I was advised that, if I felt my lavatory facilities were substandard, I should contact my local school board or the parent-teacher organization. In making this suggestion, the officials at the state department revealed just how far out of touch with public school reality they are.

Next came a call to the Occupational Safety and Health Administration (OSHA). This agency of the U. S. Department of Labor is the guardian of the health and safety of workers, right? All workers, it turns out, except teachers. The OSHA officer with whom I spoke informed me that "the federal government may go through the motions of looking out for mine workers, steelworkers, and cotton pickers." Teachers are referred back to their local boards of education—or to the parent-teacher association.

Next I called the New York State Department of Labor, Division of Safety and Health. I spoke to administrators both in New York City and in Albany. Their line was pretty much the same: "There are no restroom standards for schools." At my insistence, two officials searched the codes and came up with "an adequate supply of toilet paper should be provided." One man said that he didn't care if said paper were in working dispensers, on the backs of the toilets, or scattered around on the floor. The other said that if I sent in a complaint that an adequate supply did not exist he doubted that he'd send out an investigator. He told me that if I had complaints about toilet paper dispensers I could write my congressional representative about getting provisions added to the Public Employee Health and Safety codes.

By this time I had gone far beyond the tissue issue. I had discovered something far more depressing: despite myriad government agencies and a web of rules to protect workers, teachers live on a plantation ruled by the whim of a few people whose best talent seems to be passing the buck. Teachers have no inherent right to decent working conditions, and no government agency will investigate improper conditions. Everything depends on schools being run by administrators of good will and common sense, and there are no safeguards to protect teachers from nincompoops. Every step of the way I was referred back to the manager of my school, and since he insisted that the dispensers worked, then, by golly, they must work.

I gave up. I conceded that there was no way that I was going to get working toilet paper dispensers in the lavatories. Then a new school year brought a contract dispute with the board of education, and I was officially reprimanded by the principal for wearing a (lace-trimmed) T-shirt that said "Support Troy Teachers." I was informed that my "dress attire" was not up to professional standards. The principal and I were standing in the hallway outside the lavatories when he issued this reprimand, stating that an official document from the superintendent would follow. I responded by asking, "Is the toilet paper in there of professional standards?"

He smirked and said, "I don't know. I don't use the ladies' room." Whereupon I went a bit berserk. For *four years* I'd been trying to effect a reasonable change through regular channels: the custodian, the principal, the union, the county health department, the state department of education, OSHA, and so on. And this guy could win every battle; he could smile and tell me that the ladies didn't know how to pull the paper, that he didn't have to care because he didn't use the ladies' room. I threw a minor fit and told him I was going to phone the local TV station and tell them that he said he didn't know whether we had toilet paper in the ladies' room because he didn't use the ladies' room.

Toilet paper rolls were installed in all faculty lavatories the following day.

In Edmund Burke's words, "There is, however, a limit at which forbearance ceases to be a virtue." What he meant—it is obvious to me now—is that teachers should not try to go through channels. Most definitely, they should not wait four years to throw a fit.

When my paper chase was over, and our toilet paper rolls were installed, I discovered that the paper in the students' lavatories had never worked either. Their paper was piled on the backs of the toilets, right next to the handle that they kick to flush. . . .

There's Only One True
Technique for Good Discipline

FOUR YEARS AFTER our middle school opened, teachers were grumbling about the absence of an official discipline policy. Then, in the fifth year of our discontent, the school board adopted the Discipline Code — a holy writ of conduct distributed to teachers, parents, and children. Teachers, of course, quickly discovered that official rules didn't help them achieve authority in the classroom, and the code was filed with other bureaucratic memorabilia.

Our discipline code did not leap full-blown out of the head of an administrator. It was developed by a committee of caring, concerned people — members of the school board, administrators, teachers, parents, students. They meant well; they tried hard. Authority, however, cannot come from a committee. A teacher's authority comes from her own savvy; it is a part of her style and cannot be distributed by fiat or handed out like chalk and rubber bands.

Borrowing from sociologist Max Weber's model, I see three kinds of authority operating in schools: traditional, legal, and charismatic. Traditional authority relies on sacred custom. The teacher is always right: respect the office, if not the person. I was raised in that mode: "If you get hit at school, you'll get hit twice at home." The crumbling bulwark of most principals, traditional authority is already dead for most educators outside of military academies and some parochial schools. Nowadays parents are more likely to say, "Stop harassing my child!" And if a student is suspended, she comes to the hearing with a lawyer.

With the second kind of authority, legal, committees at the local and state levels hold meetings, set policies, write guidelines. They issue documents to establish law and order in the schools. Principals rely heavily on the edicts spewed forth: "It is state mandated" is a response designed to end all discussion.

Loopholes in the blanket of legal authority have attracted some who aren't schoolteachers but ed-biz whizzes. Flitting around the country offering teachers the Holy Grail of classroom management, these trend followers provide a psy-fi fix in the form of barter systems, contracts, and the M&M exchange. Too often their programs lead to a student extortion racket: give me a verbal massage (or some candy or gold stars), and I won't drive you nuts.

The third kind of classroom authority, charismatic, is more elusive. This personal authority emanates not from a tradition or a legal document or a manipulative barter system, but from individual personality. It can survive change in reading programs, change in dress code standards, change in ethnic makeup of the student body; it can survive amidst chaos.

One does not find charisma in its pure form very often, nor are descriptions of charismatic authority usually very helpful to educational acolytes. The charismatic teacher holds her kids—in the style of the Ancient Mariner—by her glittering eye, not her handfuls of M&Ms. The charismatic teacher knows in her bones when she is right. She doesn't have checklists to prove it. She expresses herself in the work she does, not in pretty slogans and colorful charts.

Several years ago, in *Schools Where Children Learn*, Joseph Featherstone told us that "there are no educational 'models' that can be mass produced." He pointed out that the systems approach is generally inappropriate to education, where most of the problems are human, not technical. "Learning is far more complex in its sequences and motives than the simple models constructed by behaviorists, which are drawn from observations of pigeons eating corn friskies . . ." How naive, then, to suppose that a teacher can take a course, learn a set of dialogues, and parrot a sequence of sixty-three positive statements to get children to behave correctly.

School administrators intone that "in order for learning to take place, there must be order in the classroom." That may be true, but I feel the emphasis is in the wrong place. In order that learning may take place, there should be something worth learning. Sad to say, an orderly classroom is too often considered accomplishment enough for teachers. One need not take home a book, prepare a lesson, or do anything beyond assigning daily reading in class; teachers who never file disciplinary referrals make the administrative honor role.

The behaviorist ed-biz-whiz gang has moved in and capitalized on this administrative yearning for order. Once the behaviorists had curriculum whipped into shape with their lists of objectives and criterion-referenced tests and brightly colored skill packets, discipline became the obvious target. Now they offer their programs as a contract: You do this and the child will do that. Their classroom management schemes—the frozen waffles of junk pedagogy—are packaged in promises and contain few redeeming qualities. I know because I have recently read fifteen books on discipline. They have chapter titles like "The Ecology of Classroom Discipline," "Contingency Contracting," "Congruent Communication," "Assertive Discipline," "Operationally Defined Misbehavior," and

"Minimal Intervention." The self-proclaimed educational experts who write them make a good buck dispensing wisdom and conducting training sessions to show teachers how to organize their classrooms. Training and control are neatly packaged and marketed under the name of "learning." Classroom management and teaching become the same thing in the eyes of the trainers, and, I fear, too often in the eyes of the teachers.

The pseudospecialized vocabulary of child control adds to the confusion. I am uneasy when I read that a "response cost is defined as the removal of specified amounts of positive reinforcement after (contingent on) a behavior." I read that "punishment is the presentation of an environmental event, contingent on a behavior, which decreases the strength of that behavior," and my brain buzzes. I read of "compliance devices," "token economics," "deceleration targets," "alternate responses," "environmental alterations," and "terminal behavior," and I break out in a rash. I read about the teacher as "operant conditioner," "reinforcer," "facilitator," or "psychodynamicist," and I shout, "NO!" (I must confess, however, to a certain fascination with the expression "terminal behavior." If these guys could guarantee that the next time Selina snaps her gum at me it would be her terminal act, I might sign up for their course.)

The bold assertions amaze me. Without equivocation or hesitation, the behavior mod folks state that the child's "behavior extinguishes since it is no longer successful in obtaining the reinforcement (attention of the teacher) the child desires." Personally, I don't think I've ever extinguished a child's behavior. Furthermore, I agree with James Herndon that all the operant conditioning in the world won't change "simply a mean son-of-a-bitch, no matter how he got that way." Of course, the positive self-image people usually don't talk about the crazies or the six-foot hoodlum with his fist in your face. Most of their classroom dramatizations deal with children passing notes and speaking without raising their hands.

None of the books I read on classroom management addressed the issue of teacher physical prowess. For inner-city kids at least, body language is more important than sweet words. I am not talking about physical strength or abuse; I have never used physical force on any of my students. I do know, however, that Pete respects me and accepts my authority because one day I put my 103-pound body on the line against him. Pete is a big, angry seventh grader who can't read. He has average intelligence, good auditory memory, and I don't know why he can't associate squiggles on paper with words. I know only that he is in a rage most of the time.

I discovered that mine was one of the few classes in which Pete was disruptive. He was allowed to be absolutely passive in other classes. As long as he didn't cause trouble, no one bothered him. In one class he was given an 80 for "good attitude." He got a 55 in my class because he would not try language experience stories and refused all tests I gave him. One day Pete was leaning back in his chair, needling another boy who was trying to work. The second boy pushed Pete on the chest, causing him to fall over backward onto the rug.

The probability of a blow being struck was about 99 percent. No way could Pete be put down like that in front of his peers without retaliating. I dashed over and shouted, "Pete, you had it coming! You were bothering him!" Pete quickly turned his anger on me. Towering over me, he actually began to huff himself up bigger. I leaned in very close and said, "He was wrong to touch you, but don't make it worse by touching him. You were wrong, too. Calm down."

Pete huffed a couple more times and tried to stare me down. I leaned even closer and stared back. Then he walked out of the room. I followed in a couple of minutes, and he was able to talk to me and eventually to the other boy. They shook hands. I consider this incident one of the most positive things that happened between us in the first five months of school. Pete found out that I wouldn't let him get out of control, that he didn't have to hit me, and that I wouldn't let him hit anyone else. I didn't stop Pete by saying, "You are angry." I stopped him with my voice and my body.

Not long after that confrontation, Pete and I began a different kind of interaction. One day he waited for all the other kids to take their spelling tests, then said, "I'm ready for mine." Five rhyming words. He got 100. He asked me to sign the paper and carried it off. We were in the process of doing winter stories. A bank of marvelous words and phrases—like *icy misery, frozen Arctic regions, shattered water pipes, windy walloper*—stretched the length of the hallway. I told Pete to choose five words, which I'd help him turn into a story. A couple of days later he heard me tell another student to go out in the hallway and find ten good winter words. "You only gave me five," Pete frowned. "I guess I better go get another five."

Pete wrote his stories, read them, typed them, read them again, and hung them in the hallway. To me, this was worth 100,000 gold stars or "I like the way Pete is sitting down" statements. I venture to guess that Pete would rather have those stories than a whole packet of M&Ms.

I once heard Pete tell someone, "Ohanian's mean. She don't let you do nothin'." Sometimes in our daily notes he writes to me, "Get off my bak," signs his name and, in tiny letters, adds, "I am jus kidn." Pete's words are high praise. Pete is getting discipline; he is getting a bit of control over his own education; he is learning to do things because he has to.

I tell this long story because I think the teacher who gave Pete an 80 is wrong. He has given up on the kid, but for the sake of peace passes him on.

Only when teachers begin to hate themselves for their toughness are they beginning to grow and to make it as teachers, says Herbert Foster, author of *Ribbin', Jivin', and Playin' the Dozens: The Unrecognized Dilemma of Inner-City Schools.* Foster says that 2 or 3 percent move beyond the "discipline" phase to what he calls humanization. I suspect this latter phase is very similar to what I'm calling charismatic. Students can relax because they know the teacher is in charge physically, spiritually, and intellectually. I don't think it is an overdramatization to refer to this physical-spiritual-intellectual power as grace, in Weber's sense of the word. The person who possesses it must constantly revalidate it in action. It is non-transferable: one doesn't get grace in an inservice course.

Most discipline schemes, euphemistically known as classroom management techniques, reek of manipulation. Honest emotion is forsaken in the name of control and quietude. Lee and Marlene Canter, authors of *Assertive Discipline*, would even have teachers plan ahead how they will praise their students; they recommend practicing with a colleague the phrase, "I like the way you did your work." Where is conscience, responsibility, passion?

I see no need to become a different person eight hours a day because I am a teacher. I answer students with myself—with my concern, joy, pleasure, anger—not with the gimmickry of sixty-three positive responses learned from a manual. Because I regard my style as my essence, I resent it when I tell a positive reinforcer about a good classroom experience only to have her smile tolerantly and tell me, "That's one of our techniques," as if what the children and I do so well together were invented by a behavior mod guru and could best be learned through a copyrighted publication.

These social hustlers are promoting a dangerous panacea. They say, Do it because it works. But if the positive stroking is an end in itself, students may never understand the joy that can come from a job well done. In the words of educator and author Edgar Friedenberg, "Behavior modification is planned to mold desirable behavior directly, without rooting it in ethical purposes. It seeks to operate at Kohlberg's lowest level of moral judgment: behavior is good because it is rewarded. This is a serious denial of the humanity of the person subjected to it." Humanitarian people who are aghast at the suggestion that electric cattle prods would very quickly bring order to chaotic hallways might ask themselves how they can blithely administer their knee-jerk jolts of positive reinforcement.

The positive approach folks—so glib in their upbeatness—are wrong too when they insist that a teacher's vulnerability (what educator George Dennison called the "teacher's moment of doubt and defeat") can be manipulated or bargained away. My students know that they can make me cry. The greatest defense against vulnerability is not a prepackaged, fast-fix management system; it is competence. Teachers must be intellectually, spiritually, and physically competent—basically able to deal with kids. If they aren't, then all the behavior charts and checklists and magpie jingles in the world will do little good.

My teaching career began in a Queens high school in the middle of a term. To say that my classes were undisciplined is to put it mildly. LeRoy serenaded the class with a trumpet mouthpiece every day. I could never quite catch him with it, and when accused of making disturbing noises, he put on his dramatic "Who, me?" act to further entertain the class. Two of my students were blind. They didn't like each other and did their best to punch each other out. I tried to keep them apart, but if one sensed the other was near, there would be a pitiful flailing of arms and cursing. I dragged myself home every night in utter defeat and tears.

On a most memorable occasion, three quarters of the class got into an ice-cream fight. Kids who couldn't remember to bring a pencil organized themselves to come to class with piles of ice-cream sandwiches, which they promptly spread over one another and the room. Although I knew a teacher was supposed to handle her own dirty linen, I made a desperate call to the department chairman. He gave me some valuable advice. He didn't tell me to punish the kids or to barter with them or to offer them contingency contracts. He told me to become a better teacher. He gave me specific suggestions on how to improve my curriculum. I have never forgotten that discipline "technique." It worked from the very start, and I use the suggestion to this day. When a kid is in trouble in my class, I don't change the way I smile—I alter his curriculum.

That department chairman invested a lot of time in me. He came to my class every Monday and watched how I applied a suggestion for getting across curriculum from the previous Monday's conference. Then he added an item to the list. Slowly, layer upon layer, he helped me to build mastery of the material I was teaching. He borrowed veteran teachers' notes for me, he taught demonstration lessons, he arranged for me to observe other teachers. He was certainly the administrative exception; too often, administrators tell us they have no time to teach demonstration lessons—that it is their job to administer, not to teach. They demand that teacher competence arrive on the first day of school, along with the room keys.

I suspect it is their unwillingness to get involved in teaching that leads administrators to support cosmetic behavior mod schemes so wholeheartedly. Such schemes keep kids out of the office, and that is all that matters. For in their offices, many administrators are busy writing perfect and impossible statements that they expect teachers to enforce. I discovered the truth of that observation—along with other, more heartening, revelations—during my first year of teaching. From on high came a fiat forbidding students to wear denim pants. Right outside the school, kids were fighting a racial gang war. In my classroom, they were threatening to throw one another out the third-story window. And I was supposed to worry about the cotton content of their trousers? You bet I was. From time to time the assistant principal in charge of discipline would stop me and remark that he'd noticed Jerome Wright wearing denim pants and that I hadn't reported it.

The enforcement of strict dress codes has lost some importance in recent years, but every once in a while a principal will come barreling into my room and insist that a kid remove his hat. It seems a terrible waste of administrative energy to me. I'd be more impressed if an administrator came in and asked what I am doing to teach Johnny to read.

I used to think a kid couldn't learn if he was feeling lousy about himself, but now I'm convinced he'll never feel better unless he develops some skills. Control and quiet may be the administrative way of judging teachers, but that does not mean we teachers should settle for such a paltry goal. We are not plumbers; we need to know more than how to locate the on and off spigots of a child's behavior. We need to be more than mere mechanics in the classroom—keepers of compliance devices and counters of environmental events. Educational bureaucrats and their fellow travelers insist that education must be objective and quantifiable. Maybe someday soon, when parents show up at open house, the teacher—or classroom facilitator—will not need to be present at all. Parents will be able to get all they need to know from a file: Johnny's grade on the CAT, the Stanford, the whatever. They will also see a carefully kept record of how many times Johnny called out without raising his hand and how long it took to "extinguish" this behavior. Let us hope that when this day arrives, someone will have kept in the archives a videotape showing what Maria Montessori called "the first dawning of real discipline." She described this dawning as the moment "a child becomes keenly interested in a piece of work, showing it by the expression in his face, by his intense attention, by his perseverance in the same exercise. The child has set foot upon the road leading to discipline." The teacher doesn't need to say "I like the way Bill has settled down" on such an occasion.

'Yes, But Where Are Your Credits in Recess Management 101?'

WE'VE ALL HEARD about the sorry state of America's teaching profession. No less than a half dozen national commissions have given their baleful assessments of our public schools within the last year, and the poor training and the low quality of our teachers have figured prominently in their criticisms. Among the suggestions offered to correct these deficiencies have been higher salaries, merit pay, master teachers, abolition of tenure, and stiffer training requirements. While some of these reforms are better than others, all of them recognize the special urgency of encouraging the nation's best, most talented young people to forsake lives of tort litigation and commodities speculation for the far more useful occupation of helping to revive our floundering schools.

As a teacher I realize that it won't be easy; the job has some daunting occupational hazards. Even the uninitiated probably can guess the difficulty of trying to make *Silas Marner* meaningful to disaffected ghetto youth. But I doubt that anyone unfamiliar with the inner workings of our schools can fully appreciate how Byzantine the system really is, or how debilitating the innumerable irritations of daily life. Policemen on guard in our cafeteria; making sure everything on the blackboard got transcribed into braille for my blind students; begging the assistant principal not to expel the big, disrespectful man-child who writes like a dream; the relentless interrogations of the unforgiving secretary when my roll book statistics don't balance. It's not the easiest way to make a living.

Still, these aren't the reasons that I'm now thinking of leaving the profession after seventeen years. Nor do I agree with the emphasis many of my colleagues put on the usual culprits when they try to explain why talented people shun the profession and the best teachers are usually the first to leave. Low pay, burnout, pushy parents, incompetent administrators, and apathetic kids are certainly problems. But something else has driven me to distraction—more specifically, a group of people I'll call the High Priests of Certification.

Who are the High Priests? They come in many guises—school administrators, state government bureaucrats, even union officials. They mouth a common goal: to protect the citizenry from unqualified, incompetent teachers. It's a noble purpose. But having experienced firsthand the obsession of the High Priests with enforcing irrelevant regulations, their strict adherence to the letter of the law, and their zeal for bureaucratic pettifoggery, I've reached an opposite conclusion. The High Priests aren't making sure we have competent, qualified teachers in the classroom; if anything, their activities seem to be one of the major reasons such teachers never get near a classroom—or decide to leave the profession altogether.

Paper Pushing 101

I'm not suggesting that I'm a great teacher, nor do I think that standards are irrelevant. Authorities must take reasonable steps to insure two important things: that teachers know their subject matter and that they know how to teach it. But as I think my experience amply demonstrates, the High Priests are often obsessed with everything *except* these things.

My acquaintance with the High Priests of Certification goes back a long way, so let me start at the beginning. In the mid-1960s I answered a newspaper plea for people to become high school English teachers. The ad used the word "crisis," but I soon discovered that New York City's Board of Education was not so desperate as to think my master's degree in English literature qualified me to teach. The examiner acted annoyed that I was wasting his time; don't come back, he told me, until I had the thirteen units in education that were required to get an emergency teaching certificate.

Never having taught, I was hardly brimming over with confidence. So I meekly acquiesced to this bureaucratic stricture. In fact, I even told myself that education courses made some sense, and that I would become a better teacher by taking them.

Then I began the classes. For one year, four nights a week, I listened to such discussions as an overview of American education policies and practices up to 1914, taught by a professor who poured most of his energy into constructing multiple choice exams. One professor instructed us in the psychology of the adolescent—without once mentioning sex. In another class, we spent the entire term rewriting Greek myths.

Perhaps my most memorable class taught me how to pass out paper. To my professor mismanaged paper distribution was apparently the first step down the slippery slope to classroom anarchy, and he insisted that mastery of his technique would make or break a teacher. People who've never taken an education course think I'm joking when I tell this story, but it's true. In fact, amidst all the theory and meaningless exercises, the tips on paper distribution were the only practical things I encountered in that tortured year of night school.

So I completed my education classes and was certified by New York City to teach English. I taught for a year in a large urban high school in Queens, where I quickly discovered that all the theory and history I'd learned in my education courses was as useful as a water pistol in a street gang fight. (I also learned that the paper distribution technique I'd learned worked only with straight rows, and I wasn't a straight-row teacher.) I went home every night and cried, but I survived the year.

I left New York City and moved to central New Jersey when I got married. It was there that I had my next encounter with the High Priests of Certification. I applied to every village, hamlet, and town I could think of, and while many of them had openings, none would allow me to teach. The problem was that I had never been a student teacher. "But I've taught, really taught," I protested, describing my harrowing year in the urban high school—a trial by fire that I thought would count for more than practice teaching. The looks of withering scorn that I received from more than one interviewer made it clear that this matter wasn't worth discussing. Rules were rules. So I found a job at a local Youth Center— teaching kids who had dropped out of the local high school. Later, I found a job teaching college English.

In 1969 I moved to Troy, in upstate New York, and applied for a job in the public schools. I quickly learned that I had several strikes against me. The first was that I'd taught college English. "You'd be too intellectual for us," the local superintendent informed me. A second demerit was that my undergraduate and graduate degrees were not in education. When the superintendent discovered that my degree in medieval literature was from Berkeley, my fate was sealed. "You'd be too intellectual *and* too radical for us," he proclaimed.

But I persisted. Less than a week before school started I was in the district office, applying for work as a substitute, when I heard that some state funding had come through for a new, experimental program in remedial reading. The superintendent hired me on the spot because of my experience in Queens working with "those colored kiddos." It didn't seem to bother him that I had no experience teaching seventh graders or remedial reading.

"How do you teach remedial reading?" I asked my sister, who happened to teach the subject herself. She sent me boxes of texts, articles, and suggestions. I studied the texts each night and the kids each day. I made a lot of mistakes and I learned a lot—more from the kids than from the texts. Inspectors from the state department of education pronounced my experimental program a success. My boss was enthusiastic.

Three years later the funding for the program evaporated as quickly as it had appeared. A principal asked if I'd like to organize an open classroom, kindergarten through the sixth grade, with an emphasis on reading and writing. The prospect of teaching such young children was daunting, but also challenging. I accepted. I sought help everywhere I could find it, including weekend seminars, summer workshops, collaborative newsletters. And as I handed out hammers and saws to first graders as part of my effort to spark their interest in story writing, I wondered if anyone in the district office was still worrying about intellectualism in my classroom.

My years in elementary education taught me something very important: that this was the kind of teaching that made me happiest. In all modesty, I also had some talent for it. In 1973 I was given tenure, and the next year I was named Teacher of the Year for Troy. I went on to become one of five finalists in New York's Teacher of the Year program. No one in the state department of education seemed the least bit concerned that a teacher who originally had been certified in secondary English could be tenured in elementary education. In fact, several administrators at the state education department wrote me letters of commendation and congratulation.

But the good times were not to last. The open education concept was canceled in favor of some other fleeting fancy, and I was out of a job once again. So I helped establish a curriculum for a new, alternative high school for students who had dropped out of the regular program. Two years after that, I started a new — experimental, of course — program for seventh and eighth graders with low reading ability. By some miracle of administrative apathy, this program lasted for six years, until the spring of 1982. At that time an administrator who had a way with words informed me that I'd been "liquidated."

Doing the Transcript Tango

It was at this point that my problems with the High Priests of Certification really began. For thirteen years I had been toiling on the educational fringes, working in experimental programs where no one had mentioned certification requirements. If one were willing to work with "those" kids, any troublesome requirements apparently could be bent. But my "liquidation" brought me into the educational mainstream for the first time, and I was in for some rude surprises.

I must admit I was partly at fault for the pain and suffering that followed. After my job was eliminated, I was assured that a position awaited me at the local high school. But I told my superiors that I didn't want that job, that I wanted to do the kind of teaching I liked and did the best — in elementary school. (Though my longest stretch of teaching involved remedial work with seventh and eighth graders, I deliberately used the warm, close-knit elementary model rather than the more formal, statistical curriculum necessary in high school where one is required to process over one hundred students a day.) Little did I realize that my avowal of pedagogical preference would brand me a troublemaker and a malcontent—and subject me to six months of bureaucratic misery.

The first big surprise was the reaction of my union, the American Federation of Teachers. I had been a member for more than ten years, and had dutifully paid my sixty-eight dollars in annual dues. I was also the editor of our union newspaper. I'm not sure I expected the union to help one of its own, but I certainly didn't expect it to throw up road-blocks in my path.

How wrong I was. To the union, my proposed defection to the ranks of the elementary school teachers suggested willful abandonment of twelve years' seniority, assorted "vested rights," and other mysterious but valuable commodities. The union representative told me they just couldn't allow that; they had to "look out for my best interests." An exasperating exchange of letters between the union and me followed, to little avail; everything came back to the union's insistence that I take the job at the high school because it preserved my seniority. "I'm not a very good high school teacher," I protested, observing that I hadn't taught regular high school since my first year in the profession. "That's not the point," the union representative told me; regardless of my elementary teaching talent, he insisted that I could not afford to succumb. "Your pri-mary concern must be job security," he insisted. When I offered to sign a statement testifying to my willingness to sacrifice job security for satis-faction, he curtly replied, "We can't let you do that."

I never did learn why the union was so adamant. In fact, if there'd been some ulterior, sinister motive—say, fear that my decision would establish a precedent that the administration could use against my colleagues—I at least could have given my friends an explanation. But to this day I can't fathom it; I felt a bit like a captive in some Kafka novel, thrown into prison and prosecuted without ever being told the charges against me. And union officials weren't kidding about looking out for my "best interests." They began going through my file, making copies of documents to build a case as to why I had to remain in secondary school. Through the grapevine, I heard that they also met with the superintendent, urging him to press me on taking the high school job that I didn't want.

The school district's administrators likewise were suspicious of my desire to move "down" to elementary school. Besides, there were the certification rules. The superintendent told me he couldn't let anyone teach elementary education who wasn't certified in that field. He agreed that my having received tenure from the district in an elementary education job was somewhat at odds with that rule, and conceded that my status made a "potentially interesting legal point." But *he* hadn't been superintendent when I was granted tenure, so he wasn't about to champion my cause. He said he'd have to rely on the advice of the state education department's Bureau of Certification.

This actually struck me as reasonable, all things considered. I figured that obtaining elementary certification would be little more than a formality. At best, the state would accept my tenure as proof that I should be allowed to teach elementary school again. At worst, I thought the bureau might require a course in the history of New York State and perhaps in the methods of teaching elementary math and science. These were subjects I knew little about, and if the state was going to insist on my learning more about them, it would be hard to get indignant about that.

I lived close to the bureau's headquarters, so I decided to pay them a visit, taking along copies of all my college transcripts. (I was trying to make this as painless as possible; a decade ago, when my application to be certified as a secondary school teacher had been absolutely straightforward, it had taken more than a year of sending forms back and forth in the mail before I was approved.) An examiner at the bureau agreed to look through my papers and let me know—informally—where I stood.

It wasn't long before he'd spotted a problem. The transcript *copies* I'd brought weren't good enough. "For actual certification we must have official transcripts," he told me. This struck me as a silly excess of bureaucratic caution, but I thought that it shouldn't be too much trouble to comply. I'd sent official transcripts when I was recertified in New York City, and again when someone at the bureau insisted on checking on my status as a reading teacher. I told the examiner he need only consult my file. "We discard our files every four years," he replied, leaving me stunned by the audacious irony of it all. Who would have suspected that some of the greatest paper pilers in the world could also shred with such abandon?

My next mistake was in appealing to logic and common sense. "Can't you look at my permanent certificate from the New York State Education Department, which qualifies me to teach English, and accordingly conclude that I couldn't have received it without having presented my official transcripts?" Wrong again. A basic tenet among the High Priests of Certification is that nothing can be taken on faith, not even the previous approvals of certifiers in their own bureau. I still had to bring them official transcripts.

Back in the school district office, the secretary offered to help. The district had its own set of my official transcripts, and she suggested sending them to the Bureau of Certification. But it turned out that wouldn't do either. Transcripts are "official," she was told, only when they come *directly from college registrars.* This wouldn't be easy; like most teachers, I'd taken a course here, a course there, and compiling all the necessary transcripts would be an exasperating chore. Still, I resigned myself to the bureaucratic imperative. For the fifth time in my thirteen years of teaching I responded to the official directive, writing the necessary letters to faceless college bureaucrats so I could prove to some state bureaucrat who'd never seen me in a classroom that I was, indeed, fit to teach.

Pedagogical Purgatory

Then the bomb fell. Assuming my transcripts were finally in order, the examiner told me I still needed to take some college courses. The math and science problem, I assumed. I couldn't have been more wrong. My obvious shortcomings in these areas apparently were of no concern to the state of New York. They wanted me to spend a semester student teaching and take two more education courses—in reading. "But I've taught reading for thirteen years," I protested. "I even have a certificate of continuing eligibility, allowing me to teach reading forever and ever in New York State." It didn't matter. "You can't enter an elementary classroom without six more units in reading," the examiner told me.

This made absolutely no sense. Reading was my strength. I was certified to teach high school English. I was further certified to teach reading to anyone. On several occasions the state department of education had hired me as a consultant on reading problems. Now I was being told that I couldn't teach elementary school, for one simple reason: I didn't know enough about reading.

If the examiner found this odd, he didn't let on. In fact, his reaction to my pleas illustrated another striking attribute of the High Priests: they don't have much of a sense of humor. He curtly informed me that the state wasn't claiming I didn't know enough about reading, it was merely a matter of meeting the certification requirements. I tried to compromise. "It's late in the year. Can I get an extension, a year in which to complete these courses?" I asked. He replied that teachers were now a glut on the market, and that there were scores of recent graduates already qualified for the job I wanted. "There's no way you will be allowed in a primary classroom before you have earned six units in reading." By now his tone was menacing; I could almost see the state troopers blocking me from the classroom door, protecting innocent children from my incompetent clutches should I try to foist myself upon them without those six units.

As for the requirement that I take a course as a student teacher, I was able to wear him down on that one. Even to the most obstreperous bureaucrat, thirteen years' experience in the classroom is a convincing argument that you at least know the business end of a chalk eraser. The examiner handed me a form that would waive the student teaching requirement, although it still required my superintendent to attest to my having successfully taught elementary school for two years. (Getting the signature was no trouble—and wouldn't have been even if I had been a raving incompetent. The bureau, in typical fashion, always seems to demand such oaths from the people least likely to know of the candidate's worth; they never ask for testimonials from principals, fellow teachers, or students.) This minor victory at least provided some consolation as I left the bureau, wondering if all this grief was really worth it. I was rapidly realizing why most teachers I knew stuck with the same job, year after year, however much they might complain about "monotony" and "burnout." To change fields is to risk coming into direct contact with the High Priests of Certification.

So I had to take some reading courses. What kind? This only added insult to injury: the bureau couldn't have cared less. In fact, the classes didn't even have to remotely involve reading instruction for elementary school children. If I could find an accredited course on teaching Serbo-Croatian folk tales to left-handed senior citizens of Aleutian descent, that would be just fine. All that mattered was that the class have a course code that belonged to a university department of reading.

I decided to make one last-ditch effort to escape this bureaucratic purgatory. I knew a few people in high places at the department of education. I had letters of commendation about my work as an elementary teacher. I'd given speeches at conferences on elementary education sponsored by the state department of education. Surely these top-level specialists who had expressed respect for my work would help me cut through the sticky morass of officialism.

Once again, a major miscalculation. My friends offered little more than a few phrases of token sympathy about how ridiculous the situation was before telling me, "I wish I could do something, but you know those guys in certification."

They'd beaten me. So I found a sympathetic university professor— "You know those guys in certification," he commiserated with me, using what by now had become a standard refrain. He agreed to waive some of his own requirements to admit me into his doctoral seminar on reading. This was helpful to me because I could take the course over the summer and be ready to teach the coming fall. (Of course, to be admitted to summer school I had to order another set of official transcripts, but that's another story.) The seminar was everything I'd always found education courses to be: dull, pedantic, filled with lofty theorizing and totally devoid of useful advice on how to really teach eight-year-old children to read. Still, it gave me three credits (I picked up the other three by paying $270 tuition to enroll in an "independent study" program and write a magazine article). The class also served my professor's interests. He got a tuition-paying body so that the university could pay his salary. I realized just how important my presence was when I found the professor pleading whenever one of his students betrayed the slightest hint of dissatisfaction, "Please don't drop this course. We have the minimum number to keep it going." The seminar gave me a new insight into why education schools are such rabidly enthusiastic allies of the High Priests of Certification: without all these requirements, a lot of their professors would be pounding the pavement, having to seek honest employment.

Finally, I could pass official muster. There was just one final problem: finding a job to match my new credentials. Just a few weeks before the new term was to begin, the union renewed its campaign to force me into a high school teaching job. The union representative trotted out a new argument: if I moved to primary education, a young teacher without secondary certification would be without a job. My first impulse was to snarl, "Well, why didn't she spend her summer the way I did—getting certified?" Then I realized it's exactly this attitude that keeps the circles of hell burning—once they've suffered the trials of certification, teachers feel little urge to grant absolution to other hapless souls. Catching myself, I instead asked to see a list of precisely how many positions, like mine, had been "liquidated," compared to the number of openings that had occurred through attrition. The union representation couldn't provide me with a list, confirming my suspicion that there were more than enough jobs for the teachers in my predicament. Still, he insisted that he was absolutely, positively sure that accepting a position as a secondary teacher was in my "best interests."

By now it was the end of a long, tortured summer, and I phoned the superintendent. I told him I didn't want the union offering me jobs or trying to pressure me into taking one I didn't want. "If you have a job to offer, please tell me directly," I pleaded. And then I burst into tears. It was at this point that the superintendent offered me the third grade job I really wanted.

Was it a coincidence? Was the job there for me all along? I don't know. I only know that after I was offered the job, no one ever asked to see the certificate that made it legal for me to teach those third graders. They just took my word for it.

Looking back, from the perspective of a year's leave of absence, I'm not bothered so much by the hundreds of dollars I had to spend on the reading courses or the endless wasted hours I spent stalking my new certificate. What upsets me most is the knowledge that I was just one victim of a giant, little-acknowledged conspiracy against the good will and sanity of dedicated, committed teachers. I've talked to several colleagues who've left the profession for good, hounded into exasperation over certification rules. And I'm constantly hearing of new strategies education schools and state bureaucrats have devised to make certification rules more onerous and even less relevant to good teaching than they already are. For example, the state of New York no longer believes that a master's degree in reading is sufficient for children with "learning disabilities." Many who've been teaching these kids—whose major problem is not being able to read—must now take thirty-six new, improved units in order to keep teaching. Nationally, many well-meaning reformers are offering similar prescriptions. John Goodlad, a noted professor of education and author of numerous tomes that are required reading for education majors, recently urged the creation of a new position called head teacher. To qualify for this position one can't be just an excellent teacher; one must also have a Ph.D. in—you guessed it—education. Goodlad assures us that the means already exist "for providing a continuing supply" of such persons, and I don't doubt it. Nor do I doubt that the High Priests will rise to the challenge of figuring out how to certify them. Meanwhile, the additional requirements will, I suspect, be one more reason why potentially good teachers steer clear of the profession altogether.

There's one final irony. For all the hassle I've been through, and for all the certification requirements, none of the administrators, union officials, or state examiners that I've mentioned has ever seen me teach. For all they know, I could be the best teacher in New York State—or the worst. If we're truly concerned about improving the profession, then evaluating teachers according to meaningful standards—Do they know their subject? Can they teach it?—is perhaps the most important reform we can make. Unfortunately, that's the last thing that the High Priests and their apologists seem interested in.

Huffing and Puffing and Blowing Schools Excellent

THE GOOD GRAY managers of the U. S., the fellows who gave us Wonder Bread, the Pinto, hormone-laden beef wrapped in Styrofoam, and *People* magazine—not to mention acid rain, the Kansas City Hyatt, $495 hammers, and political campaigns—are now loudly screaming that we teachers should mend our slothful ways and get back to excellence. I would invite the corporate leaders, the politicians, and the professorial consultants to climb down from their insular glass towers before casting any more stones of censure at, or even giving advice about, my lack of excellence in the classroom. Life is complicated. All of us are, in Thomas Hardy's words, "people distressed by events they did not cause." There is no reason for teachers alone to shoulder the blame.

The various commissions and task forces on educational excellence seem to exemplify one of those laws of human nature: you can tell what a community thinks of you by the committees you aren't asked to join. All of this education commission razzle-dazzle is nothing new; it constitutes just one more in a long, histrionic string of repudiations of teacher savvy and sensitivity. When national leaders decide that it's time to find out what's going on in the schools, they convene a panel of auto dealers and their fellow Rotarians. Individually, these folks are undoubtedly witty, astute, and kind to cats. Collectively, they produce a lot of bluster and blunder; their notions of reform are, at best, spongy. They say, in effect, "I'll huff and I'll puff and I'll blow your schoolhouse excellent."

Would that they could. But most schoolhouses are built of brick, and, though the people behind those brick walls may listen to a little corporate whistling in the dark by adding a course in computer literacy here and one in consumer math there, they remain impervious to real change, especially since no real change has been called for. If you want real change you must talk to teachers, maybe even listen to them. For without teachers real change will never happen.

I confess to feeling about most committees the way Lord Palmerston felt about delegations: they are "a noun of multitude, signifying many but not much." In line with this description, the multifarious state-of-education groups have employed the popular "ready, fire, aim" approach—relying not on the firsthand observations of teachers and students but on the collated reports of other report writers. I propose a national lottery for education consultants. Instead of listening to pronouncements from every state, county, block party, and gathering of the Moose, why not choose just one? We could then syndicate the banalities of this lone lucky consultant and be done with it.

As things now stand, the U. S. would be better served if these commissions and task forces developed a master plan for getting rid of Astroturf and saving the spotted bat, a species as endangered as the science teacher. The education community is ill-served by their unilateral advice pacts. One can't help but wonder why our corporate brethren don't go off and figure out how to run an airline or a steel mill. Not that we teachers wouldn't welcome them into our classrooms. I'm sure that any teacher in the land would extend an invitation to any member of the many commissions on excellence to come to the classroom and show him or her how to make efficient use of school time on the day before Halloween, during a snowstorm, on the morning after an X-rated movie on cable television, during the first half hour after a child vomits in class, or immediately after the school nurse checks the group for head lice.

I can glean a few crystal moments from my own years in the classroom, but I suspect that the pestiferous pedagognosticians will have a hard time fitting my treasured moments on their graphs of excellence: watching a scruffy, smelly, foul-mouthed sixteen-year-old emerge from six months of solitary Scrabble playing to write a letter to a dictionary publisher; seeing a deaf child understand a knock-knock joke for the first time; sharing gravestone rubbings; judging an ice-cube-melting contest; publishing a forty-five-page student anthology of cat stories. I can almost claim that I never met a curriculum I didn't like—at some particular time, for some particular child. And that's my problem: all I can offer are particulars. When the one-size-fits-all, spray-and-use planners gather together, I run for cover. Any good teacher will tell you that a curriculum or an instructional approach can't be standardized and remain effective, even within a single classroom. There's always that child who needs something different.

In my first year of teaching, one of my ninth graders refused to read *Silas Marner*. Wishing I had had the guts to refuse to teach that particular novel, I gave him a different book. I figured I had enough troubles without carrying the added weight of failing someone for saying no. In my more optimistic moments, I even hoped that this particular ninth grader was exercising literary taste.

As I look back on that incident twenty long years ago, I marvel that I had the good sense to avoid that battle. It is fairly easy to see now that *Silas Marner* was not worth bloodshed or even tears, but I marvel that I sensed it then. The burdens of teaching are heavy; the joys, fleeting. Occasionally, good judgment and even excellence can be recognized in retrospect, but in the classroom you usually just hope that you can get through the day without having to apologize for anything.

We are ill-served by the present hardening of the categories, the separation of academic life into the real subjects and the frills. To hear some people tell it, a herd of basic skills escaped from the schoolhouse a few years back, apparently chased away by frivolous, fuzzy-headed electives. Now, if our economy, national security, and petrochemical life-style are to dominate, we need corporate help in corraling the wayward critters once again. Balderdash. All of this basic skills rumble-bumble is a smoke screen; whenever folks bring it up, check to see what they're selling. Mom, apple pie, two cars in every garage, and basic skills. Who could possibly be against such things?

People who talk about basic skills are expressing, of course, not a theory but a mood. Calling for a return to basic skills has the moral imperative of eating turnips; it is akin to the plaintive cry for law and order. Sure, we all want peace and quiet, a chicken in every microwave, and everybody reading at grade level. But these are weasel words, as easy to pin down as a whirling dervish.

Discussing absolute curricula for high school is about as productive as talking about best diets or sharing theories on how to restrain proliferating zucchini. For all their technological pizzazz, our mandarin advisors don't seem to understand that you simply do not educate children by the same methods employed to build rockets or harvest tomatoes.

I dropped out of high school English teaching (the first time) after just one year. Outside the school, students were terrorizing subway passengers, buying and selling dope, having babies. Inside, we gave departmental exams on Tennyson. Even when I did manage to figure out ways to supplement the curriculum, I had to sneak in early so that I could steal ditto paper and other supplies. Not to mention staying up until midnight weeping my way through 150 themes and survival plans for the next day. In the ensuing two decades things have gotten not better, but steadily worse.

I wonder if concerned commission members and community leaders have any notion of just how debilitating it is for teachers, having figured out what to teach and even how to teach it, to then be forced to beg, borrow, and steal—and mostly do without—basic supplies. I wonder if the report writers have ever been in charge of a classroom for which it takes two weeks to secure enough chairs for the students. And even then the teacher has to fight hard to convince the janitor that leftover eighth-grade chairs simply won't do for fourth graders. I know a lot of teachers who would cheerfully give up their copies of the reports on excellence for a ream of paper, a handful of #2 pencils, or a box of staples that fit the stapler.

As I look back over two decades of teaching, I am rather amazed that my goal has remained constant since my second day: to help students believe not only that they have the skill to read but that they might actually *want* to read one day. My teaching career began midway through someone else's lesson plan, and I still have nightmares about that first day—that gruesome moment when I told the students to open the text to the next selection, "Hiawatha." I was out on the pavement that same afternoon, scouring bookstores for used paperbacks. I sensed that I had to encourage students to read for their own information and pleasure, and I carefully watched their choices so that I could find out where to go next with them. When I could steal enough ditto paper, I typed up selections from some of my own favorites for us to read together. It may surprise those who are convinced that excellence must be imposed from above to know that the students' favorite literature was my laboriously typed excerpt from *The Once and Future King*. Interspersed with their rather eclectic curriculum was "real" school—the stuff of departmental exams and blue-ribbon commission recommendations.

Once, while I presented for my supervisor a required lesson on *Julius Caesar*, a belligerent girl (whose attendance had improved dramatically since the appearance of self-chosen books) steadfastly read her novel. My department chairman leaned over and whispered to her, "Don't you think you should put that book away and pay attention to the teacher?" "Who the hell are you?" demanded the girl. "If she wants me to put it away, let her tell me." She went back to her book, and I continued my performance. Later, it was hard to convince my boss that the girl's devotion to that book was an excellent moment for me, much more valid than my gyrations on *Julius Caesar*. Six weeks previously she had claimed that she hated reading. Wasn't this progress? Do 100 percent of the students have to play the game? Her very presence in my class was a victory of sorts, and she was not, after all, painting her nails; she was reading.

Ten years later and hundreds of miles away, the students had changed but the official expectations had not. An investigator from the state education department complained because all my students were reading different books. He dismissed the fact that delinquents, dragged into our alternative program by truant officers and probation officers, were reading at least half an hour every day, with the query, "What major work do your sophomores read?" He was uncomfortable with and even hostile toward a classroom filled with Dick Francis, S. E. Hinton, Thomas Thompson, John McPhee, Edward Abbey, James Thurber, fix-it books, almanacs, sports and car magazines, and the *Daily News*. He was not placated by the fact that the *New York Times* was also in the room, as were copies of standard classics of literature. He wanted workbooks that focused on skills and thirty copies of *A Tale of Two Cities* or *Our Town*. We could have gotten away with Paul Zindel, if we'd had thirty copies. Experts on how schools should be run make it easier for teachers to pose clever comprehension questions about different drummers than to respect them.

Stan dropped out of high school the day he turned sixteen because he "hated the damn bells, always making you stop what you're doing to go someplace else." Stan found a job as a carpenter's assistant in a Neighborhood Youth Corps program; by all accounts he was clever, industrious, and dependable. That's what his boss told me, and I certainly found him to be all those things in the GED class the Corps required Stan to attend. He whizzed through all the GED sections except math. Although his common sense made him efficient at estimating, approximating, and making good guesses, Stan refused to learn the finer points of multiplication and long division.

It may be fitting and proper that a student who won't cooperate to the extent of learning long division should be denied any sort of high school seal of approval. But, if that is the way it's going to be, we should stop requiring such bureaucratic seals of approval for carpenters' assistants.

As Stan said when the Corps fired him for refusing to take any more classes in math, "All I ever wanted to do was work." If we are going to require college degrees for jobs that people once handled without an eighth-grade education, let us admit our reason: we are much more concerned with delaying entry into a glutted job market than with striving for excellence in education.

But the writers of reports on school reform don't know about Stan. Theirs is a too-narrow outlook on education—concerned with the dearth of foreign-language proficiency among incoming college freshmen, but not with the increasing numbers of young women who must drop out of school because they are pregnant or with the disaffected youths who neither need nor want a college-prep curriculum. I am disappointed that the commissions and task forces did not examine the lives of these students. But then, I'm prejudiced. I think that the needs of children should take precedence over the needs of Harvard and even over the needs of General Motors.

The reports on school reform imply that, if we teachers would just become more efficient and use class time more wisely, our students would score better on standardized tests, measure up to the Japanese in auto production, or whatever. What the writers of these reports fail to acknowledge is that in schooling, as in baseball, all moments are not of equal value. You have to put up with a lot of foul balls in the classroom.

Of *course* we need to evaluate teachers. But the current systems, which approach teacher evaluation with a meat inspector's outlook, are doomed to failure. Evaluating teachers is not like grading eggs or beef. We need to encourage the proliferation of a variety of teaching styles, instead of setting up only two acceptable categories: Grade A and Grade B.

Maybe it is time for a doctoral student or a governor's aide to examine the fact that teachers, by and large, are decidedly unenthusiastic about the idea of merit pay. We aren't scared off by so-called standards; we are distressed by the fact that teachers are once again being told how to do their job by people who have never done it. Merit pay will reward once again the politician and the showman among us. Expertise is too easy to fake. The Duke of Wellington once remarked that he liked the Order of the Garter because there was "no damned nonsense about merit" connected with it. If the state legislators and other politicians are so interested in rewarding merit, let them go first. If all teachers were paid a decent wage, maybe the notion of merit pay could be buried in the nearest landfill, along with all the other deadly sludge.

No one intimately involved in a classroom can appreciate the subtle interplays, the minute changes that take place among people in that setting—and, when things go very well, between a student and a text or an idea. So, when we are told to get ready for the lessons-by-appointment that are arranged every six months and duly noted in our personnel files, we go for the grand slam. Most of us can do this on schedule (and we have contracts stipulating that no one dare try an unscheduled visit), but lessons-by-appointment don't reveal tiddly-pom about our real strengths and weaknesses over the 180-day season. It always amazed me that students ham up such lessons as much as their teachers, cooperating in the production of show-and-tell tinsel for the benefit of visiting administrators. For fifty minutes twice a year, we all pretend that school is what everybody outside the classroom claims it should be. No student even asks to go to the bathroom.

After a while I stopped playing this game of gray-flannel excellence. I decided, "They want to evaluate me? Well, let them see me in action"—which is often, to the unknowing eye, very close to inaction.

So my boss—the one who gets to lay down policy, write curriculum guidelines, and consult, no doubt, with important people from education commissions—sat in my classroom while three seventh graders read joke books to one another, four students read notes I had written to them and wrote replies, two students quizzed each other for a social studies test in some other teacher's class, Charlie (left behind from the previous class) remained asleep, Sharon announced she was in love and got a pass to the library to find some poems honoring the event, Raymond picked up his novel where he had left off the day before, and Pete went through his daily litany about "not doing no friggin' work in this friggin' school." Interestingly, on another occasion, when I did perform a "show" lesson for an administrator, Pete played his role of model student. But since I wasn't faking it this time, neither did he.

A good teacher makes important decisions. Does Charlie need his sleep more than he needs reading? Do certain students need a review of social studies more than they need punctuation? A good teacher savors watching youngsters read joke books, when a few months earlier they refused to believe that books could ever be funny or worth sharing. A good teacher needles the obnoxious to get to work and encourages the light-hearted to view the library as a storehouse of infinite resources.

But after ten minutes of this, my boss couldn't stand it any longer. She gathered up her agendas and her checklists and announced, "I'll come back when you are teaching." I noted that she'd been sitting across the table from Ron, who had gotten a good start on writing a poem. Three times he had called me over for help. I had nudged him to reexamine the sense of a metaphor, persuaded him to stop going for the easy rhyme, and helped him locate the thesaurus when he decided he needed a big word—one that "nobody else would know." I thought Ron's work nothing short of miraculous, but you won't find any record of these magic moments in my personnel file.

Even for the best of practitioners and observers, the teachable moment is fleeting; if you don't have a good eye, you are likely to miss it. Despite the claims of the mastery-learning crew and others of their ilk, teaching, like truth, is never pure and rarely simple. Too many expert witnesses mistake fluff and flutter for consequence. I figure that the only way to teach is well, and just how you do it is your own damn business. If my style doesn't fit on somebody else's checklist, too bad. We teachers must not be railroaded into pretending that we should be responsible for managing the timing and flow of education as efficiently and regularly as assembly-line workers produce toasters. We don't have to jump every time someone else rings a bell.

The various commission and task force reports released a flood of public sentiment for improving our schools—and a lot of cynicism in the faculty room. We knew what would happen. The flurry of public interest would soon be displaced by the next day's headline, and we teachers would be left with the nasty residue—the slush and slime of still more negative messages about how we do our jobs. The reports were so neat and precise, so self-confident in their delivery. And now here we sit in what has been portrayed as a very sloppy profession, never sure from one moment to the next that we are doing more good than harm. We are ill-served by cheap shots from the corporate and political remittance men and their consulting mercenaries whose words are akin to a nasty swarm of bloodsucking mosquitoes. Their bites may not kill, but they sure don't help us do our job.

I wish that the members of those commissions and task forces could realize how frustrating it is for us teachers to be pursued like horse thieves. There are so many witnesses for the prosecution on how we measure up in the classroom: the bus driver, the newspaper reporter, the mayor, the colleague across the hall. And now the professors and politicians are at it again. Teachers, it seems, are never acquitted. The best we can hope for is a hung jury.

Part of the problem is that we have no special skills, no secret rites all our own. Just about anybody can teach a lesson or two—perhaps even cope for a week or a month or a year. A few might even do it well. But the real test is to stick with teaching ten years or more and *still* do it well, maybe even get better at it. Teaching, done well, can drive you crazy. I have taught for eighteen years, sixteen in the public schools, and I don't think I had one single comfortable day in the classroom. There is always that tension that you'll miss something important, fail to respond correctly to a student's unspoken need. Thirty years after the fact, my sister is still pained and even intimidated by an English teacher's red-penciled comment on her theme. I worry about how my students will remember me in thirty years. We don't teach a child for just one year; our message lingers for a lifetime. God knows, the temptation is always there to react badly to innumerable provocations: wacky kids, fetid curriculum guides, maggot-brained bureaucrats, sanctimonious reports on excellence.

I like to write about my crystal moments in teaching. The savoring of these times is, I think, what keeps me going. But the call in the current wave of education reports for greater efficiency in the classroom helped me realize that my exuberant vignettes are misleading. Maybe some folks get the impression that I spent eighteen years passing efficiently from one crystal moment to another.

Forget efficiency. Not enough attention is paid to the lag time in schools, the interminable length of some of those days. Thomas Boswell writes that a typical baseball game "is primarily dead time begging to be condensed. Any game that has more than a dozen key moments is one whale of a game." He might have been describing teaching—except that we have even more dead time. Any school *year* that has more than a dozen key moments is one whale of a year. Like baseball, teaching needs to develop a system for rewarding what Boswell describes as "a phlegmatic stability—a capacity to endure long aggravation and ignore many losses and embarrassments." Have any of the good consultants come up with a checklist to assess a teacher's response to embarrassment and aggravation?

There is, of course, an important difference between teaching and baseball: we teachers usually don't know when we've scored a run. Often we realize only months or years later that something we did might have been important, might have made a difference. Too often, we never know.

This fact was brought home to me a few years ago, when I was asked to write an article on discipline ["There's Only One True Technique for Good Discipline"]. I was singularly unenthusiastic. I don't know anything about discipline and don't care anything about discipline, I told myself. Only my disgust with all the wretched writing on the subject—plus my overweening desire to see my name in print—led me to agree to do the article. And then a fantastic thing began to happen: as I read other people's tomes on discipline, as I began to observe my own classroom routines and recall incidents from past years, fairly clear patterns began to emerge. Not only did I find that I have pretty strong convictions about discipline, but I decided that I had reacted rather well to some difficult circumstances in my own classrooms.

Thus my work as a writer helped me discover my craft as a teacher. But most teachers don't have this luxury. Ordinarily, teachers have neither the time nor the inclination to pause and reflect on what they do day after day, year after year. Maybe they're too tired from dodging missiles launched by the outside hordes. Certainly the system seems to be set up to keep teachers isolated, lonely, and defensive.

My own school district, for example, no longer lets anybody go out of town for professional purposes—not even if they pay their own expenses. No conventions, no seminars, no workshops, no chance to meet other professionals. I can't figure out if the people in charge keep us isolated more because they are scared we will *say* something or scared we will *hear* something. This is not to say that my district is not at the forefront of the excellence movement. Officials bought multiple copies of the report of the National Commission on Excellence in Education and offered them free to any teacher who would write a summary for the board of education. The pity is that we would have learned more about excellence had we been allowed to visit other classrooms right in our own buildings. But no one in charge believes that teachers can learn excellence from other teachers, especially not their own colleagues. Excellence is something that travels 'round the country first-class, on a 747. And if you can't afford first-class excellence, it will eventually be packaged and available by mail. But always, always, words about excellence in your classroom come from somewhere else.

Enough of the phenomenology of excellence. Let's look at specifics. Our august advisors offer us fearful choices: four years of English or ignominy, more science and math or the collapse of the American dream. What the fellows spouting this doom fail to acknowledge is that it matters little if Johnny takes two years of English or six, if his teacher cannot do the job right. If ever an impossible task exists in this land, it is that of the high school English teacher.

To avoid being forced back into a high school English classroom, I fought local administrators, the union, and state certification officials. After sixteen years of teaching and forty-eight graduate credits beyond my M.A. in English, I filled my summer with the dreaded course requirements for primary teachers rather than face *Horace's Compromise* (Theodore Sizer, *Horace's Compromise* [Boston: Houghton Mifflin, 1984]). It is one thing to dream the impossible dream; it is quite another to be overrun by students and curriculum mandates. Until such time as union leaders or district administrators are willing to recognize and admit that merely mortal English teachers, given responsibility for one-hundred-plus students, can do little more than herd the flock, I will find something else to do.

A lot of pompous words are circulating these days about something called scientific literacy, and something else is snowballing along under the name of computer literacy. Writers of the current wave of reports insist that requiring another year of science, another year of math, and a few months of computerese will somehow keep us in the forefront of the technological revolution, insuring a rising GNP, and so on. But does another year of the same old stuff really make sense? Most often, more of the same merely produces more of the same. The prestigious panels seem intent on fostering endurance, not excellence. They count minutes-on-task but ignore crucial questions of content.

Not to mention connections. If those panel members had bothered to talk to students, they would have uncovered a recurring complaint: nothing makes sense. Students don't see how given courses connect, either to their own lives or to other courses. I'm not talking about "relevance" — about teaching biographies of rock stars or cash-register math. I'm talking about showing students that learning can enrich their lives.

A rather rigid sequence of courses makes sense for a student who's headed for Harvard. Surely, however, such phenomena as the complex topics researched by winners of the national science competition and swelling enrollments in Advanced Placement classes attest to the availability of traditional academic challenges for those who are ready to accept them.

But what about the others? Do they really need to sit in more math classes, grinding out more solutions to problems on mortgage interest rates for homes they can no longer afford? Does algebra really teach these students to think? Does the inclined plane hold the secrets of the modern industrial state? I suspect that the number of people whose lives might be enriched by knowing about vectors or studying French is extremely small—smaller by far than the number whose lives might be enriched by listening to Vivaldi. Unfortunately, I did not notice any reports extolling the virtues of Vivaldi in our schools. Art, music, and physical education (as contrasted with brute competition) have traditionally been given short shrift by our educational planners. Maybe this is because what students get out of an art class is less readily available to the scorekeepers. It's hard to know at a glance if national art appreciation is up or down by 1.43 percent in any given year.

I know that science is important. So are music and art and good books and skilled carpentry. Then what is this nonsense about getting rid of high school electives? Since when do U. S. students forfeit individual freedom when they enter the hallowed halls of high school?

I think of my own high school days, when my counselor kept reminding me that home economics was a requirement for graduation and I kept on signing up for music theory—even after they refused to give me any more credit for the course. Just before my senior year, my mother begged me to give in. "All they do in home ec is make white sauce," I complained. She pointed out that I didn't know how to make white sauce, but I took music theory for the fourth time anyway. I was corresponding with professors from across the U. S. on the theoretical necessity for the triple flat, and I could not be bothered with white sauce.

This story has two points. First, despite official requirements, I graduated on schedule. I doubt that most experts on education would have deemed my high school an excellent one, but the people in charge of my school—to their everlasting credit—knew when to look the other way. More important, they allowed me to pursue an interest that had no resale value. Even some of the professors of musicology with whom I was corresponding indicated that they thought it outrageous that a high school curriculum should deal with such esoterica. I didn't bother to explain that my teacher hadn't included triple sharps and triple flats in his lesson plans. In fact, he did not know that they existed. But he introduced me to music theory and honored my desire to travel narrow paths. When he couldn't answer my question about the triple flat, he suggested that I write the letters.

And that is where the important learning took place. I learned that it's okay for a person in charge to admit to not knowing everything; I learned that letters put the wisdom of the world in your mailbox; I learned that experts sometimes disagree. I also learned that the most satisfying learning comes when you do it simply because you want to. The course content doesn't matter. With teacher savvy, student cooperation, and a little luck, such excellence can occur in history class, in biology, in shop—anywhere.

High school should be a time of exploration, of trying on different hats—not a time of cramming oneself into a corporate mold. If Harvard wants its freshmen to have two or three or six years of a foreign language, that's fine. But it's not enough reason to make everyone else take two or three or six years of a foreign language too. The attitudes that students carry away with their diplomas are much more important than their SAT scores. If students can learn how to learn during their first twelve years of school, then anything is possible for them later on, and we teachers can feel that we have done our job. But if all that we give our students is more of the same—discrete facts disconnected from meaning or purpose—then we are in trouble.

We must be ever wary of wasting some youngster's life just because of a dubious notion that a rigorous, regimented curriculum will help restore to the U. S. a better balance of trade. As Nobel-Prize-winning economist Paul Samuelson once noted, man does not live by the GNP alone. At best, the recommendations of the commissions and task forces on school reform are hallucinatory; at worst, they are soul-destroying. Let us teachers not succumb to the temptation of asking what we can do for General Motors; let us continue to ask only what we can do for the children.

On Stir-and-Serve Recipes for Teaching

THE NOTION THAT just about any Joe Blow can walk in off the street and take over a classroom is gaining ground. It makes me nervous. No, more than that: it infuriates me. We should squash once and for all the idea that schools can be adequately staffed by thirty-two bookkeepers and a plumber. The right teacher-proof curriculum is not sufficient; children need real teachers, and real teachers must be trained.

Having sat through more stupid education courses than I wish to recall, I am not altogether comfortable defending schools of education. But I suspect that the blame for worthless courses lies as much with the teachers who take them as with the professors who teach them. As a group, we teachers are intransigently anti-intellectual. We demand from our professors carryout formulae, materials with the immediate applicability of scratch-and-sniff stickers. We are indignant when they try instead to offer ideas to grow on, seeds that we have to nurture in our own gardens.

We teachers frequently complain that education courses do not prepare us for the rigorous, confusing work ahead — that they do not show us how to run our classrooms. We refuse to admit that no course or manual can give us all the help we crave. We should not expect professors to set up our classroom systems, as though each of us were heading out to operate a fast-food franchise. There is no instant, stir-and-serve recipe for running a classroom.

Too often, teachers judge the success of education courses by the weight of the materials they cart away — cute cutouts or "story starters," all ready for immediate use. One popular journal for teachers promises one hundred new ideas in every issue. "You can use them on Monday" is the promise. No one gets rich admitting that genuinely good ideas are hard to come by.

I understand only too well this yearning for the tangible, the usable. We are, after all, members of a profession ruled by pragmatism. People who sit in judgment on us don't ask about our students, "Are they happy? Are they creative? Are they helpful, sensitive, loving? Will they want to read a book next year?" Instead, these people demand, "What are their test scores?"—as if those numbers, though they passeth understanding, will somehow prove that we're doing a good job.

During my first twelve years of teaching I was desperate for new ideas, constantly foraging for schemes with which to engage the children. My frenetic activity was due, in part, to the fact that I was given a different teaching assignment every two years. I figured, "Different children require different methods, different materials." So I would race off to the library or to the arts-and-crafts store. I'd buy another filing cabinet and join another book club for teachers.

But even when I settled in with the same assignment for a six-year stretch, my frenzy did not abate. My classroom became a veritable curriculum warehouse, stuffed with every innovative whiz-bang gizmo I could buy, borrow, or invent. I spent hundreds of hours reading, constructing, laminating. My husband gave up reminding me that I had promised to put the cut-and-paste factory in our living room out of business once I figured out what to teach. When I wasn't inventing projects, I was taking courses: cardboard carpentry, architectural awareness, science process, Cuisenaire rods, Chinese art, test construction and evaluation, curriculum development, and so on. I even took two courses in BASIC computer language. (I thought maybe I'd missed the point in the first course, so I took another—just to be sure.)

I didn't take those courses on whim, any more than I invented curriculum because I had nothing better to do. I chose my courses deliberately, trying to inform my work as a reading teacher. Although I now look back on much of my frenzied search for methods and media as rather naïve, I don't see it as time wasted. I learned a lot. Mostly I learned to simplify. And then to simplify some more.

But the path to simplicity is littered with complexities. And I suspect that it is hard to figure out how to simplify our lives if we haven't cluttered them in the first place. Sure, we teachers clutter up our classrooms with too much claptrap. The fribble is often alluring at first, and it is hard to recognize that the more gadgets we rely on, the poorer we are—at home as well as at school.

People probably always yearn for gadgets, especially if they haven't had much chance to fool around with them. A university research project makes this point rather nicely. The researcher decided to investigate the effects of computer-assisted instruction in English-as-a-second-language (ESL) classes. He set up a computer-taught group and a control group. Both were instructed in ESL for one year. And guess which group had the more positive attitude about computer-assisted instruction at the end of that year? The youngsters who *didn't* get to use the computers.

Not surprisingly, we teachers are compulsive pack rats. Fearing the vagaries of future school budgets, we hoard construction paper until it is old and brittle and unusable. We worry that we may need that paper more next year than we need it today. Have you ever known a teacher who could throw away a set of ditto masters? Or half a game of Scrabble? For years I had a gross of tiny, childproof, left-handed scissors. Childproof scissors are a horror in the first place. Those designed for left-handers are beyond description. Why did I keep them? Hey, they were mine, weren't they?

Most of us never use 80 percent of the materials jammed into our classrooms, but we cling to them "just in case." Because our job is hectic, pressured, stressful, we seldom have a reflective moment to clear our minds, let alone our cupboards. Maybe every teacher should change schools every three years and be allowed to take along only what he or she can carry. However, I must add to this suggestion my own statement of full disclosure: the last time I changed classrooms, after thirteen years in the district, it took six strong men and a truck to transfer my belongings. And that was *after* I had filled two dumpsters.

The good professors must stop yielding to our acquisitive pressures; they must refuse to hand out their one hundred—or even ten—snazzy new ideas for the well-stocked classroom. They must offer fewer methods, fewer recipes. We teachers need *less* practicality, not more. We need to have our lives informed by Tolstoy, Jane Addams, Suzanne Langer, Rudolf Arnheim, and their ilk—not by folks who promise the keys to classroom control and creative bulletin boards, along with one hundred steps to reading success.

We need a sense of purpose from our professors, not a timetable. Better that they show us a way to find our own ways than that they hand out their own detailed maps of the territory. A map isn't of much use to people who don't know where they're headed. The only way to become familiar with the terrain is to explore a little. I nominate the professors to scout ahead, chart the waters, post the quicksand. I know that I still have to climb my own mountain, but I would welcome scholarly advice about the climbing conditions.

Critics of schools of education insist that prospective teachers would profit more from observing good teachers at work than from taking impractical courses on pedagogy. Maybe so. But what are those novices going to see? Is one observation as good as another? After all, a person can look at *Guernica* and not see it, listen to the *Eroica* and not hear it. E. H. Gombrich says that every observation we make is the result of the questions we ask. And where do novices get the questions? How can they ask intelligent questions without knowing something about the subject? Can anyone really *see* a classroom without some theoretical, historical, developmental savvy?

No one enters a classroom as a *tabula rasa*, of course. We all know something about schools because we have, for better or for worse, been there. We know how schools are supposed to be. At least, we think we do. So we judge schools, as we judge anything, with a notion—or schema— of reality in our heads. Most of us don't just look *at* something; we look *for* something, because we have a hypothesis, a hidden agenda. We observe and evaluate with our minds, our memories, our experiences, our linguistic habits. Obviously, the more we know, the more we see.

But teachers cannot walk into classrooms and simply teach what they know. First, they don't know enough. Second, even this seemingly restrictive world—constrained by bells, desks, and textbooks—contains a rich stock of themes from which teachers must choose their own motifs. They must be flexible and inventive enough to modify the schema they carried into their classrooms.

I was one of those people almost literally picked up off a street corner and allowed to teach in New York City under an emergency credential. I walked into the middle of someone else's lesson plan, and, though it didn't take me ten minutes to realize that a round-robin reading of "Paul Revere's Ride" was not going to work, it took me quite a while to come up with something much better.

All I could manage at first was to teach as I had been taught. But as I learned more about the students and about ways to get around the assigned curriculum, a more ideal classroom began to emerge in my head. It remains a shadowy image—one I glimpse and even touch occasionally, but one I have long since stopped trying to file neatly in my planbook. That's okay. The bird seen through the window is more provocative than the one in the cage.

Teaching, like art, is born of a schema. That's why we need the professors with their satchels of theory, as well as our own observations and practice. Those who hope to be effective teachers must recognize that teaching is a craft of careful artifice; the profession requires more than a spontaneous overflow of good intentions or the simple cataloguing and distribution of information. It is possible, I suppose, to have an inborn talent for teaching, but I am sure that those teachers who endure and triumph are *made*—rigorously trained—and not born.

Much of the training must be self-initiated. People who have some nagging notion of the ideal classroom tickling their psyches probably look more for patterns that appeal than for practices that are guaranteed to produce higher standardized test scores. Such teachers probably have a capacity for ambiguity; they look for snippets of familiarity but do not insist on sameness. Such teachers have a greater need for aesthetic and psychological satisfaction than for a neat and tidy cupboard. But they also have a willingness to practice the craft, to try out new brushstrokes, to discard dried-out palettes.

Most of us, children and adults alike, have a strong need to make sense of the disparate elements in our lives, to bring them together, to find patterns, to make meaning. This desire for meaning is so strong that some teachers, tired and defeated by the system, rely on ritual to get them through the day, the week, the year. External order and ritual are the only things they have left to give. And these things usually satisfy the casual observer, who believes that teachers who provide clean and orderly classrooms are providing enough.

This is one reason I want the professors in on the act — out of their ivory towers and into our dusty school corridors. Maybe well-informed people, good observers who are not bogged down by school minutiae, could convince us that a tidy desk is far from enough. The professors need to promote the search for a different order, a subtler pattern — one that lies not in behavioral checklists but rather, to use Chia Yi's words, in constant "combining, scattering, waning, waxing."

It was my own search for pattern that led me to try using science as a way to inform, enhance, and give order to my work as a reading teacher. The children and I were far too familiar with the rituals of remedial reading for those routines to fall much short of torture. I've never understood why students who have trouble with a certain system of decoding should be made to rehearse that system over and over again. A few times over the course of a few years, maybe. But surely there comes a time to try a different approach. Reading had already been ruined for my students by the time they came to me. I needed to see how they approached pedagogic puzzlement, and such puzzlement would never occur if I persisted in making them circle blends on worksheets. That's why I learned how to mess around in science.

Tell a poor reader that it's time to read, and watch the impenetrable curtain of defeat and despair descend. So my students and I spent our time on science. All year. We made cottage cheese, explored surface tension, built bridges, figured out optical illusions. And not once did my students associate experiment cards, books on the theory of sound, or my insistence that observations be recorded in writing with the onerous task that they knew reading to be. Children told me that my room was a good place. Too bad, they added, that I wasn't a real teacher.

That reading room, where children were busily measuring, making — and reading — received full parental support and had its moment in the limelight. There were a lot of visitors. The teachers among them invariably asked, "How did you get this job?" Clearly, they intended to apply for one like it.

Get the job? Only in the first year of my teaching career was I ever handed a job. Ever after, I've made my own. No job of any value can be given out, like a box of chalk. We get the jobs we deserve. Maybe that's why so many teachers are disappointed. They believe all those promises that someone else can do the thinking for them.

I held seven different jobs in my school district, and I earned the right to love every one of them. That's not to say that I didn't have plenty of moments of anger and frustration. But I also experienced deep satisfaction.

Because my seven jobs required some pretty dramatic shifts in grade level, people were always asking me, "Where is it better — high school or the primary grades?" It's a question I have never been able to answer, mainly because the more grade levels I taught, the more similarities I saw. Sure, high school dropouts enrolled in an alternative program are harder to tune in to the beauty of a poem than are seventh graders. Third graders cry more, talk more; seventh graders scale more heights and sink into deeper pits. But a common thread runs throughout, and it was that thread I clung to.

Maybe I see this sameness because my teaching is dominated less by skill than by idea — the secret, elusive form. I have a hard time reading other people's prescriptions, let alone writing my own. I always figure that if you can get the idea right the specific skill will come. Teaching is too personal, even too metaphysical, to be charted like the daily temperature. Teaching is like a Chinese lyric painting, not a bus schedule.

We need to look very closely at just who is calling for "the upgrading of teacher skills," lest this turn out to be the clarion call of those folks with something to sell. The world does not come to us in neat little packages. Even if we could identify just what a *skill* is, does *more* definitely denote *better?* What profiteth a child whose teacher has gathered up an immense pile of pishposh? We must take care lest the examiners who claim they can dissect and label the educational process leave us holding a bag of gizzards.

We teachers must recognize that we do not need the behaviorist-competency thugs to chart our course. For us, reality is a feeling state, details of daily routine fade, and what remains is atmosphere, tone, emotion. The ages and the talents of the children become irrelevant. What counts is attitude and endeavor. That's why, even when we try, we often can't pass on a terrific lesson plan to a friend; we probably can't even save it for ourselves to use again next year. It's virtually impossible to teach the same lesson twice.

I'm afraid that all of this sounds rather dim, maybe even dubious. But this is where the professors might step in. There are so many outrageous examples of bad pedagogy that it's easy to overlook the good—easy, but not excusable. The professors need to shape up their own schools of education first—getting rid of Papercutting 306, even if it's the most profitable course in the summer school catalogue. Then they need to get out in the field to work with student teachers, principals, and children.

Is it outrageous to think that the professors might even pop into the classrooms of veteran teachers now and then? Wouldn't it be something if their research occasionally involved real children and real teachers (and if they had to face bells, mandated tests, bake sales, and field trips to mess up their carefully laid plans) instead of four children in a lab staffed by sixty-three graduate students? That's probably a scary thought for some professors.

I know of one school of education that relegates the observation and direction of student teachers to the local school district. The district, in turn, passes this responsibility on to an administrator who has never taught. In such a situation, pedagogy gets turned upside down and inside out. The outcome is empty platitudes, not effective classroom practice. The student teacher, who is paying for expert training, is being defrauded. The children are being cheated. The system is stupid and immoral. We need teacher trainers who know educational theory and who are savvy about children. Those professors who won't help us should be replaced by ones who will.

But aspiring teachers have a responsibility too. They must heed the advice of Confucius:

> If a man won't try, I will not teach him; if a man makes no effort, I will not help him. I show one corner, and if a man cannot find the other three, I am not going to repeat myself.

We teachers must stop asking the education professors for the whole house. I know plenty of teachers who are disappointed, indignant, and eventually destroyed by the fact that nobody has handed them all four corners. But the best we can expect from any program of courses or training is the jagged edge of one corner. Then it is up to us to read the research and to collaborate with the children to find the other three corners. And, because teaching must be a renewable contract, if we don't keep seeking new understanding we'll find that the corners we thought we knew very well will keep slipping away. There are constant subtle shifts in the schoolroom. One can never be sure of knowing the floor plan forever and ever.

In trying to renew my faith in myself as a teacher, I find little help in the "how-to" books, those nasty little tomes that define learning in eighty-seven steps. I like to think of learning as a wave that washes over the learner, rather than as a series of incremental hurdles to be pre- and post-tested. I reject *How to Teach Reading in 100 Lessons*, relying instead on *The Mustard Seed Garden Manual of Painting*, which advises that "neither complexity in itself nor simplicity is enough" — nor dexterity alone nor conscientiousness. "To be without method is worse."

What can we do? What is the solution? In painting, there is an answer: "Study 10,000 volumes and walk 10,000 miles." One more thing is required of teachers. We must also work with 10,000 children.

'Just the Facts, Ma'am': Tests vs. Intuition

MY CAT WAS driving me nuts. After five years of impeccable personal habits, he stopped using the litter box. Before facing the ultimate decision of choosing between husband and pet, I lugged the (four-legged) beast off to the vet's. The vet looked into the cat's ears, stroked his own chin, and said, "Well, it's hard to tell about these things. It could be behavioral or it could be medical. Let's wait and see." For that, the vet charged me seventeen bucks and advised me to have a good day. It's called professional services.

Would that we teachers had that kind of chutzpah. Or is it, rather, the confidence to admit there are certain things we cannot know, not right this minute anyway? We need the courage to say that we and the children need some wait-and-see time before passing judgment. If the vet hadn't been confident in what he did know, he could have given me a stack of computer printouts showing my cat's age, heart rate, reflexes, and so on. If he had really wanted to snow me, I guess he'd have shown me how the length of my cat's tail compared with those of other felines around the country. And I might have been so impressed by all those numbers that I'd have forgotten that the cat was still not using the litter box.

Americans love information, but it's one thing to play silly games in your own living room and quite another to allow children's academic lives to be taken over by the national mania for trivial and tedious factification. In resigning ourselves to keeping track of each child's so-called skills pretty much the way handicappers figure the horses, we must be wary that we don't lose faith in our own observations, our own intuition. We must ask ourselves just what we know when we know a student tests out as a 3.2, and if we know something different when that number is 2.8 or 3.6. We must remind ourselves that as teachers we come to know quite a lot about the students in our charge—long before we look at the test results.

If knowledge is to develop into understanding, it will be not as a result of standardized-test scores, but as a result of teacher observations, our ability to sort information, our sensitivity, tenacity, and plain old savvy. Most important of all is the teacher's ability to wait, to stand back and watch children—nudging and prodding, yes, but mostly giving them the time and space to grow, and having the faith they will.

But these days teachers are being pushed for judgments, instant assessments, precise placements. No longer can we admit that "Johnny's failure to complete assigned tasks could mean he's immature, or it could mean he's lazy, or it could mean he's thinking about more important things." No, that kind of waffling must go. It bespeaks an indecisiveness and even an ignorance that is positively, absolutely unprofessional. These days teachers are running scared; we feel compelled to pretend that what we do is more science than art and intuition. When asked about the children in our charge, we feel compelled to offer numbers, not opinions or anecdotes.

Joseph Featherstone, an astute observer of schools, once wrote: "Our schools assume the worst of teachers as well as children." This is probably why school districts give an average of seven standardized tests a year. The financial burden for all this testing is $100 million; nobody has tried to measure the psychic burden.

Our politicians and education bureaucrats are working hard to eliminate the vagaries of teacher judgment by making standardized testing and accountability and excellence synonymous. They refuse to recognize that much of the important matter in schoolrooms can't be ticked off in *a, b, c,* or *d* choices. A former head of the Educational Testing Service once listed the virtues of standardized tests: accuracy, objectivity, comparability. Standardized tests, he said, measure "sheer accomplishment." That ponderous term has a decisive ring. We can only wish we knew what it meant.

One of my students did not score at grade level on the standardized test at the end of the year. Does this mean that in terms of "sheer accomplishment" she and I failed the year? It was Leslie's first time in public school, and I would rate her accomplishment as nothing short of miraculous. Severely hearing-impaired, she had been educated in a very restrictive environment before she entered my third-grade class. The adjustment was very difficult—for Leslie, for her parents, and for her teachers. I've lost track of the number of hysterical scenes I took part in, both in the classroom and in the faculty room.

But Leslie learned to work and play (and fight) with other children; she learned to conform to school rules, to adapt to varying demands from various adults; she made notable progress in that crucial area nobody can measure quantitatively: learning how to learn. She learned not to be scared of new things, to jump right in and give it a try. One of the high points of the year came when, after many attempts and many failures, Leslie read a knock-knock joke to the class—with the emphasis in the right place. Anybody who thinks this was a small achievement should have seen the tears of joy streaming down her face (and mine) as she exclaimed, "I get it! I really get it! Let me read another one!" Doubting quantifiers should have heard her classmates cheering.

Such triumphs, alas, are not objective or comparable or provable. They won't appear on anybody's standardized norms or be presented to the board of education in neat little graphs to attest to the fact that I did a good job that year. What does appear on the computer printouts and the graphs is the bare, cold fact that Leslie scored six months below the magic grade-level number. Never mind that I trained her to stick with a book, to read silently for an hour each morning. Forget that this deaf child memorized poems and recited them for the principal, that she took the leading role in a play performed in front of her seventy-five third-grade peers, that she learned the value of sending people personal notes, sharing in their pain and their joy. The only thing entered on Leslie's permanent-record card is her standardized-test score.

Value, for a McDonald's customer, is a predictable, standardized product. We in education had better stop trying to pretend that we, too, can deliver a streamlined product, one that is capable of being mass-produced and mass-judged. Ours is not a neat and tidy calling. The schoolroom is full of smeary surfaces and dark, hidden depths. We can't reduce what we do to multiple-choice answers; and we shouldn't let other people try. We need to remind the politicians and the professors and the test makers that the important things we do with children are not instantly available in some sort of automatic, pop-up, pull-out, stick-on score. Bureaucrats don't like ambiguity, and so they go for the quantitative knockout punch. No anecdotes, please. Just the facts, ma'am. But as teachers, all we have are our anecdotes.

David Hawkins, philosopher as well as practitioner of education, reminds us that the teacher who is skillful at observation can tell you a great deal that's quite important about a child; she can show you how children really are.

Bureaucrats demur: "Well, we'd like to try some sort of anecdotal system of evaluation, but it just isn't practical." Hawkins answers, "Nonsense! In thinking, the important question is whether it's true or not, not whether it's practical." That is ever the question we must ask of all manner of testing. Don't tell us whether it's practical or efficient; tell us instead whether it's true.

And my cat? I fed him pills and I tickled him under the chin and pleaded with him to mend his wicked ways. Finally, I got him a new litter box, brown instead of blue. And the cat started using it. So the vet was right: it was either behavioral or medical. Mostly, it was a mystery.

Testy Thoughts of May

T. S. ELIOT wrote that April is the cruelest month, but he probably never took a standardized test. I think the evil month is May.

May, after all, is for Measurement. Don't tell me that Chaucer compared his "parfit gentil knight" to the fresh month of May or that Shakespeare penned love sonnets about those darling buds of the same month. They didn't do it with #2 pencils.

I admit to having a built-in antipathy for #2 pencils long before I ever sat behind a teacher's desk. They cut short the life of Henry David Thoreau, didn't they? Henry David followed in his father's footsteps as a pencil maker early in life and then died of weak lungs before his prime. Nobody will ever convince me those pencils didn't have something to do with it.

It's as clear as the water in Walden Pond used to be that questions requiring answers with #2 pencils are killing our curriculum. We used to be able to take the tests in stride. One day of testing in the spring did little harm, and a teacher got to know how her students rated in comparison with other kids across the nation — on that one test. But now that outsiders — professors and politicians and Rotarians and TV anchorpersons and numerous other excellence-in-education parvenus — have deemed the test an absolute measure of the child, there's trouble in River City. And elsewhere.

Nowadays standardized testing isn't limited to one day in May. Nowadays we must *get ready* for the test. I know of classes where the sole curriculum is drilling children for the spring achievement test. And English classes that devote one day a week to practicing for the PSATs. For that matter, PSAT practice is no longer limited to high school. It has filtered down to sixth grade — and even lower.

Teachers don't talk much about this *pre*testing. The months of practice. The substitutions in curriculum. We teach rounding off to third graders and plot and setting to fourth graders, for example, not because we think they're ready for it but because we know it's *on the test.*

Pretesting is one of those nasty little secrets we'd prefer not to think about. But everybody feels the pressure, and by October there's hardly a teacher in the land who doesn't select her material with at least one eye on the dreaded test coming up in May.

The fault is not so much with the test makers as it is with the folks who haven't been inside a classroom since they outgrew pimples. They're the ones who make a fast buck with their traveling road shows decrying the decline and fall of American education. They use standardized test results as proof positive that teachers are ignorant, students are illiterate, and the country in general is going to the dogs. These educational sharp-shooters insist that test scores are the sole judge of the worth of the kids, the teachers, the school, the community, the nation. After all, they warn us, the Japanese are selling more and more cars these days. And Japanese fifth graders scored higher on a standardized math test than did their American counterparts. Forget Z Theory and Circles of Excellence and Japanese salarymen and import quotas. The reason the Japanese are beating the socks off us in the balance of trade is those fifth-grade test scores. Or so claim the roving band of consultants.

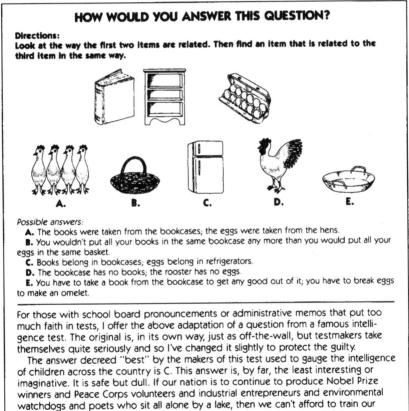

HOW WOULD YOU ANSWER THIS QUESTION?

Directions:
Look at the way the first two items are related. Then find an item that is related to the third item in the same way.

A. B. C. D. E.

Possible answers:
   A. The books were taken from the bookcases; the eggs were taken from the hens.
   B. You wouldn't put all your books in the same bookcase any more than you would put all your eggs in the same basket.
   C. Books belong in bookcases; eggs belong in refrigerators.
   D. The bookcase has no books; the rooster has no eggs.
   E. You have to take a book from the bookcase to get any good out of it; you have to break eggs to make an omelet.

For those with school board pronouncements or administrative memos that put too much faith in tests, I offer the above adaptation of a question from a famous intelligence test. The original is, in its own way, just as off-the-wall, but testmakers take themselves quite seriously and so I've changed it slightly to protect the guilty.
   The answer decreed "best" by the makers of this test used to gauge the intelligence of children across the country is C. This answer is, by far, the least interesting or imaginative. It is safe but dull. If our nation is to continue to produce Nobel Prize winners and Peace Corps volunteers and industrial entrepreneurs and environmental watchdogs and poets who sit all alone by a lake, then we can't afford to train our youth that this is the best answer. No matter what the experts say.—*S.O.*

JEAN GARDNER

Why do teachers sit still for such hogwash? We could just as well blame our negative balance of trade on the divorce rate, the ozone layer, or the consumption of Twinkies. If Detroit wants to sell more cars, they should stop pointing their fingers at schoolteachers, tighten their belts, and build better cars. This country has a long tradition of education for everybody, a tradition not to be sacrificed for the sake of looking good on somebody else's graph. Our tradition of tolerating the eccentric and encouraging the creative shouldn't have to boost the Dow Jones average to prove its merit. We teachers accept and even savor the responsibility of guiding the intellectual, social, and moral growth of students. That's plenty. We must reject responsibility — and blame — for any troubles of the Fortune 500.

The first standardized test I ever administered was a measure of reading readiness. Inner-city kindergartners trying to gain admission to first grade were asked to identify pine trees, ferns, and bamboo. Someone undoubtedly had ascertained that Phi Beta Kappas at Harvard knew about such things, so bamboo became the measure of potential scholastic success.

The temptation is always there to cover the type of material and the style of questioning children will encounter on the test. The teacher is ever in a quandary; there's only so much time in the day, and any coaching for tests must drive out other curriculum. So what price are we paying for our students' test savvy? More important, what price are the students ultimately paying?

Standardized testing can be helpful — within limits. But the classroom teacher must impose those limits, not allowing tests or experts or media hoopla to push the individualism, the spark, even the tolerance for whackiness out of her curriculum. Remember, one failure by all measurable school standards turned out to be Thomas Edison. Another was Albert Einstein. We can never know for sure who our students will turn out to be.

Not-So-Super Superintendents

THE 121ST CONVENTION of the American Association of School Administrators (AASA) in Orlando, Florida, had it all: appearances by Mickey Mouse and Shamu, racist jokes by one keynote speaker, and imitations of a cerebral palsy victim by another. For the 122d convention, in San Francisco, the cast of characters changed slightly, but the message remained clear: If you want to get school administrators into the convention hall, you'd better have a sports figure. In 1989, George Steinbrenner; in 1990, Roger Staubach.

For card-carrying AASA members, the convention fee is $280, for nonmembers it's $380. Not that the prices mean much to the attendees — they're on the expense account all the way. To help justify that, the AASA calls the fee *tuition*.

When I phoned AASA headquarters for help in finding accommodations, a very pleasant person asked me if I wanted an inexpensive, moderate, or quality room. When I replied, "As cheap as possible," she sighed. "That's good. We're running out of the deluxe — $150 and up." When I expressed surprise, she let down her hair and said, "You should hear these guys. They phone up and say, 'I don't want to be stuck in some dump like the Radisson.'" Laughing, she said, "Who do they think they're kidding? Do you think they'd stay in a place as nice as the Radisson if it was coming out of their own pockets?"

For seventy dollars you can get a one-day pass into the AASA exhibition hall, a stunning sight for a first-time visitor. When I walk into a room filled with buses and bleachers, I figure I'm in the wrong place and start to leave. Then I realize the buses are yellow, so I look around some more. I get so caught up in the stainless-steel recessed handles for lockers (in sixteen designer colors), circuit-training obstacle courses, and toilet paper dispensers promising 50 percent savings on tissue consumption, that it takes me quite a while to realize there are almost no books in the place.

Of the more than 250 exhibitors showing their wares, 53 are selling athletic equipment, bleachers, and gymnasium maintenance products; there are just 3 companies selling textbooks. Now that's not surprising, since superintendents don't choose schoolbooks — that's usually done by teacher committees — but one look around the exhibition hall makes it clear that basketball salesmen think superintendents care a lot about basketballs.

221

On the other hand, *Cliffs Notes* is here. Judging by the "Exhibitor's Directory," AASA must believe *Cliffs Notes* does it all. The company's products are mentioned under Books, Magazines & Periodicals, Curricular Materials, Reference Books, Teaching Aids & Materials, and Textbooks.

License to Sell

The AASA convention is a cheerful place. The seventeen thousand-plus administrators gathered here seem to be having a whole lot of fun looking at synthetic turf, choral risers, preportioned school lunches, cast vinyl multipurpose sport flooring, wrestling-mat holders, and electronic scoreboards.

But does any of this explain why a teacher must obtain a special license to be an administrator? Are there graduate courses in trench drain specifications? Courses in how to choose an intercom system? Lab classes providing training on selecting basketballs, file cabinets, and venetian blinds? Has anybody ever questioned why a school district needs to send its leader to Florida one year and San Francisco the next to look at toilet paper dispensers?

Somebody has to choose this stuff, you say. But should school districts be paying that somebody eighty thousand dollars a year—to select basketballs?

An examination of the "Job Bulletin" section of the AASA newspaper, *Leadership News*, raises certain questions about just what districts expect from their superintendents. The qualifications listed most often in job ads are "administrative experience" and "doctorate preferred." Despite superintendents' pivotal roles, I came across only one ad that asked for "thorough knowledge of curriculum/instruction, current research, and human growth development."

Scanning these listings reminded me of an interview I once had with a district superintendent for a job teaching remedial reading to inner-city seventh graders. The superintendent satisfied himself as to my qualifications by my affirmative reply to his question, "Would you be willing to teach colored kiddos?" Then he got down to important matters: deciding where I should be placed on the salary scale. It didn't faze him that my master's degree was in medieval literature or that I'd never had a course in how to teach reading.

As a longtime teacher, I am struck by how much higher the stakes are at AASA conventions than at the meetings designed for teachers. At the main annual meeting for reading teachers, educational consultant Lee Canter hawks his assertive discipline teacher guides for $7.95. But at the AASA convention, Canter's selling his video package, *Assertive Discipline for Bus Drivers*—for $349. There's also *The Caring Administrator Positive Resource Guide,* containing samples of such essentials as notices for teacher appreciation day, acknowledgment of a faculty member's marriage, and so forth. Price tag: $49.95.

The line between information and promotion—hazy enough in the AASA program of events, where many of the speakers billed as "Distinguished Lecturers" promote their commercial videos and training programs from the lectern—is completely obliterated in the exhibition hall, where many of the featured speakers set up booths, selling their services as consultants.

And it doesn't seem to hurt a superintendent's standing as an AASA featured speaker and consultant to have been run out of town. After failing to have any positive effect on the disastrous state of the Chicago system, Ruth Love was let go from her job as superintendent of schools there. But she is a staple on AASA programs. Her presentation at Orlando is definitely hard sell. After she acknowledges her introduction as a noted educational leader, Love says, "I can't be every place at once, so I have developed videos which are available to school districts." For those conventioneers unable to attend, Love's lecture is also available on tape cassettes. People who buy the tape get to hear an audio of Ruth Love's video.

Inside the exhibition hall, I'm pushed away from my examination of hardwood floors and U. S. Navy Recruiting Command booklets by people rushing from booth to booth exclaiming, "Got any stickers?" In general, they don't seem to care about the wares the booth's displaying. They just grab their stickers and rush on to the next booth with the same question, "Got any stickers?" I finally found out what was behind the sticker frenzy: conventioneers who fill a certain card with stickers win the right to participate in a drawing for a free trip to the next convention—not of much direct use to administrators since the district pays their way, but of great use to spouses, who attend AASA conventions in large numbers. And just think—at that next convention, the lucky winner could fill another card with stickers. . . .

Guns and Rodents

Even so, the most popular booth here is not the one giving out the most stickers. It's not even the one giving away Coca-Cola. American Air Filter draws the biggest crowd every day with a carnival-style barker who demonstrates the old find-the-peanut-under-the-shell con game.

And yes, the National Rifle Association is here too. Noting that "with the roles of society changing, educators have found it necessary to establish programs that satisfy the need for lifetime activities which provide enjoyment, relaxation, fulfillment, and meaning," the NRA proposes that schools should institute shooting sports education programs. To this end, the NRA offers an across-the-curriculum guide for integrating shooting sports into the education process. "With a little imagination," states the guide, the teacher "can link some aspect of shooting with almost every subject taught in our nation's schools."

I wondered if it was only coincidental that the convention was held during National Frozen Food Month. Eating certainly is at the forefront of convention activities, with *food functions* sponsored by everyone from the American Desk Manufacturing Company to Control Data Corporation to the Kansas Association of School Administrators to the Women's Caucus.

But AASA conventions are not just display booths and food extravaganzas. There are also five days of speeches. I guess I wasn't really surprised to see the first general session kicked off by the Magic Kingdom's royal couple, Mickey and Minnie Mouse. This is, after all, Orlando. (There's an entertainment prelude to each general session; later we're treated to the Singing Superintendents joining their voices in "Climb Every Mountain.") After the rodent pair dances a jig and does a spiel hyping the educational benefits of Disney World, the AASA president delivers a message I hear repeated throughout my five days: "We've had too much criticism. We have the greatest public education system in the world." Applause. Applause.

Huge video screens dominate the front of the hall, so you can watch the real thing on stage or the larger-than-life video representations. The audience rises to sing "The Star Spangled Banner," to recite the Pledge of Allegiance, and to hear an invocation. The executive committee of the AASA is introduced. Each committee member and spouse walks on stage hand-in-hand, the woman of the pair carrying a bouquet of flowers. First-time convention attendees are asked to stand and are entreated to strive for the twenty-five-year attendance pin.

Play Ball

And then comes the star attraction: introduced as a business man, a fierce competitor, a man who dearly loves our great country and supports our political system, a vice president of the Olympic Committee, the 1977 baseball Executive of the Year, and "great lover of young people"— George Steinbrenner.

Steinbrenner tells his AASA audience that he recently advised officials at his alma mater, Williams College, "Honor the student like me—the C-, D+ student. Someday I will return here and give you a new chemistry building."

The owner of the New York Yankees goes on to brag about his fines for being a loudmouth—"more than all my players put together—$425,000." He says that when he bought the Yankees, they were such a sorry lot. "The team picture looked like a poster for birth control." Such remarks play to a receptive house. When Steinbrenner delivers the tasteless, racist remark that "Sanchez was so lazy he thought manual labor was the president of his country," the crowd of educators roars in delight.

Then George Steinbrenner looks directly at this audience of several thousand and says, "I love teaching. Nothing is more important to me than education." America's school superintendents sop this up. They believe him, not noticing that later in his remarks he admits that he ranks breathing No. 1 and winning No. 2. And the superintendents vigorously applaud his message of keeping our foreign aid at home instead of sending it to other nations, "some of whom burn our flags. Let's keep it here and take care of our young. There's something wrong about giving it to other nations."

The audience clearly loves this beefy despot who can stand there and brag, "I do it my way"—a man who has fired sixteen managers. He was, after all, speaking to a group that knows how tough it is to get rid of just one troublesome teacher. People whose big decisions ordinarily focus on preportioned school lunches love listening to this paunchy peacock drop the names of his industrialist friends—the fellows who, he tells us, share his $120 lunches at Twenty-One.

"The most important people in this nation today are not politicians or industrialists," Steinbrenner then intones, "they are educators." Applause. Applause. When Steinbrenner adds, "You are the chosen few," they applaud again. They give him a standing ovation.

Immediately following Steinbrenner on the program is the announcement of the Superintendent of the Year. Although the master of ceremonies insists that "the suspense builds" to learn the name of the distinguished winner, hundreds of superintendents jam the aisles trying to get to the exit. Superintendents came to hear Steinbrenner the celebrity, not one of their own. And they don't care that a consultant named Zacharie J. Clemens is a featured speaker.

Clemens starts off his speech by saying "how downright awesome" it feels "to have the opportunity to address the CEOs of America's schools." Boy, do superintendents like being referred to as CEOs.

Clemens tells lots of ethnic jokes and speaks in various dialects to portray uplifting conversations he's had with everyone from superintendents to crippled children in hospital wards. He imitates the pronunciation of a person with a serious speech defect and of a child with severe cerebral palsy. He informs his audience that he knows a lot about difficult students—like Big Brenda, with her 44W bosoms, and another kid with "his fly down and his underpants in his back pocket." Using a high, squeaky, mincing tone, he quotes a first grader: "Sex education—first, you gotta avoid intersections, and second you gotta buy condominiums." Applause. Applause.

Afterward, members of the AASA audience rush forward to tell Clemens how moved they were by his performance, especially that cerebral palsy kid.

The next general session speaker, Theodore Sizer, author of *Horace's Compromise* and chairman of the Coalition of Essential Schools, does not pack the celebrity draw of George Steinbrenner or attempt the pull-at-the-heartstrings of Zacharie Clemens. After all, Sizer really is working full-time to fix America's schools. But unfortunately, the convention format takes its toll on him too. He opens with a joke about Wade Boggs' sex life that falls flat. And it doesn't help any that he has a plane to catch. As a result, his presentation is minimal, and he doesn't even stay for the ensuing panel discussion organized around it. All in all, a pretty shoddy appearance—but maybe Sizer was the only one here who gave the AASA meeting the time it was really worth. I figure that, even counting the drive to and from the airport, he must not have been in Orlando for much more than an hour.

What Makes Whittle Qualified to Do High School TV News?

THE NEW YORK STATE board of regents has again rejected Whittle Communications' request to bring Channel One, its twelve-minute news show enhanced by two minutes of commercials, to high school students.

The *New York Times*, ivory-tower sages, and assorted legislators are anxious to let Channel One into the schools, citing the big payoff: Whittle gives fifty-thousand dollars worth of TV equipment to cooperating schools.

Back in 1989, just before the regents voted for the first time on this question, Chris Whittle addressed them in three full-page ads in the *New York Times*. The *Times* showed uncommon courtesy, giving Whittle op-ed space to explain his position further. The day after his third ad, the *Times* gave his project a fifty-line (plus headline) editorial endorsement.

Whittle claimed that dissenting teachers were against his plan because we aren't "primarily concerned with the welfare of students." Whittle insists we teachers are fighting against the "innovation" offered by him and his cohorts because we care only about "maintaining [our] monopoly on the educational process." Whittle's fellow innovators are, of course, the makers of acne cream, designer sneakers, candy bars, soft drinks, and automobiles, who buy ads on his shows.

But for me the advertisements are not the issue. I'm very disappointed that even those groups such as the Parent Teacher Association and the National Education Association, who are vocal against letting advertisements usurp classroom time, have been singularly silent on the content of Whittle's whiz-bang news show. Just as there are 613 varieties of popcorn available to the consumer, there are also news shows and news shows. Caveat emptor. We had better look long and hard at whose news show we will permit to eat up great chunks of our instructional time.

Nobody has pointed out that high school teachers who let Whittle — or anyone else — into their classroom are not yielding a mere twelve minutes from a six-hour day; they are giving up twelve minutes of a fifty-minute social studies period. That adds up to 24 percent of their instructional time with those students.

None of this bothers the *New York Times* editorial writers, ivory-tower sages, and legislators. In an editorial urging the regents to accept the news program, the *Times* said, "expensive video technology . . . can deliver quality educational programming to classrooms." I've been hearing that same spiel for nearly three decades now. The fact that it is a technological promise that has never been delivered is, however, not the question.

The real question is whether we can give Whittle Communications carte blanche on 24 percent of our instructional time. I wonder why I don't hear anybody asking for Whittle Communications' curriculum vitae. Just what are their qualifications for analyzing, synthesizing, and reporting world affairs? What does Whittle Communications know about adolescent psychology? Cognitive development? Learning styles? Shouldn't we demand some answers before we let Whittle's curriculum — or anybody else's — into our classrooms?

None of the pundits even hint about the content of the Channel One news show. Anyone who does see it cannot fail to recognize it as the progeny of a back-street liaison between Trivial Pursuit and *A Current Affair*, a snappy mixture of popular culture star-worship, world events, and consumerism. Whittle's show is no worse than what kids already see on television, but it isn't any better, either. I have based a twenty-year teaching career on the premise that I have the obligation to offer a creative alternative to the glut of shoddy TV my students see at home.

Of course the content of Channel One has never been the issue for its supporters. They concede that the only reason to let this whiz-biz news show into classrooms is to gain the promised payoff. Fifty thousand bucks ain't peanuts, no siree, Mabel. This is, after all, the American way: You pay your money and you get your banana. But if the keepers of the schoolhouse are going to sell themselves so cheaply, I wonder how they will react when the National Rifle Association, Greenpeace, the Palestine Liberation Organization, Planned Parenthood, Daughters of the American Revolution, The Flat Earth Society, The Gay Alliance, vivisectionists, vegetarians, Rotarians, Rosicrucians, Scientologists, or the local skinheads show up at the schoolhouse door with fifty-thousand dollars and a curriculum to save America.

I am appalled that members of the media, the universities, and legislature once again put so little value on education, urging teachers to give up 24 percent of our instructional time for a few bright baubles. Instead of warning us about Roman bread and circuses, these pundits act as barkers for the show. And next week they'll be back to make proclamations on the erosion of teenage ethics.

Contrary to Whittle's claims, no video will help our youth be better citizens. We will help our youth to become good citizens not by exhortation but by demonstration. We adults must provide good models; we must live good lives. In an era of congressional payoffs, savings-and-loan scandals, big business stealing apple juice from the mouths of babies, we teachers must not sell ourselves short. We must stand up and be counted. We must take responsibility for the content of the courses we teach. We must just say no to Cracker Jack prizes.

Inside Classroom Structures

In order to get an emergency teaching license in New York City twenty-five years ago, I had to take an education methods course in which the professor demonstrated how to pass out paper. At first I thought it was a joke. Not being experienced in educationese, I was not aware that professors of education did not kid around. Insisting that this paper parceling was the make-or-break principle on which a new teacher's success might well rest, the good professor became upset when he discovered that not only were some of us in the back of the room giggling but also we had moved our chairs out of alignment. Muttering about the need for straight rows, he insisted that we get in line so he could proceed with his demonstration.

Only a person who has never taken a methods course would ask, as did my husband, if that story is true. Not only is it true, it's not even my best teacher-training story. At that same college a professor would not dismiss his class when a fire alarm went off because (1) he didn't smell smoke and (2) the class was taking an exam and he was afraid he couldn't control collusion if he let them out of the room. Anyway, I don't know how to write fiction; the great thing about education commentary is that you never have to make anything up.

I confess that although I am meticulous about fire alarms in my own career, I've never been much good at efficiency: paper distribution and record keeping and time-on-task have pretty much eluded me for the past twenty-odd years. Nonetheless, when I say I'm not a straight-row teacher, I'm not talking about where I put the chairs. I've taught where student desks were bolted down in neat and tidy rows and I've taught where the students and I bought a big red velvet sofa at the Salvation Army store. It matters not; I don't measure my worth by how many times I get the kids sitting in a circle. William Blake reminds us, "A fool sees not the same tree that a wise man sees." No place is this more true than in the classroom. One of the most retrogressive principals I know harangues teachers she catches sitting at their desks, as though being on your feet were equivalent to being on your toes. Classroom structures that really count are internal, not only hidden from the casual eye but also hidden too often from our own selves. We grow so accustomed to being judged on our external structures that we forget to nurture our inner selves, to build on our own foundations. And once we lose faith in our own best instincts, then all we can do is worry about where to put the chairs; we start relying on somebody else's notion of good books. Everything about this insecure calling we call teaching teases and tempts us to tack on one more addition from somebody else's floor plan.

Structures. The word itself has come to be synonymous for me with teacherliness. I'd been teaching what we used to call remedial reading for a couple of years when I stumbled across an Elementary Science Study (ESS) manual called *Structures.* That forty-seven-page guide wiped remedial reading out of my life and changed my very notion of what a teacher is. "Why don't we help these kids find a reason to read?" I asked my boss, who recognized — and supported — a revolution when he saw one. Fortunately, we were moving into a new building, and at the same time I scrapped the contents of the remedial-reading lab, I also wiped out labels and timetables. I announced that henceforth I was a media-resource teacher. I thought I'd invented a new term, one carrying no negative baggage. I wanted people to associate me with the library and in those days we'd never heard of the *resource room.* Because we needed to collect the Title funds New York State provided, I was still a reading teacher on the books but nobody told the kids. Teachers had a list of children who, by law, had to meet with me for the required contact hours per week. But because I opened my door to everybody in the school, no child had a label. All children who could persuade their teachers to let them out of the room were welcome to come to my room for as long as they needed. "Gifted" children showed up right alongside the not-so-gifted, and the students formed remarkable cross-age, mixed-ability partnerships. Because we ignored the bells, children weren't interrupted; they had the time they needed for messing around and making discoveries. Daryll, a boy repeating first grade whose official records labeled him as having "short attention span, difficulty sticking to a task," for example, worked for three hours straight on his proof that sixteen bottle caps on one side of a balance beam weighed the same as sixteen bottle caps on the other side. He set up this proof and then tested it and tested it and tested it. I did not go near him during the entire three hours. His moment of realization was private but profound. Just to make sure, he came back two days later and weighed those bottle caps one more time.

Parents heard so much about the messing around that they asked if they could hold a PTA meeting in my classroom. They didn't want a slide show of our projects; they wanted to come and mess around themselves. And they did.

People cringe when they hear of upward of thirty children scattered all over a room doing different things. "Where's the structure? The accountability?" are questions I'm often asked. In point of fact, it's much easier to recognize—and account for—what's happening with children involved in twenty-five individual projects than to figure out the significances when twenty-five children work through the same ditto sheet. Or read the same novel.

A crowded room filled with children messing around is in my mind's eye forever. Several children were working on *Structures*. They had contests to see who could build the strongest clay bridge, the highest tower of straws. They watched a film I'd borrowed from the Rensselaer Polytechnic Institute physics department about a bridge collapsing because of wind resonance. They loved that film, watching it over and over. (The PTA also asked to see that film their children talked about nonstop.)

Jeannie, a fifth grader, was not involved in *Structures*. When she wasn't helping a third grader construct a dinosaur mobile, she was working on her own sound experiments. But so much of our learning is sideways. Although students were held responsible for keeping project notebooks, they were free to "waste time," to nose around other kids' projects. Jeannie watched the bridge film half a dozen times and then commented, "Isn't that like the rice experiment?" I still get chills when I recall that moment. Weeks before, Jeannie had taken an oatmeal carton, cut a hole in the side, stretched tissue paper over the top, and put grains of rice on the paper. She noted that when some children shouted into the hole, the rice jumped. Other voices could not make the rice jump. The experiment card directed her to readings that explained how the frequency of some sounds matched the natural frequency at which the air in the box vibrated, causing the rice to jump. Jeannie must have had fifty-three kids shout into her carton before she wrote up the experiment. Weeks later, she was prepared to make the intellectual leap associating the convoluting bridge with the jumping rice. Jeannie needed the shouting and its attendant tomfoolery; she needed the repetition; she needed the freedom and the space to explore, to play, to work—in preparation for that impressive intellectual leap. And what *was* she doing, anyway? Was it science? reading? writing? math? Was it gifted? remedial? cooperative? solitary? Does it matter?

People traveled from other cities to see that classroom; the state education department gave me a couple of awards; the library school gave me money; an official at the U. S. Department of the Interior phoned one day to tell me I was terrific. But educational hoopla has a shelf life shorter than that of cream puffs, and one year's innovation is next year's limp noodle. Two years after I created that classroom, a newly hired deputy chief administrator who needed to establish her own priorities assigned me to supervise criterion-referenced tests throughout the district.

I lasted three weeks as a pencil pusher, and then I went to the superintendent and insisted on a transfer. I did not quite quote e. e. cummings'

"There is some shit I will not eat"—but I came close. I told the superintendent I would take any *teaching* job in the district, but I had to teach. And thus it was that I came to set up a storefront classroom for forty extremely disaffected high school students who had been excluded from the regular campus.

A lot of people thought that assignment was my punishment for rocking the boat. The people who thought it most of all were my students: they were convinced that something must be wrong with any teacher who had to work with *them*. How wrong they were. We were given an empty building, and we created a school. Not only did we choose the chairs, but choice of the curriculum—from reading, writing, science, and social studies to risk taking and responsibility—was ours too. After the students and I bought the overstuffed red velvet sofa, I ordered lots of periodicals, lots of paperbacks, and lots of ESS supplies. Students accompanied me on visits to used-book stores. They enjoyed giving me a hard time because I wouldn't order the *National Enquirer*. Anyone who teaches reluctant readers of any age knows that their most frustrating quality is their ennui. Those kids firmly believed there is nothing (legal) under the sun that will spark their attention, never mind their enthusiasm. I had faith that the daily paper, some blockbuster books, and the investigation of the structural capabilities of an index card could surprise, amaze, and maybe even delight and challenge my students.

I'll never forget the excitement and wonder on the faces of those turned-out teenagers when Mike's toothpick bridge held forty-five pounds of books before it began to sag and creak. Staring at his bridge, Mike said, "I didn't know I had the patience to do anything like this."

Even an architectural graduate student at Rensselaer Polytechnic Institute was impressed. I invited her in as a "structures consultant" and she told us that not even RPI requires bare-bones toothpick bridges; they use pea connectors. "Oh god," moaned Mike, "You mean there was an easier way?" And he puffed up more than ever—knowing that not only had he succeeded, but he'd done it the pure way, the tough way. And he'd done it all by himself.

How many times in our curricular planning do we allow the time and space for a seven-year-old and a fifteen-year-old to discover that they have patience? That they can achieve without shortcuts or props? Without remediation? There is no question but Mike was Daryll's older soul brother. Mike echoed his fellow teenagers when he said, "The one thing I hated about the regular school was every time you started something, the bell would ring and you'd have to go start something else." The structure of regular school seldom gives you three hours to weigh bottle caps or three weeks to build a bridge.

Don't look to the ESS *Structures* manual if you want a recipe for making toothpick bridges. Toothpick bridges aren't even suggested in the manual. But other bridge projects are, and, as with all undertakings worth their salt, one thing leads to another. Students who think they don't like to read, be they nine years old or fifteen, find informational books irresistible. We had books about killer bees and motorcycles; we had books about bridges. While he was reading about bridges, Mike noticed an article in the newspaper about a man who built a toothpick model of the Eiffel Tower and wondered if he couldn't build a toothpick bridge. The marvel of the ESS manuals is that they are not "how-to" documents; instead, they nudge and prod and provoke teachers and students to think for themselves, to extend themselves.

Yes, there was a bit of luck that Mike saw the newspaper article. But serendipity comes to people who can recognize sparks of illumination. If I have had any core reading list through the years, then newspapers are it. If your goal is to help students become lifetime readers, then newspapers are a great place to start; hook a fourteen-year-old on newspapers and you've hooked him for life. I required seventh graders to start the period by reading newspapers for ten minutes. Convincing the administration that I didn't want newspaper kits, not watered-down student newspapers, but fifteen subscriptions to the local paper, plus one copy each of the *New York Times, New York Post,* and the *Daily News* was not easy. I required my high schoolers to read the newspaper fifteen minutes a day — in addition to their half hour of extended reading. I carry in my mind's eye a host of beautiful serendipities that this newspaper habit provoked over the years.

And the routines of basic experimentation as well as the bursts of discovery in *Structures* showed me that teaching first graders and sixth graders and high school and college students is much more the same than it is different. Roland S. Barth revealed the basic premise under it all. When he was still a principal he described his first visit to Elementary Science Study. He asked a lot of questions and seemed to get few answers:

"Can I see the lesson plans for a unit?"
— We have none.
"How does a teacher teach without plans?"
— You put the materials out and see what children do with them. When children ask a question or need something, you help them. (1972, xvii)

It's easy to see why such a philosophy would drive most administrators nuts. Most teachers too. What's hard for teachers is not passing out paper or maintaining time-on-task or choosing good books. The hardest thing for a teacher is to keep her hands off. And her mouth shut.

Structures is no longer available from Education Development Center, the folks who received National Science Foundation funds to develop the ESS manuals; they're scrambling for a $24 million payoff for subverting their good idea. When I read recently that the National Science Foundation had granted Educational Development Center (EDC) nearly $24 million to come up with a new hands-on elementary science curriculum, I phoned EDC and asked what was wrong with the old hands-on ideas they had developed more than two decades ago. They didn't like the question. After all, if you can get megabucks to improve an old idea, then that idea *must* need improving; that's the American way. After being transferred, put on hold, and disconnected, I still wouldn't let go of the question and finally reached a cheerful woman who explained the need to make things neater, more straightforward, the need to give teachers frameworks and strategies so they can present lessons to their students and their students can produce outcomes. In short, they're designing things so teachers know ahead of time what they will teach and students know what they're expected to learn. When my informant found out I hold in sacred trust half a dozen of the original EDC Elementary Science Study teachers' guides, she admitted, without flourish, "You old diehards are not going to like the revision." (The original *Structures* manual is still available: Delta Education, Box M, Nashua, NH 03061. While you're at it, you may want to ask about the other thirty-five ESS manuals they sell.)

Donald Graves worries about why bad things happen to good ideas. Graves suggests that the reason science and social studies processes died on the vine was that the teacher was reduced to a spectator role. When somebody hands you your structure—tells you what you should teach and what the kids should learn—then you are a spectator. Graves expresses concern that writing and reading processes may fare no better if teachers allow themselves to become spectators. Graves is the first to lament that when teachers worry whether they should do the five-step Graves or the seven-step Graves, they have misunderstood the point. They are spectators, not teachers.

In my darker moments I wonder if any idea can succeed if it can't be linked to textbooks and worksheets. Certainly few people are anxious to make *restructure* synonymous with *simplify* or *inexpensive*. There's something about an educationist that loves a system, a forty-six-step plan, a checklist, a core reading list. And teachers who try to subvert neat and tidy structures never have an easy time. When I taught third grade, my district decided to invite teachers into the book-selection process, and I served on the language arts textbook selection committee. At our first meeting we discovered that middle- and upper-grade teachers wanted a bigger and better grammar book, one with lots of drills. Third-grade teachers seemed more open to the idea of abandoning student textbooks in favor of a teacher-resource pack of half a dozen professional books about language acquisition and development. And so we third-grade teachers split off from the pack and formed our own subcommittee.

Certain high administrators must have heard what was afoot because three of them showed up at our next meeting, one that brought together all the third-grade teachers in the district. The deputy chief administrator, the very same one who selected me to administer criterion-referenced tests, insisted we needed not just a grammar text but a spelling text too. In a tone implying that only good spellers will pass through the Pearly Gates, she announced, "A child doesn't need to be able to read a word to learn how to spell it correctly." If there were such a thing as a text devoted to commas, I'm sure she would have insisted we buy that too.

With this kind of pressure from the top, you might think there was no hope. But teachers have a way of surprising you, especially when the vote is by secret ballot. When the vote was taken, the majority favored the teacher-resource packs over individual student texts. Months went by. Some of us sent suggestions for teacher-resource books to the deputy chief administrator's deputy. Finally, the third-grade teachers were called together again — to vote on the textbook issue. When we muttered, "We thought we already voted," we were told that vote was "unofficial." This time we voted by a show of hands and the outcome was closer, but the "no text" people won again. The next day the deputy chief administrator's deputy issued a memo calling for a signed ballot from every third-grade teacher. She said this was "in fairness to the teachers who were absent from the meeting." Results of that tally were never announced but the third-grade teachers were called to meet one more time. At last, I caught on: we were going to vote until we got it right. The deputy chief administrator's deputy made an impassioned plea that we be sensitive to "our image of excellence as perceived by the public." She asked us, "How can the public have faith in our commitment to excellence if we don't even have a language arts textbook?" Whereupon third-grade teachers voted to provide every student in the district with a language arts textbook. My only satisfaction was that even in the face of all that pressure, the vote was close.

Months later, my third graders asked if we were ever going to use those new books stacked on the window ledge. I told them they could use them whenever they wanted. And they did. Every time we had choices, five or six children would choose to "play school." Someone would be teacher and pass out either the language arts texts or the basal workbooks. (Although I did not use a basal, in the name of excellence and standards a classroom set of workbooks was delivered to my classroom.) The teacher would wave the pointer and yell at the students to "do their pages." They loved using the teachers' manuals to correct those pages. Sometimes I wonder if it's like my friend who carefully excludes sugar from her children's diet. Every chance those kids get, they binge on junk food. Given the chance, my students binged on the forbidden workbooks.

That experience has made me quite sympathetic to the folks in California who have come up with a literature plan. Bad things happen to good people. Bad things happen to good literature too. Last year I was invited out to California to take a look at the California Literature Project. Good things are happening: teachers are excited about literature. They are themselves reading and talking. But bad things are happening too. In developing lists of books to fulfill the official plan of "a systematic, well-organized core program in which the overlap of selections at more than one grade span level is avoided," there is a whole lot of argument among teachers over who *gets* particular books. Second- and third-grade teachers, for example, come close to shedding blood over who gets *Charlotte's Web.* And ninth graders get *Great Expectations.* Honest. I met a lot of teachers in California who, in the name of a new, innovative structure, have decreed that *Great Expectations* is the book that every ninth grader in the district must read: gifted students and not-so-gifted students all read this book so that they have a common piece of literature they can discuss. If this doesn't make you weep, what will?

I wonder why otherwise reasonable people go sort of crazy when book-choosing time rolls around. For one thing, terminal hypocrisy sets in. The same people who swap copies of Judith Krantz and Stephen King and Irving Wallace in the faculty room put Dickens on their core lists. Core lists, it seems, are made by people who feel confident in their knowledge of what *other people* should read. In 1969 I made a case that the execrable reading taste revealed in best-seller lists is a direct result of the artificiality, sentimentality, and just plain bad writing of basal readers in "To Hell with Rip Van Winkle" [p. 96]. Why would we expect things to have changed in just two decades when, as Larry Cuban reminds us, for all the periodic hustle and bustle, the pedagogy in schools hasn't changed much in the past one hundred years?

I've never met a required book list I liked. Such lists are always prescriptive and retrospective. They keep us looking over our shoulders, maintaining a static rather than a dynamic notion of culture. And the worst part is that once you let a core list into your life, it's very hard to dislodge it. Asking a faculty to change a recommended book list and getting a new list approved by administrators and the board of education is like asking someone to move a graveyard. If you're persistent, stubborn, and intractable, you may get a few new items added; you'll never get old bones removed.

Who's afraid of Charles Dickens? I am! Putting Dickens on a required core list, insisting that every eighth grader must read *A Christmas Carol* and every ninth grader must read *Great Expectations*, victimizes children. I have nothing against Dickens as literature of choice. If individual teachers know and love Dickens and know and love their students—and feel they can make a match—then God bless those teachers, every one of them. But California teachers I talked with lamented that Dickens is not a personal choice; traveling under the name of standards and excellence, it is simply what is required. Others defended the choice on the grounds that it is meritorious for every child to have a classic in common, that not-so-able children are invited into a community of learners and share this experience with all their classmates. I see it as a heartbreaking requirement. Force-feeding students Dickens will exclude many of them from knowing the personal joy that literature can bring, a joy that is their right. I worry not just that those vulnerable students will never try Dickens again; I worry they will be scared off from dipping into any literature again. Remember that bromide from some years back, "This is the first day of the rest of your life"? We need to choose our books as though today were the last day of our lives—and theirs—if we hope turn kids on to reading.

Poet-farmer-teacher Wendell Berry gives us a wonderful image of what happens when people insist on unanimity over diversity. He gives us "crazy old Mrs. Gaines who sang of One Lord, one Faith, and one Cornbread" (1989, 26). Wendell Berry never even hints that crazy old Mrs. Gaines might have been a high school English teacher, but certainly the irony of high school is that students' literary choices become ever more restricted. I can sympathize with teachers who regard it as an excess of diversity to say to their students, "Choose your own books," but surely when the core book is *Great Expectations* we must recognize that such lists are taking us too far in the direction of received dogma. And as Wendell Berry points out, they had to lock up crazy old Mrs. Gaines in a room because "for her, to be free was only to be lost."

I used to ask teachers, "What would happen if you were shut up in a room with thirty of your colleagues and not allowed to leave until you'd all read the same book?" But that's exactly what happened in California. The California Literature Project brought teachers together during the summer and subjected them to an intensive, rigorous study of James Joyce's *Ulysses*. The next summer another group studied Proust. When I met those teachers at a weekend reunion, I heard lots of groans and laughter, lots of talk about "surviving" Joyce and "surviving" Proust. I both admire and am appalled by the notion. I can acknowledge and even applaud the power of their intellectual endeavor. I witnessed firsthand the sense of community and joint accomplishment it engendered. But I wonder if *survival*—getting through a book—is the literary model we want for our classrooms. I wonder how many of those teachers have, on their own, read more Joyce, more Proust. How many of them have read more Irish writers, more French writers?

As an English major I avoided courses on eighteenth-century literature because I'd discovered on my own that *Tom Jones* was just about the greatest book ever written, and I was afraid some professorial pedant would ruin it for me. Even though I was led through *Moby Dick* by one of the best professors I ever had, and even though *Moby Dick* was his passion (how many teachers build an altar—complete with lighted candles—in the front of the room with *a book* in the place of reverence?), I felt only relief when we finally got through it. My only real emotion for the book was, "I made it; thank God it's over." I never looked at Melville again—until about five years ago when, piqued by a scholarly comment, I decided to take another look. I'm not at all surprised that my eighteen-year-old self couldn't appreciate Melville's grand passion, couldn't see his humor. My recent pleasure in the book convinces me I just might even be ready for George Eliot. A few years ago I asked some people I respect a lot what books they would commend to teachers. Katherine Paterson and Robert Coles both spoke so eloquently of the richness of *Middlemarch* that I know one day I'll have to relinquish my school-forced detestation and give it a try.

I don't want my students to survive literature. I want my students to read out of curiosity, out of a need to be informed, out of an anticipation of fun. I want my students to read widely—and fairly casually. Time enough for them to plumb the depths of literary analysis—if they want to do that sort of thing—when they get to college. Since my first year of teaching, when *Silas Marner, Julius Caesar,* and *Johnny Tremain* were on my school's required list, I've never been able to bring myself to tell a student he *had* to read any particular book. Students are so diverse. And as publishing imprints abound, we have available a bountiful supply of limitless possibility, books as diverse as the children in our care. What is the need for "one cornbread"?

For me, coaxing students into reading is rather like growing African violets. Twenty years ago my husband and I ordered some seeds. The seeds were so infinitesimal we thought the packet was empty. And by the time the seeds finally germinated months later, we had almost given up hope. I forget the exact timetable but we didn't have flowers for several years. And young readers are a whole lot like African violet seeds. They need a good environment; they need to be given space and time to develop. They need, in Jane Hansen's (1987) words, to be led "from behind," their language learning capabilities supported indirectly through the environment we offer them. We can't force readers; we must nurture them. My violets are still in brilliant bloom. And Denise is still blooming too. Denise is proof that classroom habits can last a lifetime. One of my articles of faith has been to exchange notes with my students every day. Even at her angriest, Denise, the student so recalcitrant she had the distinction of failing seventh grade twice, always wrote, and she still writes today. Denise writes of taking her kids to the library every week. She says her kids like *Flat Stanley* almost as much as I do. Denise writes about introducing her children to the Stupids, Frog and Toad, and Madeline, as well as Stanley. Denise writes, "I can't wait until they're old enough for Gilly Hopkins. I want to read that book again." I like to think Denise learned something important in my class—and it has nothing to do with whether or not she ever read someone else's notion of a classic. I measure my success not in how many children I can push through *Great Expectations*, but in the Denises who are tempted to read a book twenty years after they leave my care.

There's another *structures* kind of moral to this story. I was so convinced that our classroom letter exchange was the best pedagogical tool I'd ever used that in 1978 I sent an article about it to a professional journal. When it was rejected, I sent the article to another professional journal and another. Not even half a dozen form-letter regrets could deter me from a good idea. My students let me know every day that the experts were wrong. Letter writing might lack pedagogical pizzazz but my students let me know it was crucial in our lives. Of course, my error was not in the process but in the nomenclature. There is something about our profession that loves a two-dollar word. Nonetheless, to this day I can't stomach calling letters between a teacher and her students *interactive journals*.

Too much of what travels under the banners of official excellence bespeaks a contempt for students and for teachers too. Core lists show a lack of trust in teachers, in students, and in literature. Core lists have a way of turning into literature laws, hemming teachers in and fencing kids out. Core lists have a way of telling students that the only good authors are the dead ones. Literature that becomes itemized, formalized, and, most dangerously, standardized, dies. What we have left is a graveyard of books. What we need is a dynamic model of literature, one that encourages our students to become lifelong readers, one that encourages them to become parents who read to their children. This won't happen if *student choice* is not central to the program.

I stressed this idea of student choice in a talk to the California Literature Project and a number of Project members wrote me notes accusing me of anarchism. Student choice, they insisted, is fine and dandy for recreational reading, but for *literature study* the teacher must choose. Left on their own, teachers insisted, students won't move beyond *Sweet Valley High* books.

I know for a fact that this is not true. It's not true with first graders; it's not true with high schoolers. When you surround children with the sounds and sense of wonderful language, they respond. They make good choices. When my third graders and I won one hundred free books in a paperback book contest, I told them they could each choose a book to keep and then choose four each for our classroom library. No blue-ribbon book-selection committee could have taken their charge more seriously, and the list the children came up with was impressive. No one wasted a choice. They chose fiction such as *The Little House* books, *Owls in the Family*, *Frog and Toad*, *Ralph S. Mouse*; they chose mysteries, poetry, nonfiction; they chose hard books and easy books. "But not too easy," they reminded one another. Over and over I heard a book dismissed with the comment, "You'd only want to read that one once."

The same thing happened with seventh and eighth graders. When I was still a remedial reading teacher with an inherited lab filled with ugly little controlled-vocabulary paragraphs, I decided the best way to revitalize the program was to give each of my students a book coupon redeemable for a paperback once a month in a local bookstore. I took my students for their first visit. They quickly passed over *Snoopy* books, hairstyling books, and series romances. Amazing to me, 90 percent of those inner-city remedial students chose such classics as Shakespeare, Twain, and Hawthorne—yes, and Dickens too—for their first book. They'd pick up Shakespeare and say, "Oh yeah, I've heard of that." They seemed to like the idea of owning an important book even though they had no intention of reading it. After that, students visited the store on their own. They brought back sports biographies, young adult novels, mysteries, fairy tales, and adult best-sellers. Two sisters pooled their coupons and saved up until they had enough for a hardback cookbook. Sylvia complained that every time she chose her book she had a fight with her mother over who got to read it first. I told Sylvia she must be making good choices. One day Sylvia's mother visited my classroom, wanting to see if I had any more good books she might borrow.

Isn't that what education is all about? Helping people to make their own choices? Helping them establish some sort of criteria for making good choices? Who's going to provide the core books for our students when they're on their own? I hear a lot of talk in California about giving teachers *a sense of ownership*. There's no mention of the students' ownership and I'd certainly put money on my supposition that no student was included on the vote for *Great Expectations*. Anyway, I have grave doubts about this thing called *a sense of ownership*. Either it's yours or it ain't, and twenty years messing around in schools has shown me that if you want it, you gotta grab it. Anybody starts talking about a sense of ownership in my house and I'm going to count the silverware.

In our restructuring for real literature, aren't we taking things just a bit too seriously? Over and over I see that word *worthy* in connection with literature in the classroom. My third graders learned a whole lot about how language works from riddle books, Amelia Bedelia, and Morris and Borris. When short-story writer par excellence Tobias Wolff was in high school, his older brother Geoffrey wrote him a letter from Princeton, advising him on the great core books he should read if he ever hoped to amount to anything. The rather pretentious and pedantic Geoffrey was ahead of his time with his core list for his brother's enlightenment. Recently, Tobias sent his brother a copy of that long-ago letter with a note, "OK, Mr. Smarty Pants, I'm a professor and I still haven't read this stuff."

The real issue is not whether the literature we bring to our students is worthy; the real issue is whether we are willing to take risks in the classroom or not. Edward Abbey was a wonderful gadfly and, for me, a mentor. When he died recently, I knew I'd lost a friend. He wrote often of the need for self-testing. He warns us not to become settled in our ways, "content as pigs in a warm manure pile." Abbey wrote that to be alive is to take risks. To be always safe and secure is death. In Abbey's words:

> The permissive society? What else? I love America because it *is* a confused, chaotic mess, and I hope we can keep it this way for at least another thousand years. The permissive society is the free society, the open society. Who gave us permission to live this way? Nobody did. *We* did. And that's the way it should be—only more so. The best cure for the ills of democracy is democracy. (1977, 230)

It comes as no surprise that Abbey liked to quote Walt Whitman. "Resist much," advises Whitman in his Preface to *Leaves of Grass:* "Love the earth and the sun and the animals. Despise riches. Give alms to everyone that asks. Stand up for the stupid and crazy. . . . Take off your hat to nothing known or unknown. . . . Re-examine all you have been told at school or church or in any book and dismiss whatever insults your own soul." Who would dare to put this on a core list? And yet the best cure for the ills of education is to risk much, to resist much. The best cure for the ills of education is more diversity, not less.

In a deep sense students are more the same than they are different, but on the surface there is a whole lot of diversity. How can we choose our curricula ahead of time? How can the same books be altogether "right" year after year after year? One group of third graders loved *Amelia Bedelia*, but next year's crew, a more sophisticated bunch, thought that was "baby stuff." *Trumpet of the Swan* is on California's fourth-grade list. I would have fought to my last gasp anyone who tried to prevent me from reading it with one of my third grades. Much as we all loved it, I read the book with children only that one time. New years bring new seeds, new books. How about *Sarah, Plain and Tall?* Who *gets* it? Do the rest of us just have to sit there smoldering with envy?

In his poem "Traveling at Home," from his book by the same name, Wendell Berry reminds us

Even in a country you know by heart
it's hard to go the same way twice.
The life of the going changes.
The chances change and make a new way.
Any tree or stone or bird
can be the bud of a new direction. The
natural correction is to make intent
of accident. To get back before dark
is the art of going. (1989, 23)

A teacher whom I've never met but with whom I've developed a friendship through correspondence put it this way: "I've taught first grade for twenty-three years and I've never done it the same way twice." I mentioned this to a longtime colleague who has taught fourth and fifth grades for more than twenty years and she agreed. "The year I get things right, the year I'm satisfied, I'll know it's time to quit."

Borrowing from Judith Viorst (1984), I offer my version of "If I Were in Charge of the World":

If I were in charge of the world
I'd cancel facilitators,
Friday spellings,
Pizza bribes, and also
Questions at the end of the story.
If I were in charge of the world
You could read *Charlotte's Web*
In any grade you wanted.
You could even read it twice.
If I were in charge of the world
There'd be a million million
Pages of delight,
Instead of thirty-two copies
Of three novels
Somebody else chose.
If I were in charge of the world
Nobody under age forty would be encouraged to read *Moby Dick*,
No books would come by decree.
And a person would said knock-knock riddle books with pop-up
    pages are a quintessential part of a reading program

Would still be allowed to be
In charge of the world.

References

Abbey, Edward. 1977. *The Journey Home.* New York: E. P. Dutton.

Barth, Roland S. 1972. *Open Education and the American School.* New York: Agathon Press, Inc.

Berry, Wendell. 1989. "Meditation in the Spring Rain." In *Traveling at Home.* San Francisco: North Point Press.

———. 1989. "Traveling at Home." In *Traveling at Home.* San Francisco: North Point Press.

cummings, e. e. 1955. "I Sing of Olaf." In *The New Pocket Anthology of American Verse,* edited by Oscar Williams. New York: Washington Square Press.

Hansen, Jane. 1987. *When Writers Read.* Portsmouth, NH: Heinemann.

Ohanian, Susan. 1969. "To Hell with Rip Van Winkle." *Intersections.* Troy, NY: Center for Urban and Environmental Studies.

Viorst, Judith. 1984. *If I Were in Charge of the World and Other Worries.* New York: Atheneum.

Whitman, Walt. 1959. Preface to 1855 Edition of *Leaves of Grass.* In *Complete Poetry and Selected Prose of Walt Whitman,* edited by James E. Miller, Jr. Boston: Houghton Mifflin.

. . . .

THIRTEEN WAYS OF LOOKING AT MASTERY LEARNING

I

Among twenty behavioral objectives,
The only puzzling one
Was mastery of Learning.

II

I was of three minds,
Like a desk
On which there are three pencils.

III

The Learning sat in the publishing mist
It was a small part of the program.

IV

A child and a teacher
Are one.
A child and a teacher and Learning
Are one.

V

I do not know which to prefer
The beauty of Mastery
Or the beauty of Learning,
The student mastering learning
Or just after.

VI

Learning filled the long blackboard
With barbaric scrawl.
The shadow of the student
Crossed it, to and fro.
The mood
Traced in the shadow
An indecipherable cause.

VII

O thin publishers of tests,
Why do you imagine Mastery?

245

Do you not see how learning
Lurks in the classrooms
Of the teachers about you?

VIII

I know noble accents
And lucid, inescapable rhythms:
But I know, too,
That the student is involved
In what I know.

IX

When any learning is acquired
It marks the edge
Of one of many circles.

X

At the thought of students
Mastering Learning,
Even the bawds of euphony
Would cry out sharply.

XI

He walked past classrooms
Without looking.
Once, a fear pierced him,
In that he mistook
The shadow of his equipage
For learning.

XII

Times are changing
Learning must be mastered.

XIII

It was competency time
It was testing
And it was going to test.
Learning sat
With the publishers.

With apologies to Wallace Stevens, who wrote "Thirteen Ways of Looking at a Blackbird."

Credits

· ·

THE AUTHOR AND PUBLISHER wish to thank those who have generously given permission to reprint borrowed material:

"Stacks of Letters" originally appeared in *Learning*. Reprinted with permission from the February issue of *Learning* 1981. © 1981 Springhouse Corporation, 1111 Bethlehem Pike, Springhouse, PA 19477–0908. All rights reserved.

"Love, Leslie" originally appeared in the *Whole Language Catalog* (1991).

"The Tantalizing Vagueness of Teaching" originally appeared in *Learning*. Reprinted with permission from the July/August issue of *Learning* 1986. © 1986 Springhouse Corporation, 1111 Bethlehem Pike, Springhouse, PA 19477–0908. All rights reserved.

"Collaboration, Silence, and Solitude" originally appeared in *Vital Signs 2: Teaching and Learning Collaboratively*, edited by James L. Collins (Boynton/Cook Publishers, Inc., Portsmouth, NH, 1991). Reprinted by permission of Susan Ohanian.

"Notes on Japan from an American Schoolteacher" originally appeared in *Phi Delta Kappan*. Reprinted with permission of the *Phi Delta Kappan* (January 1987).

"P. L. 4–142: Mainstream or Quicksand?" originally appeared in *Phi Delta Kappan*. Reprinted with permission of the *Phi Delta Kappan* (November 1990).

"To 'Pete,' Who's Lost in the Mainstream" originally appeared in *Education Week*. Reprinted with permission from *Education Week*. Volume 4/Number 28/April 3, 1985.

"Question of the Day" originally appeared in the *English Journal* (November 1983), a publication of the National Council of Teachers of English. Reprinted by permission.

"Will You Recognize the Ready Moment?" originally appeared in *Learning*. Reprinted with permission from the September issue of *Learning* 1984. © 1984 Springhouse Corporation, 1111 Bethlehem Pike, Springhouse, PA 19477–0908. All rights reserved.

"Okay to Be Different" originally appeared in *Learning*. Reprinted with permission from the February issue of *Learning* 1985. © 1985 Springhouse Corporation, 1111 Bethlehem Pike, Springhouse, PA 19477–0908. All rights reserved.

"Reading for What?" originally appeared in the *English Journal* (January 1981), a publication of the National Council of Teachers of English. Reprinted by permission.